Kickstar
Your Corpor

Kickstart Your Corporation

The Incorporated Professional's Financial Planning Coach

Andrew Feindel

WILEY

Library of Congress Cataloging-in-Publication Data

Names: Feindel, Andrew, 1981- author.
Title: Kickstart your corporation : the incorporated professional's
    financial planning coach / Andrew Feindel.
Description: First Edition. | Hoboken : Wiley, 2020. | Includes index.
Identifiers: LCCN 2020028485 (print) | LCCN 2020028486 (ebook) | ISBN
    9781119709138 (hardback) | ISBN 9781119709145 (adobe pdf) | ISBN
    9781119709121 (epub)
Subjects: LCSH: Corporations—Canada—Finance. |
    Corporations—Canada—Taxation. | Incorporation—Canada.
Classification: LCC HG4090 .F45 2020 (print) | LCC HG4090 (ebook) | DDC
    658.150971—dc23
LC record available at https://lccn.loc.gov/2020028485
LC ebook record available at https://lccn.loc.gov/2020028486

Cover image: © Sahara Prince/Shutterstock
Cover design: Wiley

Printed in the United States of America.

SKY10021363_092320

For Tina, Jake, and Sophie & For Mel, Julia, Sophie and Sam.

Contents

Utilizing Tax-Efficient Strategies 237

Acknowledgments

I would like to thank my business partner and good friend Kyle Richie. Since working together in 2004, we have shared a vision for improving wealth management, and have implemented many of those ideas mentioned in this book. Kyle was ranked #1 by Wealth Professional in 2018 and has been a keynote speaker at investment conferences globally. As a top ranked advisor in Canada, he has successfully mentored many young financial advisors. We are both fortunate to work with each another and I look forward to many more years together.

Thank you to all the clients we have worked with over the years for their support and validation; Alexandra Macqueen for her help with streamlining the writing and asking "Why don't you write another book?"; Paul Matthews and Alexander Herman for their help with this book's title; Volt Chan, James King, Frank Santelli, Dan Collison, Sue Neal, and Ermos Erotocritou for their leadership; Serena Dang and Harpreet Wadehra for their sound accounting advice; Martin Houser, Mark Fox and Alison Minard for their legal advice which always challenges; Ty Wehrenberg and Glen McCrum for all their opinions; Jeremy Enwright, Ryan Shoemaker, Rachelle Allen, Tara McCue, Rob Gray, Erin Blair, and Edwin Pavey for making work fun; Alex Loh, Lisa Johnson, Yola Guo, Jennifer Olvet, Dylan Biggs, Coby Tiffin, and all our administrative team—thank you for putting up with us; Jack Courtney, Blair Evans, and Christine Van Cauwenberghe for their always diligent insights; the welcoming teams at Richardson GMP, especially Craig Bassinger and his team; the Horwood sisters and Bakish brothers; and the supportive team at Wiley for their input and revisions. Lastly, thank you to my family and friends, especially James Obaji for his perspective on these financial issues and our late best friend Joe Magnotta, who always wanted people around him to succeed. It was Joe's idea to hold our first financial planning seminar titled "Wealth and Wine" at his parents' winery—the first step in our journey.

100% of the proceeds of this book will be donated to charity.

About the Author

A **ndrew Feindel** CFA, CFP, CLU, CSWP, CIM, FMA, CSA, FCSI, HBA (Ivey) Senior Vice President, Investment Advisor Andrew.Feindel@richardsongmp.com

Andrew Feindel is a Senior Vice President and Investment Advisor at Richardson GMP.

Andrew is a co-author of *Kickstart: How Successful Canadians Got Started* (published 2008, Dundurn) where he interviewed 70 prominent Canadians including former prime ministers (Brian Mulroney), Native leaders (Matthew Coon Come), physicians (Dr. James Orbinski), business owners (Jim Pattison), cartoonists (Lynn Johnston), astronauts (Dr. Roberta Bondar), and ballet dancers (Karen Kain).

He built his career around understanding both the nuances of wealth and, perhaps more importantly in his chosen profession, the nuances of people when it comes to wealth.

A graduate of Upper Canada College's class of 2000, Andrew went on to graduate from the Richard Ivey School of Business and the Stockholm School of Economics with an honours degree in business administration. Sixteen years ago he joined Kyle's physician and dentist-focused practice and brought his deep understanding of the medical field with him — his father is a cardiac surgeon in Toronto, his grandfather was a neurosurgeon inducted into the Canadian Medical Hall of Fame, and his wife is a nurse.

Andrew has regularly appeared in the media, including the Financial Post, Globe and Mail, Reader's Digest, and CBC. He was also recognized by Wealth Professional magazine in 2017 and 2019 as one of a small group of up-and-coming young advisors poised to lead Canada's wealth management industry into the future.

Andrew holds many professional certifications, including the Chartered Financial Analyst (CFA), Certified Financial Planner (CFP), Chartered Life Underwriter (CLU), Chartered Strategic Wealth Professional (CSWP), Chartered Investment Manager (CIM), Financial Management Advisor (FMA), Certified Senior Advisor (CSA), and is a Fellow of the Canadian Securities Institute (FCSI).

Introduction: The Value of a Coach

"Another financial planning book," you may be thinking. "What value will this be to me?"

The shelves of your local library and bookstore are already filled with every imaginable book on finances: budgeting, business planning, investments, retirement planning, tax planning, planning your estate, how to save money, best practices for businesses, and more. What value could one more provide?

The truth is, this book is unlike any other you've encountered. Whereas most other books provide copious amounts of information and detail about financial topics, very few provide concise, targeted, and pragmatic guidance with a boots-on-the-ground perspective from a team that's "been there, done that."

And even fewer are written for you, the incorporated professional.

This book aims to change all that. From whether and when you should make the decision to incorporate, to the proper place of insurance in your financial plan, to how and where to invest and how to keep the taxman at bay, to the use of trusts and charitable donations, what you're holding is a complete, yet concise, guide to everything that matters in your financial life as an incorporated professional.

I wrote this book because I saw a gap in the advice that's available to people like you. Together with my business partner, we've built a very successful financial planning practice serving the needs of incorporated professionals, and now is my time to give back.

In our practice, I see a lot of misconceptions and even mistakes that need course-correcting. These blunders happen because people don't have a reliable and accessible source of the guidance they need—and, I would argue, deserve—for organizing and managing their financial lives as incorporated professionals.

As you're reading along, think of this book as your own financial planning coach. Like any good coach, the book will help you look at your current state of affairs, and then provide direction to enhance the results you're getting—now and in the future. Working through the ideas in this book may involve some unlearning on your part, whether that's related to how and where you invest or the way you think about how to accomplish the goals you have for yourself and your business.

My only request is that you enter with an open mind, ready to discard some rules of thumb that you may have heard for decades but, in reality, don't work for you and your situation.

Chapter 1
Incorporation 101

If you're reading this and you're not incorporated, you need to call your financial planner *right now* and ask them why they haven't recommended that you incorporate. One of my best friends is a very successful family doctor in Ontario. We made sure that as of day 1 in his career—before he'd even received his first Ontario Health Insurance Plan (OHIP) payment—his medical professional corporation was set up and properly structured. Over the course of his career, this single move has saved him hundreds of thousands of tax dollars. *So if you're a practicing professional, and you're not incorporated, why not?*

What You'll Get Out of This Chapter

This chapter covers the basics of incorporating for the professional and business owner, including a review of the process and costs to incorporate, as well as the likely benefits. We also review when incorporation may not be beneficial, and how buying a house meshes with your corporate structure.

(continued)

> (*continued*)
>
> In this chapter, you'll learn about shareholder loans, the lifetime capital gains exemption, how a corporation can provide creditor protection, and what to do with your corporation when you transition into and through retirement.

Why Incorporate?

Here's the answer: the rationale for incorporation is the difference between paying income taxes at your personal rate, which can be as high as 53.53% (Ontario's highest marginal rate in 2020 after $220,000 of income), or your corporate small business deduction (SBD) rate of 12.2% (Ontario's combined federal and provincial tax rate). But in addition to the (potentially substantial) tax benefits of incorporation, you will also get increased flexibility in choosing the government programs in which to participate and invest.

A good financial planner should acknowledge that they have absolutely no control of the markets. While we do all try our best to spot trends and mispricings, in some form or fashion, we are always riding along with the ebbs and flows of market movements.

Taxes, in contrast, we have complete control over (within the rules and parameters of the tax code). Taxes are factual, they are mathematics, they are "known knowns." This means that we can master and control them. While we cannot avoid them, we have the ability to plan and mitigate some taxes. In our financial lives, our focus should be on controlling the controllable—and the corporation is a powerful tool that allows us to control our tax bill.

What Does It Cost to Incorporate?

Setting up your professional corporation using a lawyer should cost you less than $2,000—and less than $1,000 if you take a do-it-yourself approach. Organizing the corporation—issuing shares and creating by-laws and shareholder agreements, for example—can drive up costs, but keep in mind that you can deduct up to $3,000 of costs related to incorporation. And while it's possible to incorporate using a DIY approach, consulting with a professional can help ensure that you're set up appropriately from the get-go.[1]

To be frank, however, I view the cost of incorporation essentially as a "sunk cost" (a cost you have already incurred and cannot recover), as you will likely incur these organizational costs at some point in your career—the only question is when.

Also, in my conversations I always stress that you shouldn't be fooled by the myth that higher legal costs will produce better outcomes for your corporation. Incorporating is simple. The only "trick" to watch out for is ensuring you create enough classes of shareholders at the outset so your spouse (or future spouse) and/or your kids (or future kids) can all have shares—they each need to have a letter in front of their shares (Class A, Class B, and so on) so the corporation can pay them different amounts, if you like. That's the (only) "secret sauce" for your Articles of Incorporation. (With that said, if this issue has to be fixed later on, it can be, but your legal costs may be much higher.)

In general, your yearly corporate accounting fees might be in the range of $1,000–2,500/year, and ongoing maintenance fees could be as high as $500 (with a lawyer) or $150 (if you file yourself). These fees can be much higher if there is significant active and passive income. Additionally, each year, you'll need to renew the certificate of authorization, and you'll also need to keep the corporation's minute book up to date.

What's the Process to Incorporate?

(If you're already incorporated, skip ahead to the section "How Does Purchasing a Home Fit into My Incorporation Timeline?")

We all know time is money, and addressing the added complexity of a corporation will take some of your valuable personal time.

The good news, however, is that most of this extra time commitment is required only once, during the initial stages of incorporation.

The following is the basic process to incorporate.

Written Consent

In some provinces, it is required that written consent be obtained before you can license your corporation. Each province has its own rules and standard applications, which can be obtained from its appropriate provincial licensing body.

Articles of Incorporation

You will need to prepare a shareholder agreement and your articles of incorporation, usually using legal counsel. You will also need to establish a corporate bank account, advise your respective association (e.g., the Canadian Medical Protection Association (CMPA)) of your incorporation, and assign your medical services billing number to the corporation. (Professional corporations, as defined in section 248(1) of the Income Tax Act, must notify the relevant professional regulatory body of their incorporation.) You should also advise all employees, patients, suppliers, creditors, and insurers that you've incorporated your professional practice.

Payroll Remittances

Once you receive your Canada Revenue Agency business number, which will look something like 12345 6789 RP0001, the number for your corporate remittances will look something like 12345 6789 RC0001. (The two numbers will be identical, differentiated only by the RP, RT, or RC program accounts.) You do not need to make corporate remittances in the first year, but you are required to make payroll remittances. It is important to note that enrollment for payroll and/or HST accounts is not automatic—this is something your accountant will be able to help you with.

Employment Contracts

Upon incorporating, a new written contract will need to be created for the new employee/employer relationship you'll be entering into as an employee of your professional corporation. Additional contracts for your spouse, children, and any other employees will also need to be developed. Establishing written contracts may be important for future reasonability reviews, given the new tax on split income rules (more on that later).

Transferring Assets

When you incorporate, you should consult with your accountant and/or financial advisor about which assets, if any, need to be and/or should be transferred to the corporation. (Keep in mind you are, in fact, selling your practice to your corporation.)

You can transfer assets, including goodwill (an intangible asset that's made up of the value added by your reputation and customer lists to the value of your practice), tax-deferred to your corporation by filing an election with the Canada Revenue Agency—called a "section 85" election, as the rules are set out in section 85 of the Income Tax Act. This election will ensure you avoid having to pay taxes if the fair market value (FMV) of your assets exceeds their adjusted cost base (ACB).

While the greatest benefit of the section 85 election is to transfer eligible property on a tax-deferred basis (at the lower of cost or the undepreciated capital cost) to a taxable Canadian corporation, there is an opportunity to trigger a gain if it is beneficial to the individual's circumstances. Also, whether the transfer is tax-deferred or not, it is nevertheless a disposition and must be reported on the transferor's tax return.

Before you transfer any other assets to the corporation, such as real estate or insurance policies, a careful cost–benefit analysis should be carried out. The following are some high-level considerations.

Real Estate

An individual can simply sell an existing rental property to their corporation in exchange for assets or debt, but the sale would trigger any unrealized capital gains, as well as a possible recapture of any capital cost allowance previously claimed on the rental property in the hands of the individual.

An individual may also transfer personally held assets to a corporation on a tax-deferred basis by taking back shares (and possibly debt) of the corporation in exchange for the property. The value of the shares received would reflect the value of the property transferred to the corporation. Then, when the property is eventually sold by the corporation, any accrued capital gains would be taxable to the corporation and distributed to the shareholder, likely in the form of dividends.

There are other factors that would need to be considered as well before assets are transferred to the corporation. For example, in the case of real estate, you would be required to pay a land transfer tax if the property is not used for the active business of the corporation. While I have seen some lawyers work around these issues using a trust structure, it's best to assume these taxes are to be paid. It is also important to determine whether the goods and services or harmonized sales tax (GST or HST) applies.

It should be noted that some real estate transactions do avoid land transfer taxes. These include gifts for no consideration (including no assumption of a mortgage). Although the tax is triggered and a tax return should be filed, as the tax is based on the consideration, the actual amount of the tax will be nil (as the consideration is also nil).

Insurance Policies

If you're thinking about transferring a personally held insurance policy to your corporation, you need to proceed with great care, specifically comparing:

- The corporate savings of the corporation paying the insurance premium (note that life insurance premiums are not a deductible expense unless specifically required as part of collateral on debt) minus the income tax due on the cash surrender value (CSV) minus the adjusted cost base (ACB) at the transfer; and

- The cost of paying a lump-sum bonus this year so that, after personal income tax, you have enough remaining to pay the tax due on the taxable income.

While the March 2016 federal budget reduced the benefits of transferring insurance policies to a corporation, it recommended that consideration which is at least equal to the higher of the CSV and the ACB of the policy be paid. If this recommendation is implemented, the policy's new ACB will be the highest of the following amounts: the value of the policy (CSV), the fair market value of the consideration paid, and the ACB. This new ACB will affect the taxation of the insurance plan. If the policy is surrendered before death, there is a gain to the extent that the CSV exceeds the ACB. On death, any life insurance proceeds received, assuming the corporation is the beneficiary, are added to the CDA account, and can be paid out as a tax-free capital dividend.

Choosing Your Corporation's Year-End and Maintaining Your Corporate Records

Once you are incorporated, you will need to designate a fiscal year-end for your corporation. If you're looking to keep things simple, choose a corporate year-end of December 31, the same as your personal tax year-end.

There can be some advantages, however, in choosing an off-calendar year-end. For example, with an off-calendar year end of July 31 or later, you would be able to defer paying taxes for up to 179 days. This means you could declare a bonus in the company fiscal (non-calendar) year, but not actually take the money into (taxable) personal income into the following (calendar) year.

Your professional corporation will file its own return and pay its own taxes. The corporation's tax returns are due six months after your designated corporate year-end, but the final balance of any tax owing is due two to three months after your corporate year-end.[2] As you will now be an employee of the corporation, and no longer a self-employed individual, your personal taxes will be due by April 30—and not the deadline of June 15 granted to self-employed individuals and their spouses.

A mistake that's often made in the first year of incorporation is failing to file for dividends, recorded on T5 slips, by February 28 of the following year. This oversight will result in a late fee of the greater of $100 or $10 per day.[3] February 28 (or 29 in a leap year) is also the date for filing T4 slips. You will need to keep your company records for at least seven years—including invoices, receipts, cheques, and documentation of your salaried employees' duties and hours worked.[4]

When Does It Not Make Sense to Incorporate?

Although there are powerful potential benefits to incorporating your professional practice, there are also some (limited) situations in which it is advisable not to incorporate.

If you are retired and have no intentions of ever working again, ever, then incorporating won't be the right choice. To be crystal clear: I don't mean if you are retiring in one year, or slowing down or moving to part-time work. That's because there could still be many thousands in tax savings in those final years that could significantly change your corporate/RRSP mix, estate plans—and reduce your future tax bill, once you really are retired, as well.

In 2014, I started working with a physician in his 70s. Although he was in the process of reducing his working hours, we still had him incorporate his medical practice. By taking this one action, over the five remaining years of his working life, he achieved the following results:

1. His RRSP balance was reduced by $200,000, reducing the income he would take in the form of RRIF withdrawals (and thus the taxes he would eventually pay);

2. His corporate investment account balance was $250,000—giving him more control and lower (eventual) taxes;
3. The expected taxes payable on his estate were reduced, increasing his children's inheritance; and
4. He received five years of government benefit payments totalling close to $40,000—none of which he would have received had he not followed our advice.

If you plan on working less than a year in Canada and then move permanently to a new country, then you should not incorporate.

Notice I didn't say "if you plan to move to another province," as your corporation can be portable. That is, the benefits of incorporation all hold true if you work in Ontario for, say, one year and then work in Alberta for the following 20 years. While oftentimes a share restructuring may be required (given the different rules in different jurisdictions), unless you are planning on working in both provinces, in most cases it is a better option to have one corporation that moves from Province A to Province B than to set up a brand-new corporation. This is called "continuing" the corporation—a corporation is said to have continued when it has moved from one jurisdiction to another. Keep in mind, however, that different regulatory bodies may have different requirements.

If you make less than $50,000 per year and you do not have a partner who earns an income, you should not incorporate. In situations where your partner does have a high income and you can incorporate, there are ways to make this beneficial for you as a collective unit.

If you are an American citizen working in Canada, you should not incorporate until you understand the pros and cons, including excessive filing requirements—as the United States and Eritrea are the only countries that tax based on citizenship, resulting in annual filings for the prorated share of the passive income earned. Before you make the decision of whether to incorporate, you will need to understand which investment strategies can be used, *but also cannot be used,* given your citizenship and tax position.

Additionally, in December 2017, the United States implemented a transition tax that could be punitive for U.S. citizens working in Canada. With that said, I have worked with families for whom incorporation was certainly worthwhile—as in many other things, the devil is in the details.

If you have student debt, should you still incorporate? While student debt cannot be transferred to a corporation (given the debt is not tied to a tangible asset), it's still *almost always worthwhile to incorporate*. Why pay 20–40% more in taxes (by remaining unincorporated) to save 4% in interest (even though national student loan interest gives you a tax credit)? However, if you're facing a substantial student loan balance, you could look into federal student loan forgiveness programs that forgive up to $40,000 of debt in a five-year period if you work a minimum of 400 hours in an underserved or remote community.[5]

What If You Have No Small Business Deduction?

While many professionals do not receive the small business deduction (SBD) as they are associated with a partnership (i.e., most incorporated lawyers with a large firm), most of the benefits from incorporating still apply. (Note that the 2016 federal budget introduced a number of changes to corporate taxation when income is earned in a partnership or revenue is received from another company.)

Often I see physicians who are working in partnerships where they share the SBD have solutions put forward to fix this problem, but require a majority of their colleagues to be on board. In most cases it does make sense to enter into a cost-sharing arrangement or the advisable solution put forward by the legal team.

At first it seems costly with no SBD, as your corporate taxes go up from 12.2% to 26.5% (in Ontario; this varies per province). However, you do receive an enhanced credit on your dividends that can range from 8% to 12% less in personal taxes, making up for much of that loss in having no SBD.

How Does Purchasing a Home Fit into My Incorporation Timeline?

What if you are buying a home in six months to two years' time—does it still make sense to incorporate now? In a word, yes. Your home is a leveraged investment that grows tax-free, and, because of these characteristics that are unique to the principal residence, will likely be one of your best long-term investments . . . like a "super-TFSA," if you like.

You normally need between 25% and 35% of the purchase price as a down payment—and the fastest way to save the down payment is usually to incorporate.

(As a side note, I also advise clients that it is okay to potentially overreach a little more than normal on their home purchase price, to avoid having to purchase an intermediary home, and then eventually sell that intermediate home in order to purchase a long-term or "forever" home within a few years. That's because the transaction costs in real estate, such as real estate commissions paid on the sale, can be significant. When all the transaction costs are factored in, they might represent up to 10% of the purchase price—a cost that can be avoided if we could somehow speed up the process to get into that long-term home.)

Let's take a look at an example.

Saving for a Down Payment: Incorporated and Non-Incorporated Options

This example assumes the following:

- John is a physician earning $400,000 per year who wants to buy a condo in Toronto for $1,000,000.
- We'll assume the growth rate on the condo is 4% per year, but for the moment we'll ignore all real estate transaction costs (i.e., land transfer taxes, legal and real estate commissions, and so on).

- At a $400,000 income, John's *average* tax rate will be 44%, though his *marginal* rate will be 53.53%.
- Let's assume John needs $100,000 of after-tax ("take-home") pay to meet his day-to-day living expenses.
- John wants to save $250,000 as a 25% down payment on the condo.

With no corporation, based on these assumptions John could save $124,000 in the first year, and it would take him a total of two years and almost three months to make up the 25% down payment on a property that may well appreciate during John's "waiting period" (meaning his $250,000 no longer represents a 25% down payment).

If John incorporates, his average corporate tax rate would be 12.2%, and he could pay out $129,000 in dividends to fund his $100,000 lifestyle spending needs (at an average tax rate of 22%), allowing him to save $223,000 in the first year.

In this scenario, he will have a $250,000 down payment within a time frame of about 15 months—cutting an entire year off the time frame for saving the required down payment.

And not only does John save up the down payment more quickly, he also saves about $40,000 on the condo purchase price, given our projection about real estate appreciation over the waiting period. How is John able to realize his down payment savings strategy so quickly and effectively? The key is his use of a shareholder loan from his corporation, which we discuss next.

Can I Purchase My Principal Residence through My Corporation?

The answer is a qualified yes: you *can* purchase your principal residence through your corporation, but you usually *shouldn't*.

Why not? Because you'd be giving up one of the largest benefits the tax code allows, the principal residence exemption. This benefit allows all the gains in our homes to grow tax-free, but the benefit is eliminated if the home is owned by the corporation.

Let's look at the example of a family member of mine, who purchased their home in 1987 for $750,000. Fast-forward to 2017 and this same house was sold for $4,850,000 (a gain of $4.1 million over 30 years)—as a tear-down, believe it or not! Because the house qualified as their principal residence (sheltered under section 40(2)(b) of the Income Tax Act), they didn't have to pay even a cent of tax on the $4.1 million gain—compared to a tax bill of over $1 million if the corporation had owned the house. In a nutshell, if it's your plan to hold (own) the home for many years, or unless you think the house will not appreciate in value, it's best to own your home personally.

However, there are certain situations where one may want to consider owning their principal residence through the corporation.

Let's consider a situation in which you have almost all your funds in the corporation, which would result in a very large personal tax bill to come up with that 25%-plus down payment. Let's also assume we are purchasing a property to own for less than five years, so the likelihood of significant capital appreciation is relatively low.

In this case, the benefit of purchasing the property through the corporation would be to come up with the payments through lightly taxed corporate dollars, as opposed to much more heavily taxed personal dollars. However, given that the house is still a personal-use property (a tax concept that refers to items you own primarily for the personal use or enjoyment of your family and yourself), you would need to either pay rent to the corporation for the equivalent market rent—which results in having to pull out money from the corporation—or take a taxable benefit for the market rent.

The former (paying rent) allows further deductions in the corporation for many of the costs—such as interest, utilities, and hydro—but would likely result in a higher personal tax bill. That's because you would likely need to withdraw double the amount needed for rent in order to pay the tax due on the withdrawn income. This option could also create problems under the new passive income rules (which came into effect for taxation years beginning after 2018), as rental income (paid to your corporation) counts toward the $50,000 threshold.

All in all, the only situations in which we've seen it make sense to have the corporation own your principal residence is when you take a taxable benefit for the imputed rent. (This is a complicated area of tax law, where professional advice is most definitely warranted!)

In making your decision about whether to own your principal residence personally or through your corporation, you will need to estimate and weigh all these costs—loss of the principal residence exemption, potentially higher loan costs when borrowing corporately as opposed to personally—against the potential benefits, which are the savings of after-(corporate)-tax dollars versus after-(personal)-tax dollars.

What about Shareholder Loans?

As a shareholder, you can take a loan from your corporation. Here's how that works: you can personally borrow money from the corporation and will not have to repay the loan until one year after year-end, giving you a repayment window of up to 729 days. Shareholder loans can be helpful in situations like the one we've just discussed, when you need to take on debt for personal reasons—whether that's financing your personal residence, cottage, or vehicle.

On your corporate books, the loan will appear as an asset to your company and a liability to you. In repaying the loan, you will need to pay the daily prescribed interest rate (currently 2%) or have a deemed interest benefit, but this will be less than the current prime rate (currently 2.45%).[6] All things considered, I would much rather see you pay the prescribed interest rate to your corporation than a higher interest rate to the bank for your debt payments.

One more note about shareholder loans: it is very important to make sure you repay any loan you receive from the corporation. If you fail to repay the loan, you will have to add the borrowed amount to your personal income tax return, and you will be charged interest by the Canada Revenue Agency (CRA) for taxes owed. Also, once you have repaid the loan, you should avoid additional shareholder loans, as the CRA could potentially penalize you for a series of loans.

Does a Professional Corporation Give Me Creditor Protection?

A professional corporation differs from a "normal" corporation in that it offers no creditor protection to its directors and shareholders, and no protection from personal liability in the case of professional negligence.

While there are certain ways to ensure creditor protection for your assets, I believe the issue of creditor protection may not be as relevant in the medical industry, given that most professionals have coverage through their association. (Professionals should check with their provincial or territorial regulatory body for details on their particular circumstances.) The professional corporation can provide limited personal liability covering non-professional liabilities (such as office space lease liabilities and bank loans that are not personally guaranteed).

With that said, you can look at forming a separate holding corporation or investing in creditor-protected assets, such as segregated funds, to help provide extra measures of credit protection. Both options, however, will result in extra accounting, legal, or management fees—which is why a cost–benefit analysis should be completed with your financial advisor before you take any action.

If you own rental properties, however, we recommend using holding corporations for creditor protection. Although you may have adequate coverage through your association for your professional activities, that won't cover your rental properties, and a disgruntled tenant could lead to a creditor issue.

How Could I "Supercharge" My Charitable Donation?

Once you have incorporated, it's probably time to rethink how you donate to charity. Whether we're talking about donations that are as small as $25 to support a colleague's charitable run or tithing 10% of your income to your church, it is important to know the basics on how to maximize the tax effectiveness of your donation.

If you donate personally, you receive a 15% federal **credit** (plus provincial credit; e.g., in Ontario 5%) on your first $200, then a 29% federal credit (plus provincial credit, e.g., in Ontario 11%) after that, and finally a 33% super credit for people in the top tax bracket. Given that donations can be carried forward for five years, if your donated amount is under $200, you might as well defer it to a future year and claim all the donations together so you can benefit from the larger credit. Between 2013 and 2017, if this was your first donation—called the first-time donor's super credit—you would receive an additional credit of 25% on the first $1,000 in donations. (The first-time donor's super credit expired at the end of 2017.)

If you donate corporately, you receive a tax **deduction** from your donation. This tax deduction reduces your taxes on your active income.

Usually with professionals, tax deductions are worth more than tax credits. The exception would be if you happen to have a very low personal tax rate, with the result that you can take funds out of your corporation at a lower rate than the credit you are receiving from your donation credit. (Keep in mind, however, that we have to eventually make up every dollar we spend personally by pulling more money from the corporation.)

But beyond deductions versus credits, there are other ways to increase the tax efficiency of your donated dollars. What many Canadians don't realize is that as of May 2006, donations to registered charities of publicly listed securities are exempt from capital gains taxation on gains triggered as a result of the gift, making it more tax-efficient for donors to give securities directly to charity, rather than to sell them and give the proceeds to the charity.[7]

Let's look at an example of how this works: I work with a client who tithes to his local church, giving 10% of his income ($60,000 per year) to his church. To help him accomplish this goal, we set up a charitable account for him at no cost (note, many banks and financial institutions charge thousands for this setup/transaction).

When the time comes for his donation, I take the best-performing asset from the previous year and roll that over to the church. In the last transaction we did, it was an investment with a book value of $20,000 and a market value of $60,000. The church receives the same $60,000 they were to receive anyway, and they can sell the asset right away or hold on to it. The client, in turn, receives a $60,000 tax deduction, but this also saves him upwards of $10,000 in corporate taxes. Plus, the client can now withdraw $40,000 from his corporation tax-free through the capital dividend account (CDA). Since 0% of the gain is taxable, 100% of the gain is added to the CDA (see sections 83(2) and 38(a.1)(i) of the Income Tax Act).

Think about all the times you have donated, or will donate in the future, to see how much money is left on the table if you are not employing this specific strategy. You could even use those tax savings to donate to your second-favorite charity!

What Is the Lifetime Capital Gains Exemption (LCGE)?

The lifetime capital gains exemption (LCGE) is an exemption, valued at $883,384 for 2020 and indexed to inflation every year, that can be used when corporate shares are sold.

For example, if you sell your corporation for $883,384 as a share sale, not an asset sale, then you would have no taxable capital gain and pay no taxes.

Given every Canadian has access to the lifetime capital gains exemption, in many situations where the shares would sell for more than $883,384 (or whatever the limit is for that year), you would want to add family members, such as your spouse and/or children, to multiply the capital gains exemption. For instance, if you and your spouse each owned shares, for 2019 you would have, between the two of you, a total of $1,766,768 in tax exemptions ($883,384 × 2). You are not required to use the full LCGE all at once, however. Again, this can be a complex area requiring professional guidance.

(On a side note, a common misbelief is that this exemption is in some way related to the capital gains from the growth on your investments. While these are both forms of capital gain, their tax treatment is very different!)

Keep in mind the CGE only applies to the selling of shares, and not the selling of assets. This can sometimes lead to a mismatch between the seller and a prospective buyer, as sometimes the buyer would prefer to buy the assets, but—given the CGE—the seller would often be better off selling the shares. For example, you can see this mismatch when a seller is purchasing equipment that has already been depreciated on the balance sheet by the previous owner. As a buyer, you may then be in a position in which you are buying equipment for a higher value than you can depreciate, given the seller has already received the tax benefits from the years of depreciation. Depending on your side of this transaction, you may want to leverage this mismatch to influence the selling price.

Most physicians will not be able to benefit from this exemption, as it requires you to find a buyer for your medical practice. (A practice sale is much more common with dentists.) However, in recent years we have seen a rise in the sale of medical practices, given the value of patient rostering or family health organization (FHO) practices (using the FHO compensation model).

In order to qualify for the CGE, the corporation must qualify as a small business corporation at the time of sale. In order to qualify, two criteria must be met, the first being that you, or a person related to you, must have owned the shares for a 24-month holding period immediately prior to the sale. Secondly, 90% of the assets at the time of sale, and more than 50% of the fair market value of the assets held during the 24-month holding period, must have been used for carrying on an active business in Canada, or be shares and debt held in other small business corporations (or a combination of these two types of assets).

For corporations that will not pass this test, there is a "purification" method to allow the shares to qualify. In order to purify your shares and thus qualify for the CGE, you will need to set up a holding company to transfer assets to. It's very important to do this correctly. For instance, if you transfer funds as intercorporate debt, as opposed to an intercorporate dividend, your shares may be ineligible for the exemption. It should be also noted that while most assets can be transferred in kind, some assets—such as permanent insurance—may give rise to a taxable benefit if the cash surrender value (CSV) of the policy exceeds its adjusted cost base (ACB), though the ACB is usually negligible or nil in the earlier years of the policy. This is why it's best to plan this sale carefully, to avoid paying unnecessary tax.

Before we leave this topic, note that the lifetime CGE has evolved since its creation in 1986. It started with a $500,000 lifetime exemption on any type of capital gain, such as a cottage sale. In this early form, many Canadians could reap the rewards of the CGE. Then, in 1994, the CGE was reduced to $100,000 and subsequently restricted to the sale of qualified small business property, including farm and fishing property. As a result, many Canadians "crystallized" (or claimed) $100,000 of exempt capital gains.

This history is important as it demonstrates that tax policies can and do change. While many incorporated professionals will plan to use their CGE in retirement, in many scenarios it may make sense to use the lifetime CGE now, anticipating a potential rule change in the future. To use the exemption before retirement, you would trigger capital gains, resulting in an increase to the cost base of the shares. Then, when the shares are sold in the future the amount of tax paid would be dramatically reduced, due to the adjusted (increased) cost base.

Now That I Have Incorporated, Can I Deduct My Golf Membership Fees?

In a word, no!

Dues for recreational or dining clubs, such as golf or tennis clubs, are not deductible expenses, *even if* the expense has a business purpose, as there is a specific rule in section 18(1)(l) of the Income Tax Act that prohibits the deduction of all recreational club dues. For meals and beverages consumed at golf clubs and the like, however, the deductibility rules are the same as those that would apply at other restaurants, so long as the costs are separately itemized (they are generally 50% deductible, with some exceptions). If the full charge is shown and not itemized, the full deduction is generally disallowed.

As an aside, there was a Tax Court of Canada case involving Gillis Truckways Inc. (*Gillis v. The Queen*—2005 TCC 782) in which a golf membership was paid for by a corporation. In that case, the CRA reassessed a taxable benefit of 100% of the cost of the membership to Mr. Gillis, who brought the case to court; the judge directed the CRA to lower the taxable benefit down to 40% of the membership cost. Maybe with a golf lobby group the current tax rules could change!

What Do I Do with My Corporation When I Retire?

Assuming you do not sell your practice shares, when you retire your professional corporation needs to remove the "professional" title, leaving you with a numbered holding company. This is usually done with the help of a lawyer and your accountant, but this change doesn't require you to sell any assets nor does it trigger any taxes. In addition, this change also allows you to modify the structure of shares however you wish. When looking at estate planning purposes, for example, you may want to freeze the value of your shares and issue new growth shares to other family members, or to a trust, to transfer future growth and taxes to that member.

Real-Life Case Example of Restructuring Shares

In 2015, I sat down with a client in his late 60s who had a significant amount of assets in his corporation, which we'll call "123456 Ontario Limited."

The client ultimately wanted to pass on his assets to his daughters in a tax-efficient manner. We collectively decided any life insurance solution was off the table—and starting in 2016, new top tax rates were coming into effect, with new surtaxes.

Here are my notes for the transaction we implemented:

Redemption of Preferred Shares Prior to December 31, 2015

Background: At present, retaining eligible dividend income within an Ontario corporation defers 0.49% in personal tax (the difference between the Part IV tax rate of 33.33% and the top personal marginal tax rate on eligible dividends of 33.82%). Assuming the Liberal party platform tax rate proposals are implemented, the top personal tax rate on eligible dividends will jump to 39.34%.

- 123456 Ontario Limited has a general rate income pool (GRIP) balance of $1,295,018 (calculated as of April 30, 2015), which would allow for the payment of an eligible dividend of the same amount.
- The payment of a $1.3 million dividend would result in personal tax of approximately $439,660, but generate a refund of tax to the corporation of $433,333 (an incremental tax cost of $6,327).

Recommendation: As an alternative to paying a dividend, 123456 Ontario Limited could redeem a portion of the preferred shares issued to you.

- Assuming the preferred shares have a paid-up capital (PUC) (to be confirmed by your accounting firm), a redemption of $1.3 million worth of shares would generate a taxable dividend of approximately $1.3 million to you (the taxable dividend is the difference between the redemption amount and the PUC of the shares).

- The dividend can be designated by the corporation as an eligible dividend to the extent of the corporation's GRIP balance at the time of the share redemption.
- The advantage is that for a current net tax cost of $6,327, the future tax exposure of your estate will be reduced by a minimum of $347,880 (based on the anticipated 2016 top tax rate on capital gains of 26.76%), but more likely by as much as $519,220, assuming the preferred shares will be redeemed on your passing (and based on an anticipated 2016 top tax rate of 39.34% on eligible dividends).

While this transaction took several steps, one can see that with the easing of restrictions on corporations in retirement, there are a lot more potential opportunities for planning!

Key Takeaways from This Chapter

- In many cases, professionals and business owners who are able to incorporate should do so—and the process may cost less than you think. So if you're able to incorporate but have not yet done so, ask your professional advisors why not?
- The main benefits of incorporation include the increased flexibility and control you gain, which can allow you to reduce your tax bill each and every year you're incorporated.
- Despite the benefits of incorporation, there are situations in which incorporating your business or establishing a professional corporation doesn't make sense. If one or more of those situations applies to you, consider holding off until the time is right.
- Finally, keep in mind that the corporation isn't a "magic solution" to create tax benefits out of thin air: you'll still need to play by the tax rules within the structure of your corporation.

Top Questions to Ask Your Financial Planner

1. If you're not incorporated and believe you're able to incorporate and the time is right, ask your professional advisors why not?
2. If the time isn't right for you to incorporate now, ask your advisors when they think the time might be right for you, and for a plan to get you there.
3. If you are incorporated, ask your advisors to walk you through how the corporate structure is being used to it's full advantage for you, using this chapter as a guide.
4. If you are incorporated, do you have a plan for what happens with the corporation once you transition into retirement?

Notes

1. More information on the steps that follow incorporation can be found on the Government of Canada's Corporations Canada website at https://www.ic.gc.ca/eic/site/cd-dgc.nsf/eng/cs06646.html. Corporations Canada is Canada's federal corporate regulator.

2. Under section 248(1) of the Income Tax Act, the three-month limit is only available to CCPCs that (a) claimed the small business deduction in the current or previous year, and (b) did not exceed the small business limit on an associated group basis.

3. For more information, refer to the Canada Revenue Agency's web page on late filing of information returns at https://www.canada.ca/en/revenue-agency/services/tax/businesses/topics/payroll/penalties-interest-other-consequences/payroll-penalties-interest.html#late_filing_info_return.

4. For more information on your record-keeping responsibilities, refer to the Canada Revenue Agency's website at https://www.canada.ca/en/

revenue-agency/services/tax/businesses/topics/keeping-records.html.

5. For more information on student loan forgiveness for family doctors, refer to this Government of Canada web page: https://www.canada.ca/en/services/benefits/education/student-aid/grants-loans/repay/assistance/doctors-nurses.html.

6. Information on the prescribed rate can be found on the Government of Canada website, at https://www.canada.ca/en/revenue-agency/services/tax/prescribed-interest-rates.html. The prime rate is usually the interest rate at which banks lend to customers with good credit. It's the annual interest rate that Canada's major banks and financial institutions use to set interest rates for variable loans and lines of credit, including variable-rate mortgages.

7. For more information, refer to the Government of Canada website, https://www.canada.ca/en/revenue-agency/services/tax/individuals/topics/about-your-tax-return/tax-return/completing-a-tax-return/deductions-credits-expenses/line-34900-donations-gifts/capital-gains-realized-on-gifts-certain-capital-property.html.

Chapter 2

The Compensation Decision: Salary or Dividends?

L et's say it's a new tax year, and you're marking the start of it by asking yourself a question:

Should I pay myself a salary, should I pay myself in dividends, or should I do some combination of both?

In looking for answers to this question, there's no shortage of opinions. Your accountant may tell you one thing, your colleagues are all doing different things, advice from the big banks and accounting firms are different, and there are even articles in the mainstream financial papers—such as the *Globe and Mail* and the *Financial Post*—that completely contradict each other. What's the right advice for you?

What You'll Get Out of This Chapter

One of the biggest and most important questions you'll face as an incorporated professional or business owner is around your personal compensation.

If the corporation earns income (and not you personally, as if you were an employee), somehow that income has to move from the corporation to you—and you have a choice about how that happens.

Depending on which compensation option you select—salary, dividends, or a mix of both—you'll face different tax issues both while you're working and in retirement.

How do you decide which of the possible compensation options is the best fit for your personal situation? This chapter runs through the implications of each choice, with some examples to illustrate the impacts of different options. By the end, you should have a basic understanding of the compensation choices you face, and where to start in selecting the option for you.

Understanding the Roots of the Compensation Question

Anyone who has a corporation has likely asked these questions at some point—and while there's a lot of opinion and analysis out there, most of it looks at the issue from the perspective of just the current tax year (a tactical approach) and may ignore the long-term financial implications (a strategic approach).

It's not uncommon for business owners to pay themselves in dividends from their corporation, and we generally advise most clients to explore this approach—but only if you've considered all of the other planning points that relate to this decision. That is, your business structure, your risk tolerance in your investments, and your insurance plan should be all be interconnected to support your specific salary–dividend mix.

Sound confusing? Let's go over the basics of the salary-versus-dividends conversation, and then dive into more detail.

Salary as Compensation

First things first: salary dollars are an expense to the corporation, which lowers corporate taxable income and, in turn, reduces corporate taxes.

- Individual salaries can create registered retirement savings plan (RRSP) room, up to prescribed annual limits.
- Salaries require contributions to the Canada Pension Plan (CPP) and qualify you for CPP (retirement and disability) benefits.
- Salaries are required to apply tax credits and deductions such as child care.
- Salaries create T4 income that simplifies the process to qualify for a mortgage or line of credit.
- Salaries require regular payroll remittances (and T4s issued by the end of each February).
- Salaries are required to be "reasonable" and commensurate with the work actually carried out by the employee.

Dividends as Compensation

Dividends are paid to shareholders from the after-corporate tax dollars inside your corporation.

- Dividends receive a dividend tax credit.
- Dividends do not create RRSP room.
- Dividends do not require (and are not eligible for) CPP contributions.

- Dividends incur no payroll source deductions, and no T4 income slips are issued.
- Dividends require T5 slips to be issued by the end of February.
- Paying out dividends allow for refundable dividend tax on hand (RDTOH) to be reimbursed.[1]
- Dividends require no monthly remittance, and can be paid at any time or frequency, whether once a year or 365 times a year.
- Dividend amounts are not required to be "reasonable" unless they fail the new tax on split income (TOSI) rules.

With this basic background in place, let's take a look at the decision-making factors that will allow you to evaluate the salary-versus-dividends decision in your compensation.

Dividend-Splitting with Family Members

The Old Rules: Pre-2018

Prior to 2018, a dividend could be paid, subject to the share provisions, rights, and restrictions of the relevant classes of shares, to family members (who were 18 or older) of the owner of a Canadian-controlled private corporation. By splitting the company's income among several family members, the family as a whole could reduce the overall tax it paid.

Under the old rules, since 2006, I've been advising clients to use income-splitting opportunities, and not be shy about taking advantage of them. If you had an 18-year-old child who had no other income, you could pay that child $50,000, $60,000, or $70,000 in dividends and they would, in turn, pay very little taxes. In fact, they could even simply gift you these proceeds back, as we have no gift tax in Canada (unlike other countries).

In contrast to that advice, under the pre-2018 rules, many accountants were advising against paying too much" in dividends to children, as it could raise red flags with the Canada Revenue Agency (CRA).

In the end, while there were no CRA rulings against this particular form of tax planning, the new TOSI rules, implemented at the start of 2018, put an end to this opportunity.

Whether old rules or new, my bottom-line thinking is that *when you are allowed an opportunity to save some taxes, take advantage while you can.* I subscribe to the notion of playing legally and honestly in the rules of the game, and what is known as "tax avoidance" is fully within the rights of any taxpayer. If the rules change, we should then adapt—but until then, I think of it as our financial duty to pay as little tax as possible.

(Note: for a non-professional corporation, a child can receive dividends if they are at least 25 years of age and own at least 10% of the voting shares and value of the family business. It is safe to assume here that no dividends can be issued to children, given that we are generally dealing with professional corporations.)

The New Rules: Tax on Split Income—2019 and Afterwards

On December 13, 2017, the federal government released legislation with the intent to simplify the income-sprinkling rules (referred to as the tax on split income or TOSI) previously released on July 18, 2017. The intention of the legislation is to prevent the allocation of income to family members who are not involved in a business. The new legislation came into effect on January 1, 2018.

Under the new rules, there are still opportunities to split or sprinkle income. These opportunities relate to family members working for a corporation that carries on the professional practice of an accountant, dentist, lawyer, medical doctor, veterinarian, or chiropractor.

A family member can receive dividends from a Canadian-controlled private corporation if any of the following conditions are met:

1. The family member worked in the business for at least 20 hours per week continuously in the current tax year or for at least 20 hours per week for the five prior years; or who are actively engaged on a regular, continuous, and substantial basis in the activities of the business;
2. The amount of the dividend paid is reasonable based on the work performed; and
3. The owner of the corporation is over 65 years of age.

With the new TOSI rules, while they are more complicated for children aged 18–24, my view is that the federal government and the CRA have left the door open with respect to spousal dividends.

Here's my thinking: If it's difficult for your spouse to justify 20 hours a week of work in the current year, have they worked for five years in the past?

Keep in mind that the five years do not have to be consecutive, nor do they have to be the immediately preceding five years—they could be any five years working for your business while that business is in existence.

Looking at your spouse's involvement in your business, is there a documented track record of dividends and salary to support this? If the answer is "yes" then the rules are binary: you are in!

Therefore, you have no "reasonableness test"—meaning you can pay $1 in dividends or $1,000,000 in dividends without needing to justify the payments as "reasonable."

For those who do not meet this five-year test but are close, I would start looking at scenarios where you start building up to this case scenario, as the tax savings could be significant. In fact, there may even be situations where it's advisable for a spouse to take a leave of absence from their other paid work to work for your corporation and allow for future dividends to be paid.

In 2018, a politician asked federal Finance Minister Morneau how one would prove their past record in respect to dividend payments to a spouse, given that there was no requirement to track previous dividends. The response was that our tax system is based on the honour system. With that said, one should seek the advice of their accountant here.

A good accountant would also recommend that you start recording your spouse's contributions on timesheets on a moving-forward basis to validate these claims.

The pushback reasonable approach I hear sometimes from accountants is, why not pay yourself $150,000 in salary and your spouse $50,000 as an office manager to avoid any of the new rule changes?

This echoes accountants' recommending against significant dividends to the children prior to the TOSI rules, and the logic remains flawed:

- If you are paying your spouse a $50,000 salary and at the same time are also saying that your spouse does not work 20 hours a week, then your spouse is making more than $50 per hour in an administrative position.
- We would likely have a hard time defending $50 per hour paid to a spouse for a role that an arm's-length person would willingly do for half that wage rate.

The reason these factors are important is that if we pass the reasonableness test and can issue dividends to our spouses, this helps out the case for paying all compensation in dividends, so we can likely income-split in a less restricted way.

Conversely, with income splitting available through the corporation, if one family member is paying a much higher amount in taxes than the other, that should be a red flag that we are doing something wrong.

Let's look at an example.

Scenario 1: John and Jane with Salary

John has a $150,000 salary and pays his spouse Jane a salary of $50,000. Let's assume that both John and Jane are residents of Ontario who maximize their RRSPs and are exempt from Employment Insurance, given that they own more than 40% of the shares of the corporation; in addition, this analysis does not incorporate the Climate Action incentive. See Table 2.1.

Scenario 2: John and Jane with Dividends

That same active income instead is deposited into the corporation and taxed at the small business deduction (SBD) rate. Afterwards, John and Jane pay each other an equal amount in dividends to accommodate the same cash-flow needs as are set out in scenario 1. (Note that we've kept the same assumptions as for Scenario 1; see Table 2.2.)

Table 2.1 Ontario Scenario 1: Corporation's Income $500,000, $150,000 Salary, and $50,000 Salary

		Salary	Salary	Combination
Income:	Employment	$150,000	$ 50,000	$200,000
Expenses:	CPP	$ 2,749	$ 2,372	$ 5,121
	RRSP	$ 26,500	$ 9,000	$ 35,500
	Income taxes	$ 34,335	$ 5,667	$ 40,002
Net after-tax cash flow		$ 86,416	$ 33,961	$ 119,377
Corporation's after-tax position				
Income before salary/bonus		$500,000		
	Salary expense	$200,000		
	Payroll expense (CPP)	$ 5,121		
	Corporate income taxes	$ 36,860		
Net after-tax cash flow		$258,019		

Table 2.2 Ontario Scenario 2: Corporation's Income $500,000, $67,037 Dividend × 2

		Salary	Salary	Combination
Income:	Dividend—non-eligible	$ 67,037	$ 67,037	$134,074
Expenses:	CPP	$–	$–	$–
	RRSP	$–	$–	$–
	Income taxes	$ 7,349	$ 7,349	$ 14,697
Net after-tax cash flow		$ 59,688	$ 59,688	$119,377
Corporation's after-tax position				
Income before salary/bonus		$500,000		
	Corporate income taxes	$ 62,500		
After-tax cash flow		$437,500		
	Dividend—non-eligible	$134,074		
Net after-tax cash flow		$303,426		

Looking at Scenario 2, you can see the benefit of $45,407 more in the corporation, at the expense of $35,500 in RRSPs and CPP payments. Given that CPP can technically be viewed as a tax, this is a tax savings of $9,907.

Tax Integration

So, what if no income-splitting opportunities exist and we are looking at one shareholder in isolation with a small business deduction? Now is a good time to bring up the concept of *tax integration* and examine much of the analysis that has been done on this subject.

With perfect tax integration (between personal and corporate rates), individuals should be "tax indifferent" between:

- Carrying on business through a corporation, as a sole proprietor, or as a member of a partnership; and
- Earning investment income personally or through a corporation.

In addition, with perfect integration, total tax (corporate and personal) on income earned through a corporation should theoretically equal total tax on income earned directly by an individual.

However, tax integration is not perfect. Not only that, but much of the past analysis, I believe, makes a glaringly wrong assumption by comparing *the same salary being paid out versus the same dividend*. That analysis shows a small tax-rate advantage paying dividends in Saskatchewan, Newfoundland, and Labrador, but a disadvantage in the other provinces.[2]

The flaw I see here is that as personal tax rates are lower with dividends, you don't need to pay out as much from the corporation to meet the same cash-flow needs—and therefore you can pay out less in dividends.

When using the concept of meeting cash-flow needs as your baseline assumption, one can see there is (often) a benefit, albeit very small, in paying out dividends. The following are some examples.

Salary versus Dividend Examples

Scenario 1: John's After-Tax Cash Flow: With Salary

John has a $150,000 salary and maximizes his RRSP. Note: these numbers can slightly vary if we are considering Jane to have zero income, or if John is a single adult. See Table 2.3.

Table 2.3 Ontario Scenario 1: Corporation's Income
$500,000, $150,000 Salary

		Salary
Income:	Employment	$150,000
Expenses:	CPP	$ 2,749
	RRSP	$ 26,500
	Income taxes	$ 34,355
Net after-tax cash flow		$ 86,416
Corporation's after-tax position		
Income before salary/bonus		$500,000
	Salary expense	$150,000
	Payroll expense (CPP)	$ 2,749
	Corporate income taxes	$ 43,406
Net after-tax cash flow		$303,845

Scenario 2: John's After-Tax Cash Flow: With Dividends

In this case, that same active income instead is deposited into the corporation and taxed at the small business deduction rate. Afterwards, John pays an amount in dividends to accommodate the same cash-flow needs in Scenario 1. Note: these figures assume that Jane has sufficient income from other sources (i.e., no spousal amount or other credits allocated to John). See Table 2.4.

Overall, looking at Scenario 2 in isolation—ignoring all other factors—one can benefit by having $27,855 more in the corporation at the expense of $26,500 in RRSPs and CPP payments. Given that CPP can technically be viewed as a tax, this is a potential tax savings of $1,355.

Overall, the decision boils down this way:

- If income-splitting opportunities exist, dividends should likely be the preferred route.
- If there are no other income-splitting opportunities, I would look at other factors when considering salary versus dividends.

Table 2.4   Ontario Scenario 2: Corporation's Income
$500,000, $105,800 Dividend

		Dividend
Income:	Dividend—non-eligible	$105,800
Expenses:	CPP	$–
	RRSP	–
	Income taxes	$ 19,384
Net after-tax cash flow		$ 86,416
Corporation's after-tax position		
Income before salary/bonus		$500,000
	Corporate income taxes	$ 62,500
After-tax cash flow		$437,500
	Dividend—non-eligible	$105,800
Net after-tax cash flow		$331,700

Do You Want to Put Your Savings in an RRSP or in Your Corporation?

The next issue to resolve is *where* your saved compensation is stored. If you are paying out salary, you have RRSP room and can contribute to an RRSP and get a tax deduction. But should you—or should you save funds in the corporation?

Anyone who has been through a financial analysis has probably seen their net worth statement—and while it's true that a dollar in the RRSP is equal to a dollar in the corporation on the net worth statement, it is absolutely not true that the two are equal in practice. In fact, for many professional corporations, the dollar in the corporation is worth more.

We need to look at this from a few different viewpoints: the value in the corporation today, the tax characteristics of the expected growth on your investments, whether you expect to have assets (in either your RRSP or the corporation) at death, and certain other factors such as expectations about any future tax changes.

The Value in the RRSP/Corporation Today

If you have $1,000,000 cash in the RRSP and $1,000,000 cash in the corporation, whether you pay this out over 1, 10, or 50 years, you'll always be in a lower tax bracket with corporation money than with RRSP money.

Why? Because when we take out money from the RRSP, the proceeds are taxed as (ordinary) income (like interest or employment income).

In contrast, when we take out money from the corporation, the proceeds are taxed as a dividend and we receive a dividend tax credit. As a result, regardless of how much we withdraw, *we will always be in a lower tax bracket with dividends than with salary* given the benefit of the dividend tax credit.

In the right-hand columns of Table 2.5, you can see the difference between salary versus eligible dividends and salary versus

Table 2.5 Combined 2020 Federal and Provincial Tax Rates in Ontario

Taxable Income			Ontario Tax Rates				
			Marginal rate on:				
Lower Limit		Upper Limit	Rate on Excess	Eligible Dividend Income (EDI)	Ineligible Dividend Income (IDI)	Rate— EDI	Rate— IDI
$ –	to	$ 13,229	0.00%	0.00%	0.00%	0.00%	0.00%
13,230	to	15,714	15.00%	0.00%	6.87%	15.00%	8.13%
15,715	to	20,644	25.10%	0.00%	11.61%	25.10%	13.49%
20,645	to	44,740	20.05%	0.00%	9.24%	20.05%	10.81%
44,741	to	48,535	24.15%	0.00%	13.95%	24.15%	10.20%
48,536	to	78,786	29.65%	7.56%	20.28%	22.09%	9.37%
78,787	to	89,482	31.48%	8.92%	22.38%	22.56%	9.42%
89,483	to	92,827	33.89%	12.24%	25.16%	21.65%	8.73%
92,828	to	97,069	37.91%	17.79%	29.78%	20.12%	8.13%
97,070	to	150,000	43.41%	25.38%	36.10%	18.03%	7.31%
150,001	to	150,473	44.97%	27.53%	37.90%	17.44%	7.07%
150,474	to	214,368	48.19%	31.97%	41.60%	16.22%	6.59%
214,369	to	220,000	51.97%	37.19%	45.95%	14.78%	6.02%
220,001	and up		53.53%	39.34%	47.74%	14.19%	5.79%

ineligible dividends. But whether you are saving 25.10% or 5.79%, you will be saving by using dividends as opposed to salary.

The Tax Characteristics of Growth on the Investments

Assuming tax rates remain constant, over time, the results differ, depending on the type of income that is generated on the investments.

If you earn interest income or dividend income—especially foreign dividend income—on your investments, the tax-deferred characteristic of the RRSP allows for a tax advantage to be invested in the RRSP.

However, if the majority of your gains are in the form of tax-deferred capital gains, there is an advantage to investing through the corporation. The longer your time horizon for money being kept inside the corporation for investing, the more magnified these differences become.

Figure 2.1 compares interest, Canadian eligible dividends, realized capital gains each year, and tax-deferred capital gains on a $100,000 RRSP/corporation portfolio withdrawn 20 years later at a 6% rate of return.

RRSP Scenarios

- $100,000 invested for 20 years at 6%.
- Assumed amounts already contributed.

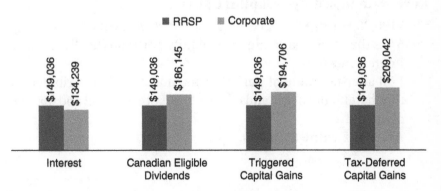

Figure 2.1 After-Tax Investment Income: RRSP versus Corporate Investing

- Full value of RRSP portfolio distributed to the individual at the end of year 20 and taxed personally at 53.53%.
- **After-tax value $149,036.**

Corporate Investing—Interest

- $100,000 invested in a corporation for 20 years at 6%.
- 6% is the interest rate on a Canadian fixed-income portfolio (no capital appreciation).
- Full after-tax value of portfolio distributed to the shareholder at the end of year 20 as a dividend and taxed personally at 47.74%.
- **After-tax value $134,239.**

Corporate Investing—Eligible Dividends

- $100,000 invested in a corporation for 20 years at 6%.
- 6% is the dividend rate on a Canadian dividend portfolio (no capital appreciation).
- Full after-tax value of portfolio (including RDTOH recovered) distributed to the shareholder at the end of year 20 as a dividend and taxed personally at 47.74% on the original capital and 39.34% on the growth.
- **After-tax value $186,145.**

Corporate Investing—Capital Gains

- $100,000 invested in a corporation for 20 years at 6%.
- 6% is the capital gain rate on an equity portfolio (no dividend or interest income).
- Full after-tax value of portfolio (including CDA) distributed to the shareholder at the end of year 20 as both a capital and taxable dividend.
- **After-tax value $194,706.**

Corporate Investing—Deferred Capital Gains
- $100,000 invested in a corporation for 20 years at 6%.
- 6% is the deferred capital gain rate on an equity portfolio (no dividend or interest income).
- Full after-tax value of portfolio (including CDA) distributed to the shareholder at the end of year 20 as both a capital and taxable dividend.
- **After-tax value $209,042.**

In drawing these conclusions, we're relying on the following assumptions:

1. You're always in the highest personal tax bracket;
2. You are fully recapturing all available RDTOH every year and the capital dividend account (CDA) account in year 20—which previous online articles have ignored; and
3. There's no change in tax laws.

Previous published analysis has concluded that based on your current portfolio structure, you should lean one way or another based on these conclusions.

I would look at this and ask: How do we get to the optimal scenario of tax-deferred capital gains (more on that in Chapter 3)? It would be nice to have a head start in our investing before we even generate a return.

Given these examples, one can see how risk tolerance comes into play here. If you're a conservative investor investing in guaranteed investment certificates (GICs) and bonds, then the RRSP has an edge here. However, if your investor profile is moderate to aggressive, and you're holding equities favouring deferred capital gains, corporate investing with tax-efficient investments is the preferred route.

(Note that passive income can vary in different provinces; specifically, if you're in Manitoba, Newfoundland, Nova Scotia, or Prince

Edward Island, these benefits may be slightly minimized given their corporate and personal rate differentials.)

Will We Pass Away with Funds in Our RRSP or Corporation?

Much of the analysis done on salary versus dividends makes the following two assumptions:

1. The tax rates today will be the same tomorrow.
2. We will spend every dollar we save in our lifetime.

Both of these assumptions are probably very wrong!

For those of us who are following policy changes, not just in Canada but in the global community, we can see the trend toward increasing personal tax rates. And unless someone's financial plan is to retire the day they have the exact amount saved up to satisfy their unchanging and exact cash-flow needs until age 95, the likelihood—especially with high-income earners—is that you will pass away with assets still available.

Today, if you pass away with funds in your RRSP, the proceeds roll over on a tax-deferred basis to your spouse (assuming they are the designated beneficiary)—potentially creating a larger tax hit during their lifetime given the higher mandated RRIF withdrawal value (but more on that later). When both spouses are deceased, then the final tax bill on the RRSP/RRIF can be as high as 53.53% in Ontario.

With the corporation, when one passes away, the proceeds roll over on a tax-deferred basis to the surviving spouse, as well (assuming, again, they are the beneficiary). When both spouses are deceased, the final tax bill on the corporate assets will likely be lower than the top rate of 48% given the benefit of the capital dividend account (CDA). (There are also other advanced tax planning strategies to mitigate this, i.e., pipeline strategies, but for most corporations these would not be applicable.)

However, the monumental difference between the two scenarios is that with corporate assets you can purchase insurance to allow for very little tax to be paid (more on that in Chapter 4), but with the RRSP, you cannot. Having a strategy to avoid upwards of taxes paid at 48% or 53% can mean your corporate dollars may be approximately 50% more valuable to your estate.

Overall, when choosing between salary and dividends, I would recommend weighing the likelihood of you passing away with assets (which involves making some predictions about your spending in retirement). If that is the scenario, then I would lean toward dividends as having some powerful tools to increase estate value.

Other Factors

Increased Financial Control

- When you turn age 71, you will need to convert your RRSP to a RRIF with mandatory withdrawals, whether you need these funds or not.
- This could give rise to an unnecessarily high tax bill and also could potentially result in a clawback of income-tested government benefits, such as Old Age Security.
- With the corporation we do not have this forced withdrawal problem and can choose to take funds or not, regardless of age.
- However, it should be noted that dividends are "grossed-up" for tax purposes—either 15% for ineligible dividends or 38% for eligible dividends. It's the grossed-up value that matters to the CRA in terms of the clawback threshold.
- Overall, in terms of revenue control, corporate assets are more favorable.

Psychological Factors

- Many accountants will point out that one is more likely to spend retirement savings if those savings are easily accessible. It's safe to say most professionals would not consider tapping into their RRSP for vacations or car purchases, but could be tempted to withdraw corporate funds for discretionary expenditures.

- If you know you are a spendthrift with your money, lacking discipline, then perhaps the RRSP is a better option to consider in the mix—simply because it reduces ease of access to already-allocated funds.

Creditor Protection

- Assuming you don't have a separate holding company or a family trust, the funds in your corporation could potentially be up for grabs if your company is sued.
- While most professionals have some type of protection or coverage at their work that would likely cover the lawsuit, the RRSP provides an extra layer of creditor protection that the corporation does not.
- While many stress this benefit, given all the other factors, I would look first into entertaining the idea of setting up a separate holding company or family trust if this is a matter of concern.

Future Tax Law Changes

- One should always be aware of the trend line in discussions of tax law changes.
- While governments can do as they wish, the rules you want to be especially well-versed on are the capital gains inclusion rate, dividend tax rates, and personal tax rates.
- Any significant changes here could swing the benefit of salary versus dividends compensation one way or the other.

Do We Want to Participate in the Canadian Pension Plan (CPP)?

As a Canadian, I fully support employees paying into CPP as a benefit for retirement. It's a forced savings program that provides a stable safety net, it helps prevent spending-out savings, and for employees it has a decent rate of return.

Additionally, there are minor disability benefits if you become mentally or physically disabled with a "severe and prolonged" disability, as long as you have contributed 4 of the past 6 years, or 3 of the past 6 years if you have contributed for more than 25 years previously.

CPP also provides survivor benefits as long as you contributed to CPP for 3 years, or if your contribution period is longer than 9 years, you must have contributed one-third of the calendar years or a total of 10 calendar years previously.

The objective of CPP (before reforms that began to be implemented in 2019) was to replace gross income equal to 25% of the average career earning up to a ceiling (currently $58,700). In 2020, the maximum pension per month is $1,175.83.

For now, let's assume most take CPP at age 65. A side discussion is the 0.6% reduction per month if you take it early (age 60) and the 0.7% bonus if you take it late (age 70).

CPP sounds okay, right? *Wrong.*

First, there is a large discrepancy between the returns earned by the Canada Pension Plan Investment Board (CPPIB), which manages the investable funds, and the returns received by individual Canadian workers in the form of CPP retirement benefits.

Specifically, in 2003, the real rate of return for CPP retirees was 6.3%. By 2015, the real rate of return for CPP retirees had declined to 3.6%. There are two major reasons for the decline in the rates of return:

1. The periods of contribution for Canadian workers has changed—originally it was only 10 years; now it's 39 years.
2. There has been an increasing contribution rate to CPP.

CPP is *even less okay* when you consider self-employed individuals with professional corporations. Self-employed workers have to contribute both the employee portion and the employer portion of CPP for the exact same benefit that "regular" employees receive, when those employees only contribute half the amount!

In 2020, that CPP premium amount is $2,898 times 2. While the benefit is okay for employees, the benefit becomes less than okay for those who are both the employee and employer.

Beware the Overpayment Trap

An interesting negative tax trap should also be noted—and avoided. If you have a spouse earning employment income from another source, and you pay them a salary, you will be responsible for their specific CPP contributions, while their other employer would also be responsible for their specific CPP salary contributions.

The CPP rules only apply on a company-to-company basis and the overcontribution rules do not take into consideration possible multiple salaries from employers.

While one can apply for a refund (the amount is refunded on Line 44800 for individuals on filing of the tax return), the spouse could potentially end up in a situation where they have overpaid the maximum CPP contribution amount, but receive no additional benefit from this overpayment.

CPP Trends to Watch

From 2004 to 2018, contributions increased 42% while benefits increased 39%. More importantly, the largest CPP contribution increase was announced in December 2018—going from a 4.95% employee contribution rate to 5.25% in 2020 to an eventual 5.7% employee contribution rate—and the benefits from these increased contributions do not hit their stride until 2065.

Also, for those who are following topics in the OECD (the Organisation for Economic Co-operation and Development), there have been conversations regarding combining government benefits. As it stands today, Old Age Security, Guaranteed Income Supplement, and the allowances are all income-tested. I would hate to see clients pay into a plan in which they have absolutely no control over the outcome and are at the whims of government policy years down the road.

Bottom-Line Considerations

For those of us who have a salary over $3,500, we have to pay into CPP as long as we are under age 65. However, for those of us who are paying dividends, we do not have to contribute to CPP.

The real question to answer is: Are you more likely to invest the difference at a better rate of return or to continue with CPP? Perhaps even more importantly, will our estate receive more from our investments . . . or from CPP benefits?

While a proper analysis for each individual situation is warranted, if past performance is at least an indicator for future performance, *I believe that for most professionals who must double up on CPP contributions, the returns are not very attractive.*

Do We Have Investments Inside the Corporation?

The more investments you have in the corporation, the more advantageous it is to pay yourself in dividends as opposed to salary. That's because with dividends, we receive all RDTOH to the tune of $1 of RDTOH refunded for every $2.61 of dividends paid out (or $38^1/_3$ cents refunded for every $1 in dividends paid).

While the benefit is capped—that is, in Ontario passive income's 50.17% interest is reduced to 19.5%, 38.33% eligible Canadian dividends is reduced to 0% and 25% effective capital gains tax is reduced to 9.75%—this could still work out to a substantial tax savings per year.

For instance, if one has a significant portfolio, paying out $150,000 in dividends personally could equate up to $57,692 in tax savings given RDTOH recapture. If in this same scenario one paid oneself exclusively in salary, one would be $57,692 worse off that year given no RDTOH recapture.

While RDTOH can be carried forward, I cannot think of many good reasons for not wanting to claim this benefit now. The value of having these extra funds work for us and grow for us over the years could see our wealth increase substantially. (With that said, if the taxpayer has significant income from other sources, it may not be as advantageous to pay out dividends for the sole purpose of receiving RDTOH.)

Lastly, how can we be sure that the government one day doesn't just choose to pull the plug on the benefits of utilizing all available RDTOH? In fact, there was a discussion piece in the federal government's tax fairness proposal July 18, 2017, drawing attention to the benefits of these credits.[3] In the end, while the government didn't eliminate the benefit, they did alternate the allocation of the benefits, separating eligible and ineligible dividends in the recording process. I would suggest claiming these benefits while we can!

Overall, the more one has saved and specifically invested inside the corporation generating passive income, the more one should be paying themselves in dividends.

What Are Some Exceptions to these Rules?

So far, these arguments have been in favour of dividends for the incorporated professional. But, as with most financial planning decisions, there are several exceptions where one should favour at least a mix of salary and dividends.

Small Business Deduction (SBD)

If you don't qualify for the small business deduction (SBD) and pay the higher corporate tax rate (26.5% in Ontario)—due to either netting more than $500,000 per year, being part of a group association that shares the SBD, failing either the passive income test, or having over $10,000,000 in assets inside the corporation—there could be a benefit to taking a salary. In these cases, one should look at all the factors discussed earlier to determine which mix makes the most sense.

Child Care Deduction

If you have young children, the government allows for child care deductions. It works out to be $8,000 per child for children under the age of seven years at the end of the year, or $5,000 per child for children aged seven to 16 years. For disabled or dependent children of any age who qualify for the disability tax credit, the amount is $11,000.

The catch here is one can only claim this deduction—and it has to be the lower-income spouse—if they have a salary (or other earned income, i.e., net income for self-employed persons or CPP disability payments). The government has a two-thirds rule, meaning that to claim $8,000 for one child, the lower-income spouse needs to earn $12,000 of salary; to claim two children at $16,000, the lower-income spouse needs $24,000 of salary.

SR&ED

Participants in the Scientific Research and Experimental Development (SR&ED) program are eligible to receive an investment tax credit of 15% or as much as 35% for qualified SR&ED expenditures. This could potentially be a significant savings that can be carried back three years, or carried forward 20 years. It's also a savings that could potentially not be here in the future.

In these situations, it is almost always recommended to have a salary to participate in these savings—albeit with the unfortunately expensive accounting bill that will come with making the claim.

Other Specific Considerations

There are also some unique tax scenarios in which paying a salary and investing in RRSPs has a larger benefit than taking dividends as compensation.

- For a first-time home buyer who requires $35,000 in their RRSP for the Home Buyers Plan, it is likely best to fund this RRSP prior to having corporate savings.
- If you use the Lifelong Learning Plan of $20,000, then contributing to your RRSP has its benefits.
- In some scenarios it's advisable to pay into a spousal RRSP to claim a higher tax deduction in your tax bracket, where your spouse can withdraw funds after three years at a lower tax bracket.

If you are eligible for the capital gains exemption upon the sale of the corporation's shares, certain criteria need to be met—and having too much in the corporation can put the corporation offside the rules. However, this can also be handled by setting up a separate holding company.

In my experience, most of these unique situations are the exceptions and are not commonly advisable.

It should be noted that these strategies should be fluid and not static. Personal and corporate tax rates are constantly changing, and investment strategies are evolving to new rules. Just because we choose to pay ourselves all in dividends today does not mean we can't pay ourselves salaries tomorrow.

Key Takeaways from This Chapter

- When you're incorporated, your compensation can be taken from your corporation as salary, dividends, or a combination of both.
- Taking compensation as dividends can give you a variety of mechanisms to attribute and distribute income for tax advantage.

- Income eventually has to migrate out of the corporation, and there are complexities that are worth examining in detail.
- Estate planning has to encompass planning for the funds and taxes on holdings in the corporation.
- Salary compensation has some undeniable attributes, but long-term planning is required.
- The Canada Pension Plan is among the factors to consider in the allocation between salary and dividend compensation.
- As a general rule, if income-splitting opportunities exist, consider using dividends as compensation; if there are no income-splitting opportunities, look more deeply at your situation to make your decision.

Top Questions to Ask Your Financial Planner

1. Should my compensation be taken in the form of salary, dividends, or a mix? How have you reached your recommendation, and have you included all of the factors relevant to my situation?
2. Should I participate in the Canada Pension Plan? If so, why? If not, why not?
3. Where will my income in retirement come from?

Notes

1. Note that the 2018 federal budget introduced new RDTOH rules applying to all Canadian-controlled private corporations earning investment income for taxation years beginning after December 31, 2018. These rules restrict the ability to recover RDTOH through the payment of eligible dividends, with limited exceptions. For more information, refer to the Government of Canada website at https://www.canada.ca/en/revenue-agency/programs/about-canada-revenue-agency-cra/federal-government-budgets/budget-2018-equality-growth-strong-middle-class/passive-investment-income/dividend-refund-rules.html.

2. See Jamie Golombek, "The Compensation Conundrum: Will It Be Salary or Dividends?" CIBC, December 2013. Available at https://www.cibc.com/ca/pdf/small-business/compensation-conundrum-nov-13-en.pdf.

3. "Minister Morneau Announces Next Steps in Improving Fairness in the Tax System by Closing Loopholes and Addressing Tax Planning Strategies" (along with draft legislation and consultation documents), Government of Canada Department of Finance, July 18, 2017. Available at https://www.canada.ca/en/department-finance/news/2017/07/minister_morneauannouncesnextstepsinimprovingfairnessinthetaxsys.html.

Chapter 3

Investing Inside Your Corporation

A mong the many benefits of incorporation is a unique financial advantage: holding investments under the umbrella of the corporation.

What You'll Get Out of This Chapter

This chapter covers the basics of how to build a tax-efficient portfolio in your corporation, taking the impact of taxes into account. We review the rules for investing in a corporation, and dispel the misconception that you need a holding corporation to invest.

We also cover how your refundable dividend tax on hand (RDTOH) and your capital dividend account (CDA) impact your investment returns and choices, and why a dollar doesn't necessarily have the same value on your balance sheet, depending on how it's earned.

(continued)

(*continued*)

We'll review examples of how different investment choices can lead to very different outcomes once tax impact is taken into account, with a deep dive into corporate-class investments and exchange-traded funds (ETFs). You'll also get up-to-date information about the new income tax rules that came into effect for tax years beginning after 2018.

Can I Invest through My Corporation?

Yes!

A common misconception is that corporations cannot hold investments, which must instead be held in a separate holding company. But this is not accurate—a corporation can definitely hold investments.

What the Income Tax Act Says about Investing through a Corporation

The Income Tax Act places no restrictions on the assets that can be owned by a corporation. Any restriction of this nature would need to be contained in the Regulated Health Professions Act or the Business Corporations Act. The Regulated Health Professions Act contains no restriction on the investment of surplus funds, and the Business Corporations Act specifically provides that a professional corporation can invest its surplus funds.

Where much of the uncertainty comes from is likely from this statement: "The articles of incorporation of a professional corporation shall provide that the corporation may not carry on a business other than the practice of the profession but this paragraph shall not be construed to prevent the corporation from carrying on activities related to or ancillary to the practice of the profession, including the investment of surplus funds earned by the corporation."[1]

We can see why the confusion exists. Simply Google the word *ancillary*: "providing necessary support to the primary activities or operation of an organization, institution, industry, or system." Technically investing surplus funds would never relate to the primary function of your business, nor does it mine. With that said, there has not been a single case of the Canada Revenue Agency (CRA) challenging the use of surplus funds. (It might provide more surety if the word "ancillary" were to be replaced with a more suitable term, "in conjunction with," so it would read, "carrying on activities related to or in conjunction with the practice of the profession.")

Structuring Investments Inside the Corporation

Most investors tend to have a focus on products: what stock to buy, what ETF to use, or how to find a five-star mutual fund.

While this is just normal investor behaviour, we like to steer clients toward stepping back and looking at investing from a strategic angle. Given that a corporation provides different ways to facilitate investing, we should determine which structures we want to use. We need to work backward from the best after-tax result to figure out what tactics to use.

Investing in corporations is very different from investing in vehicles like RRSPs and TFSAs. Why?

Growth in our RRSPs is **tax-deferred** and the growth in our TFSAs is **tax-free**. All dividends, interest, and capital gains inside these vehicles are treated equally, so the characteristics of the return are not that important. With these types of registered accounts, the conversation really should be simply about your **risk-adjusted rate of return**.

On the other hand, with a corporation, the tax is structured very differently. The conversation should be about your *after-tax* **risk-adjusted rate of return**.

The following is an example of the spread between the two different modes of investing: registered accounts versus the corporation.

Example

Assume that for an Ontario resident, taxation rates on growth look like this:

50.17% tax on interest and foreign income and dividends

- An example of an interest-earning account would be guaranteed investment certificate (GIC) or high-interest savings accounts income, or bond coupons from fixed income that are paid semi-annually.
- Foreign dividends (e.g., Apple stock with a 1.5% current dividend yield) are taxed at the highest rate, as regular passive income, and not given the more favourable dividend treatment given to dividends from Canadian source companies. Whether you pay yourself this interest or dividends or retain them in the portfolio, the CRA will not care and will issue you a tax slip either way.

38.33% tax on Canadian dividends

- An example of a Canadian dividend would be Royal Bank of Canada dividend with a 4.3% current dividend yield.
- Same as previously—whether you reinvest the dividend or not, or cash in the dividend and spend these funds at the grocery store, you will still be issued a tax slip.

25.09% tax on capital gains (due to 50% inclusion rate)

- An example would be if you purchased Shopify Inc. at $100 a share and sold it at $300 a share; you would have a capital gain of $200, of which 50% or $100 is tax free, and the other 50% or $100 is taxed at the 50.17% rate.

Simply looking at this, one can see that interest and foreign income and dividends are taxed at 100% more than capital gains, and 32% more than Canadian dividends.

But that spread can get even bigger for the investor, as there are two more factors to consider here, *RDTOH* and *CDA*.

RDTOH (Refundable Dividend Tax On Hand)

By paying yourself in dividends (as opposed to salary) from the corporation, you receive a tax credit that offsets gains in the corporation. The math works out to be that for every $2.61 of dividends you pay out, you receive $1 of refund.

The tricky part here is that the refund is capped, based on the type of investment income. For instance, even with an unlimited amount of RDTOH, you would still pay a non-refundable portion of tax on your investment income.

Assume that for an Ontario resident:

- 50.17% on interest and foreign income and dividends with RDOTH is reduced to at best 19.5%.
- 38.33% on Canadian dividends with RDTOH is reduced to, at best, 0%.
- 25.09% on capital gains (due to 50% inclusion rate) with RDTOH is reduced to, at best, 9.75%.

Your accountant should be recording this on the tax return and ensuring that these tax attributes are being used. As you can see, compared to our earlier example, the spread got larger: interest and foreign income and dividends are taxed at 100% more than capital gains and obviously more than tax on Canadian dividends, given their 0% rate.

Capital Dividend Account (CDA)

All corporations in Canada are allowed for 50% of capital gains to be tax-free, but additionally that tax-free part is able to be taken out of the corporation 100% tax-free by filing an election with the CRA.

I cannot stress enough how big a benefit that is! The tax-free component could save you up to 47.74% (the top tax rate on dividends in Ontario) on that portion of your return. Not only that, but you could save taxes on your personal income, given that you would not require as much salary from the corporation that year.

Example

To illustrate, let's say you have $1,000,000 in your corporation and have a 10% capital gain return, generating a $100,000 return.

- In this situation, not only would $50,000 of your return be tax-free, but you could take out $50,000 from your corporation through the CDA account that year (the election must be filed on or prior to the date payable in order to avoid a late-filing penalty).
- If you needed $70,000 per year in lifestyle expenses, you could potentially pay for this with 0% personal-tax-rate funds: $50,000 from the CDA account plus $20,000 in ineligible dividends, giving rise to an almost 0% personal tax rate (although the taxpayer may still be liable for health premiums).

This is why we advise clients, especially professionals closer to the beginning of their earning career, to think of your corporation as a race—a race to get to one, two, or three million dollars as fast as possible.

Once you have built a significant portfolio, your personal taxes should start to chart a downward curve as long as we have capital gains in our corporation. Because our tax system is progressive on our personal rates—the more income, the higher the tax rate—the focus should be on lowering the amount we actually need from the corporation that has to be taxed at the personal rate. If we can halve (or more) our income that is taxed at 0%, then our average tax rate will drop significantly.

For example, I've had a corporation for more than 10 years—and while my income has increased over the past decade, my average personal tax rate has decreased. The CDA is what has allowed me the luxury of this position.

New Passive Income Tax Rules

For taxation years beginning after 2018, new rules impose potentially significant adverse tax consequences if corporate-held passive income exceeds $50,000 in a tax year. ("Passive income" means corporate earnings that are unrelated to your main business.) Access to the small business deduction (SBD) may be reduced or lost in those cases, as it's ground down by $5 for every $1 of passive income (and fully ground down at $150,000 of passive income).

The new rules can bring corporate tax rates on active business income up from 12.2% to 26.5% (or even to 18.2%, given the 2020 Ontario corporate tax legislation).

One needs to keep these new rules in mind when building a portfolio inside the corporation. A couple of rules to consider:

1. **Understand how passive income is defined.**

   While $1 in Canadian dividends may be taxed more preferably than $1 in interest or $1 in foreign dividends, it all counts as $1 in passive income. However, $1 in capital gains is recognized as only 50 cents of passive income, meaning that the 2019 rule changes for passive income just made capital gains that much more attractive!

2. **Having concentrated positions in individual investments becomes less attractive.**

   For instance, if you have a $500,000 investment with $120,000 unrealized capital gains and you decide to sell that investment, you'll start grinding down your small business deduction and potentially pay more in taxes. On the other hand, if you have two $250,000 investments with $60,000 unrealized capital gains each, you can decide to sell one investment in one corporate calendar year and the other in a following year, essentially avoiding any new taxes.

   You can also see this in real estate. One of my clients is a very successful family doctor who owns multiple rental properties in his corporation. With the new rule changes, I have advised her that if she has a new $1,000,000 to spend on real estate, to purchase two properties for $500,000 each rather than one

$1,000,000 property. Bottom line, more options could ultimately mean less in taxes, even with the same return.

3. **If you are destined to fail the test one year, you might as well fail it big**.

What I mean by that is that if you are already at the $150,000 passive income mark and will have your full small business deduction limit clawed back, it may make sense to trigger more gains to avoid having this problem in future years. By failing the passive income test, you only pay more taxes in the following year. Consolidating your failures in one year is better than spreading them out!

In conclusion, when looking at these returns, you need to not only consider the tax rates on the type of income, but also take into account RDTOH and the CDA account. Thus a 4% capital gain return is greater than 8% interest, factoring every element in. Even better, a 4% tax-deferred capital gain is significantly better than an 8% interest inside the corporation.

This analysis is what I mentioned earlier: working backward to get to your desired investment structure. By working backward from your desired outcome with these rules in mind, we can really hone in on how to invest most efficiently inside the corporation—and as you can see, the focus should clearly be on capital gains, Canadian dividends, and tax-deferral mechanisms.

Reminder: Asset Allocation Still Matters

Before we jump into what different asset allocation options are out there, we will first address conceptually why asset allocation matters.

What we often see is a 40-year-old professional with a 60/40 mix of equities to bonds in both their corporation and RRSP accounts. This asset mix is the most typical one we see, whether in a moderate or average risk profile, or drawn from an age-based model portfolio like the Canadian Couch Potato.

For the purposes of this discussion, let's assume that a professional has $400,000 in their RRSP and $600,000 in their corporation, and both are invested in this 60/40 equities/bonds mix.

The problem is this: that portfolio allocation has a complete disregard for how the tax system works. If we were to assume that fixed income pays 5% in interest and equities pay 7% in capital gains for a blended rate between the two allocations of 6.2%, *this allocation could actually cost you tens of thousands per year, when you factor in all attributes and CDA accounts.*

Scenario 1
$400,000 in the RRSP @ 6.2% = $24,800.
No taxes.
$600,000 in the corporation @ 6.2% = $37,200 ($4,797 in corporate taxes net of the dividend refund, and only $12,600 addition to the CDA account).

However, if we worked backward and viewed this from a tax perspective, we can still have that 60/40 split, but invest the entire $400,000 RRSP in fixed income and the $600,000 corporation portfolio in vehicles that provide capital gains.

Scenario 2
$400,000 in RRSP @ 5% = $20,000.
No taxes.
$600,000 in the corporation @ 7% = $42,000 or $21,000 taxable ($4,095 in corporate taxes net of the dividend refund and $21,000 addition to the CDA account).

Factoring in the incremental addition to CDA, plus the delta in the net corporate tax between the two scenarios, this alone is a savings of more than $10,000, which, on a $1,000,000 portfolio is 1%.

This is what I call low-hanging fruit! If the government allows for this, then shame on us if we do not take advantage of an extra 1% return per year.

My disclaimer on the above situation is that this only works given the right portfolio values.

For instance, if a client has $50,000 in their RRSP and $1,000,000 in their corporation, I would not suggest they have less than 5% in fixed income, simply due to taxes. Your ability and willingness to tolerate risk is most important and needs to get addressed and accommodated first.

Also, whether you might potentially need funds from the corporation in the short term would also slant advice toward having more in fixed income in the corporation, simply to ensure that you are not selling any investment at a loss.

Example: What I Am Doing with My Corporate Assets

- The majority of the funds in my corporation are invested in corporate-class ETFs and pools split between using passive investing and relatively low-fee active managers such as Blackrock, J.P. Morgan, Horizons, and Purpose.
- The structure I have put in place allows for up to $5,000,000 invested in the corporation to avoid going over the $50,000 passive income threshold.
- The majority of my returns are in the form of tax-deferred capital gains, taking advantage of the earlier discussions on the lowest tax rate on passive income.
- The majority of the fees paid are deductible for tax purposes, given that expenses are deducted against the income they produce, which will mostly be deductible at the 50.17% tax rate.
- Lastly, because I am aligning my portfolio with my dividend/salary mix, I am fully taking advantage of all RDTOH (as discussed in the previous chapter) to lower my tax burden.

What Are Corporate-Class Investments?

While these investments can hold the same types of investments as a traditional mutual fund trust, corporate-class investments are held inside a corporation, which provides additional tax benefits for investors. All distributions are in the form of Canadian dividends and capital gains, the two most tax-efficient types of return, as discussed previously.

The benefits of corporate-class investments include:

- **Tax-deferred growth**

  By sharing income, gains, losses, expenses, and loss carryforwards, distributions are reduced, allowing for less tax due on a regular basis. This means fewer T3 and T5 slips for clients, and less passive income under the new rules.

  It also means that money we would be giving the government in taxes this year and in the years to follow will instead be reinvested and growing in our corporation.

  The power of compounded growth is enormous.

  Let's take, for instance, $1 saved today in taxes. Assuming a 6% return, that dollar would grow to $5.74 in 30 years. This is $4.74 you would never have seen had you paid the taxes 30 years ago.

- **Tax-efficient growth**

  Having all distributions in the form of Canadian dividends and capital gains is my personal favorite benefit. This benefit really shines if you are like me and have more investments outside of Canada than inside (given my negative view on the long-term Canadian economy as Canada's stock market is overweight energy, with 20% compared with the world index of approximately 5%).

  Take, for instance, J.P. Morgan, which at the time of this writing has a dividend yield of 2.82%.

  - If one were to own the individual stock, that 2.82% dividend would be taxed at the 50.17% corporate tax rate (less withholding taxes).

  - Instead, under the corporate class structure, that payout will likely be taxed as a capital gain at half the tax rate.

- **Tax-efficient cash flow**

  Some companies offer the ability to return a portion of your capital prior to triggering gains.

During your working years, this helps with redeploying funds without triggering excessive taxes.

In your retirement years, this could come in handy when some government benefits are income tested, such as Old Age Security.

By having a mechanism to choose between triggering gains and returning capital, we are allowing ourselves the ability to control our tax situation.

The Power of Tax-Deferred Compounding

Example

Let's take a look at some real 10-year comparisons between regular and tax-deferred compounding. The assumption we are making here is that sufficient taxable dividends from other sources (not from the investments below) were paid to the shareholders to have the RDTOH fully refunded.

iShares MSCI Emerging Markets Index ETF (XEM.TO) is a Blackrock exchange-traded fund that seeks to provide long-term capital growth by replicating the performance of the MSCI Emerging Markets Index, net of expenses.

As of June 30, 2019, the investment had performed 5.8%/year over the 10-year period and currently has a yield of 2.2%, or 37% of the return is from foreign dividends.

For comparison purposes, we are leaving out bid–ask spreads and commissions to buy/sell. (Note: **Vanguard FTSE Emerging Markets All Cap Index (VEE.TO)** has similar five-year numbers, but I am not using this due to a lack of 10-year track record given the November 30, 2011 inception date.)

versus

The Emerging Markets Corporate Class Pool currently run by J.P. Morgan Asset Management had an 8.4%/year over the same 10-year period.

However, for comparison purposes, let's assume the exact same return as above, using the 5.8%/year numbers but without having the tax drag that is created by foreign dividends.

Working through the Example

A $1,000,000 investment June 2009 in the XEM.TO @ 2.2% yield with an average return of 5.8% would = $1,687,373 pre-triggering of capital gains, with a cost basis of $1,243,108 from the dividends paid out every year. If one were to sell June 2019, then $444,265 in capital gains would be triggered, giving rise to $43,316 in taxes, and $222,133 added to the CDA account.

The net result is $222,133 personally and $1,421,924 corporately.

A $1,000,000 investment June 2009 in a tax-deferred pool with an average return of 5.8% would = $1,757,343 pretriggering of capital gains, with a cost basis of $1,000,000. If one were to sell June 2019, then $757,343 in capital gains would be triggered, giving rise to $73,841 in taxes, and $378,671 added to the CDA account.

The net result is $378,671 personally and $1,304,831 corporately.

Assuming a discount of 40% on corporate assets given that eventually these taxes are likely paid, this is $86,282 more after-tax income over the 10-year period.

(continued)

(*continued*)

Another way to look at this is that to come up with $86,282 more personally after 10 years, factoring out taxes, you would need to have an extra 1.6%/year in returns. Math: $1,000,000 @ 1.35% over 10 years = $143,803 minus the discount of 40% = $86,282.

This example assumes that taxable dividends are paid to shareholders from other sources and not from these investments. Compliments of a national tax, accounting, and business consulting firm, if we were to assume that taxable dividends are paid to shareholders from these investments, the differential is reduced to $69,970.

Example

Let's take a look at another international comparison.

iShares International Fundamental Index ETF (CIE.TO) is a Blackrock exchange-traded fund that seeks to replicate the performance of the FTSA RAFI Developed ex-US 1000 index, net of expenses. As of June 30, 2019, the investment had performed 6.9%/year over the 10-year period and currently has a yield of 3.4%, or in other words, 49% of the return is from foreign dividends.

Once again, for comparison purposes, we are leaving out bid–ask spreads and commissions to buy/sell. (Note: **Vanguard FTSE Developed All Cap ex U.S. Index ETF (VDU.TO)** would be considered somewhat similar but has an inception date of August 2, 2013.)
versus

The International Corporate Class Pool currently run by Blackrock as well and J.P. Morgan Asset Management, had a 7.2%/year return over the same 10-year period.

However, for comparison purposes, let's assume the exact same return as above, using the 5.8%/year numbers but without having the tax drag that is created by foreign dividends.

Working through the Example

A $1,000,000 investment June 2009 in the CIE.TO @ 3.4% yield with an average return of 6.9% would = $1,831,293 pre-triggering of capital gains, with a cost basis of $1,397,029 from the dividends paid out every year. If one were to sell June 2019, then $434,264 in capital gains would be triggered, giving rise to $42,341 in taxes and $217,132 credited to the CDA account.

The net result is $217,132 personally and $1,571,820 corporately.

A $1,000,000 investment June 2009 in a tax-deferred pool with an average return of 6.9% would = $1,948,843 pretriggering of capital gains, with a cost basis of $1,000,000. If one were to sell June 2019, then $948,843 in capital gains would be triggered, giving rise to $92,513 in taxes and $474,422 credited to the CDA account.

The net result is $474,422 personally and $1,381,908 corporately.

Assuming a discount of 40% on corporate assets given that eventually these taxes are likely paid, this is $143,343 more after-tax income over the 10-year period.

(*continued*)

(continued)

Another way to look at this is that to come up with $143,343 more personally after 10 years, factoring out taxes, you would need to have an extra 2.2%/year in returns. Math: $1,000,000 @ 2.2% over 10 years = $238,905 minus the discount of 40% = $143,343.

This example assumes that taxable dividends are paid to shareholders from other sources and not from these investments. If we were to assume that taxable dividends are paid to shareholders from these investments, the differential is reduced to $117,550.

For those who are wondering, the reason the second example has an even greater difference is because there is a higher dividend payout for the international ETF than for the emerging markets ETF. Bottom line, the higher foreign dividend payout ratio in a corporation is not a good thing!

Rule Changes from Federal Budget 2016

Starting January 1, 2017, corporate-class investments have lost the benefits of tax-deferred switching among the various funds held within the corporate class structure. In the past, the capital gains that would normally be triggered when units in a fund are sold at a profit could be deferred until the year in which the unit holder sells all holdings in the corporation.

However, after the end of 2016, switches among different corporate class mutual funds will result in capital gains or losses, and the tax treatment of switches between different corporate class investments will be the same as conventional investments that are structured as trusts.

What's the end result here? It means that if we are going to actively manage a portfolio where from time to time we switch value stocks to growth stocks, or small cap to large cap, having multiple investments is much less preferable than having larger pool structures where these changes can be made within the pool.

For instance, I would much prefer to have a U.S. pool where a sector rotation occurs from defensive stocks to cyclical stocks without having to trigger a gain, as opposed to manually moving from a utility mutual fund to a science and technology fund.

Considerations with Corporate Class

Fees

While the concept of corporate class structure is solid, it's all about the execution of the plan. For instance, I wouldn't pay a 3% management expense ratio for a preferred tax structure that saves me 2.5%. Given that corporate class is in a managed product structure (mutual funds, ETFs, or pools), you will likely pay a higher fee than you would when purchasing the stocks on your own. Proper analysis should be performed to demonstrate the value added of the tax structure given the fee.

With that said, I advise clients to stay away from a couple of structures. First, given all the improvements in the industry, I would recommend against holding any front-end fee structured investments—where an institution can charge up to 5% up front, or a deferred sales structure (DSC) where an institution can charge up to 5.5% as an exit penalty if you leave within a given time frame, anywhere from two to five to seven years.

When it comes to investing, I believe in liquidity. If you buy on a Monday, you should be able to sell on Tuesday without penalty. We have enough to worry about with the markets to have to worry about these additional constraints.

I also advise clients to be sure that their advisors are providing them maximum fee reductions. Many companies allow for advisors to negotiate fees down. In my experience, most advisors only offer this on a reactionary basis. I subscribe to the view that it is actually in the advisor's best interest, not just the client's, to fully negotiate the lowest fee possible, as in the long run it works out for everyone. I would hate to know I could have potentially paid a lower fee had I simply spoken up more.

Now, here is where fees get interesting. If you are in a mutual fund or a pool structured investment and you have a full fee reduction but at the same time others in this pool structure are paying a higher fee, this works out in your favour. The reason is that all the fees are lumped together and help reduce the taxable distributions—meaning there are scenarios where other investors' fees are actually aiding your tax situation.

Loss of Control

If you are a do-it-yourself investor, corporate-class investments may not be for you. Prior to Federal Budget 2019, there were Horizons swap-based ETFs, which are a type of exchange-traded funds that do not hold any stocks or bonds directly. Instead, the fund uses financial instruments called a total-return swap designed to deliver the same performance as a specific index, including any increase or decrease in price and any dividends or interest received. The ETF does not actually hold any stock, and your investments are held in cash. In a roundabout way these ETFs perform similar functions as the corporate-class structure.

I would suggest for someone picking their own stocks that it's best to stay away from high-yielding stocks, given corporate tax rates and the new passive income changes. For instance, the highest-yielding real estate investment trust (REIT) at the time of this writing is Two Harbors Investment Corp. (TWO.NYSE), yielding 14.2%. Ignoring the obvious risks to investing in mortgage-backed securities and mortgage servicing rights, a 14.2% yield here will be heavily taxed and ultimately means that a portfolio just above $350,000 could put you offside with the new corporate rule changes.

On the flip side, a company like Berkshire Hathaway (BRK.A or BRK.B NYSE), Warren Buffett's multinational conglomerate hold-ing company, pays no dividends. This means that all the returns generated in a stock like this come in the form of capital gains as opposed to dividends and interest, making it more attractive from a tax standpoint in the corporation.

It's good to note that at the time of this writing the average TSX dividend yield is 3.45% with 54 of the 60 (90%) companies paying dividends; exceptions are BlackBerry, Bombardier, CGI, Goldcorp, Kinross Gold, and Bausch Health Companies. ARC Resources is yielding the highest dividends, at a staggering 9.2%. The current S&P 500 dividend yield is 1.8%, close to its historical lows, compared to its average dividend yield at 4.3% (fun fact, it was 13.8% in 1932). 416 of the companies listed pay dividends (83%). Much of this trend can likely be accounted for by lower interest rates but also by the rise in the American growth sector, primarily the tech sector, which pays very little in dividends.

Little Fixed Income Exposure

Certain tax law changes announced by the federal government in 2013 stipulated that after December 31, 2014, income earned by yield class funds via forward contracts would be treated as ordinary income—rather than as tax-favoured capital gains. This previously was a benefit allowing for interest income to be taxed as capital gains in a roundabout way. Given the changes, it's difficult to have a high percentage of fixed income in a corporate-class structured product, and at most one may have approximately 35% fixed income in many of these funds. If an investor is very conservative or wants to construct a bond portfolio, corporate class may not be suitable. However, there are a few fixed income alternatives that accomplish a similar end result, such as BMO Discount Bond ETF (ZDB.TO), created February 2014, made up primarily of bonds trading below their par value. Since they trade below their par value the majority of their returns are in the form of capital gains and not interest. Additionally, Horizons (HBB.TO), currently being merged into a class of shares of a corporate fund structure, seeks to replicate the performance of the Solactive Canadian Select Universe Bond Index (Total Return).

Future Potential Rule Changes

With every tax and investment strategy, we will always be at the risk of future surprise announcements. The good news here is that the government has clearly looked at these strategies and already acted with implemented measures. This does not prevent them from making further changes, but I would say this only reinforces working with an advisor who is proactively adjusting to the changing investment landscape.

What If I Want to Try Investing on My Own?

If someone has a need to invest some of their portfolio on their own but also values having an active advisor, I always suggest they manage the RRSP and TFSA while they use a professional manager to invest in the corporation, the reason being that with RRSP and TFSA investments, it's all about risk-adjusted rates of returns; with the corporation, it's about after-tax rates of return. There are no tax-enhanced investments for registered accounts simply because there would be no benefit. It's okay to allow both worlds to work together here.

What If They Increase Capital Gains Taxes?

A few years ago, there were rumblings of a potential capital gains tax hike. However, nothing came of it, and since then there has been little public discussion. With that said, the government can do as they wish and if it ever came to a capital gains tax increase, then the value of corporate-class structured investments would be reduced.

However, we can say with certainty that one would never be worse off having capital gains as opposed to dividends or interest. It would not make sense in a capitalist environment to incentivize companies to pay out 100% in dividends over reinvesting the funds back in the company for future growth, which allows for capital appreciation.

Key Takeaways from This Chapter

- Corporations can be used not only to hold funds, but also as opportunities to invest those funds to grow them.
- Certain tax advantages make investments inside of a corporation advantageous, specifically capital dividend accounts, RDTOH, and capital gains.
- Corporate class is a unique structure that is available inside corporations, and may be worth investigating.
- Basic rules of investing, like asset allocation and diversification, still hold true.
- Not every investment vehicle or strategy is appropriate, depending on your time horizon, capital, risk tolerance, and professional advice can help you avoid potential bad decisions.

Top Questions to Ask Your Financial Planner

1. How have you created a tax-efficient asset allocation between my personal and corporate investment accounts?
2. Is my available RDTOH being recorded and used appropriately to reduce my tax-owing?
3. What is your plan to manage and reduce my average tax rate over time?

Note

1. Refer to Section 3.2, subsection (2) paragraph 5 of the Business Corporations Act, R.S.O. 1990, c B.16.

Chapter 4

Valuing Permanent Insurance on the Holistic Corporate Balance Sheet

I n my experience as a financial advisor, I've discovered that discussions about insurance—specifically, permanent insurance—can inspire some of the most passionate and deeply held beliefs.

Some people believe wholeheartedly that no one, ever, should purchase permanent insurance, whereas others believe just as fervently that insurance can play a critical role on your personal balance sheet for tax, financial planning, and risk management benefits.

In this chapter, we review a specific strategy for the use of insurance: corporate-owned permanent life insurance. This is a narrower discussion than the more general review of insurance that follows in Chapter 5, Risk Management.

What You'll Get Out of This Chapter

For the incorporated professional or owner–manager, the use of corporate-owned permanent life insurance is one of the most powerful—and most tax-efficient—ways to build wealth and create and protect estate value. But this strategy is frequently decried as expensive, inappropriate, and motivated by considerations other than the best interests of the potential purchaser, among other criticisms.

In this chapter, we provide a careful review of the assumptions, benefits, and qualifications associated with the use of corporate-owned permanent life insurance, especially in light of new rules for the taxation of passive income inside corporations.

We review each of the strategy's claimed benefits and disadvantages to provide clear insight into the power of properly structured, corporate-owned permanent life insurance to deliver value on an after-tax, risk-adjusted basis.

Our goal is to ensure that readers are able to isolate and understand both the potential benefits and drawbacks that may arise when using corporate-owned permanent life insurance as a wealth- and estate-building strategy.

A Review of the Basics—Permanent Life Insurance as Tax Arbitrage

Life insurance, at the most elemental level, is a hedge against the risk of premature death—and if it weren't for the Income Tax Act, there wouldn't be much more to this story, and no chapter to read.

The Income Tax Act, however, changes everything, as it introduces tax arbitrage, or the opportunity to take positions that capitalize on features of the tax code.

First, the use of permanent life insurance provides an initial tax arbitrage opportunity, as it allows for the buildup of tax-deferred savings, which can then in turn be used as collateral to provide a tax-efficient cash flow (potentially in retirement), in addition to the payment of the tax-free death benefit.

Secondly, these attributes are then multiplied for the incorporated professional or owner–manager who can pay for a policy using (lightly taxed) corporate dollars from an active business, not (more heavily taxed) personal dollars—and whose corporation can receive the death benefit tax-free.

Finally, and more recently, with the 2018 introduction of new rules regarding passive income inside corporations, this strategy offers an additional benefit to the incorporated individual who is able to use permanent life insurance to avoid the impact of passive income on the small business deduction.

We review each of these attributes in turn.

The Benefits of Corporate-Owned Permanent Life Insurance

Pay Premiums with Corporate Dollars

In Ontario, the small business corporate tax rate is just 12.2% on the first $500,000 of active business income, the lowest rate in the history of corporate taxation in Ontario. The rate in 2000, for example, was 20%, and limited to just the first $200,000 of active business income.

The corporate tax landscape in Ontario has changed significantly since 2000, and not just in terms of tax rates. Starting in 2006, many Ontario physicians became able to incorporate their practices.

As a result of that changed landscape, an Ontario physician who purchases permanent life insurance inside their professional corporation is able to use much more lightly taxed corporate dollars to cover this expense, versus personal dollars subject to marginal rates as high as 53.53%.

Holding all other parameters constant, using corporate dollars from an active business to pay life insurance premiums reduces the cost of premiums 30–40% or more, compared to the non-incorporated individual purchasing the same product.

Avoid New Passive Income Rules

Not all corporate tax is created equal. Instead, tax on passive income inside a corporation is subject to a rate that is 50.17% (assuming Ontario residence) on interest and foreign income and dividends, 38.33% on Canadian dividends, and 25% on capital gains (due to the 50% inclusion rate).

Starting January 1, 2019, new rules imposed potentially significant adverse tax consequences if corporate-held passive income exceeds $50,000 in a tax year, as access to the small business deduction may be reduced or lost. The new rules can bring corporate tax rates on active business income up from 12.2% to 26.5%, or to 18.5% with the 2019 Ontario corporate tax legislation implemented.

Investment income in a corporate-held permanent insurance policy, however, will grow tax-free and will not impact the small business deduction, meaning permanent life insurance policies provide an effective escape hatch from the new passive income tax rules when there is an underlying need for insurance.

Creating Cash Flow

There are several options for creating liquidity and cash flow from a permanent life insurance policy, some more tax efficient than others.

If a policy has cash value, it can be cashed in ("surrendered"), either partially or completely. A complete surrender eliminates the policy's death benefit and can result in a fully taxable policy gain to the extent the cash surrender value (CSV) exceeds the adjusted cost basis (ACB) of the policy. A partial surrender can result in a prorated recognition of any policy gain. Another option is to take a policy loan from the policy's CSV. A policy loan is also a disposition of an interest in a policy, but unlike a partial surrender, a policy loan only results in taxable income when the amount of the loan exceeds the full ACB of the policy.

Dividends generated under an insurance policy are generally used to pay premiums or purchase additional insurance within the same policy. When used for these purposes, policy dividends produce no immediate tax consequence.

Dividends can also be paid in cash to the policy owner; however, doing so reduces the policy's ACB and results in tax when the policy's ACB has been reduced to zero. Paying dividends in cash will also limit the growth of the eventual tax-free death benefit. Finally, an insurance policy with cash value can be used as collateral for a loan from a lender, potentially up to 90% of its cash value.

Collateral borrowing strategies are often the most tax-efficient means of creating a cash flow from a life insurance policy, but such strategies have their own issues and risks that need to be considered.

If a corporation is the owner of a life insurance policy, the tax consequences of withdrawing funds from the corporation for personal use must also be considered. Most strategies, but not all, will expose the funds to a further personal level of tax.

Provide a Tax-Efficient Financial Legacy

The death benefit from any life insurance policy is paid out and received free of tax. When the beneficiary is a corporation, it receives the funds tax-free—and may then be able to pass most or all of those funds on to heirs or other estate beneficiaries tax-free.

This outcome compares very favourably, for example, to the combined top marginal tax rate in Ontario on non-eligible dividends, which is 47.74% in 2020 (and was 24% not long ago).

By way of comparison, if an investor sought the same after-tax estate value as that provided by a death benefit of a corporate-held life insurance policy of $2 million, they would need in excess of $3.8 million in cash inside the corporation to match it—meaning an investor would need nearly twice as much saved to match the same benefit.

(As a side note, I always tell clients that if we knew the exact date they were going to pass away, we could create the perfect financial plan. For example, if you knew the date of your passing, to create the most optimal financial outcome, we would make sure you spent your last RRSP dollar and all of your corporate savings on that day, in order to avoid the 53.53% and 47.74% tax rates at death, leaving every other dollar in tax-efficient insurance!)

In summary, the benefits associated with the use of corporate-owned permanent life insurance include:

- Tax-efficient cost through the use of corporate, not personal, dollars to purchase the policy
- The opportunity to avoid the impacts of new corporate tax rules for passive income
- A mechanism to create potentially tax-efficient cash flow in or before retirement
- A way to create a tax-efficient financial legacy

A Real-World Example: My Plan in Action

Let's look at my own plan. Using a Canada Life Estate Achiever participating life insurance policy, I've structured my plan to, with a high probability, be paid up in 8–10 years, depending on interest rates. I have maximized the deposits up to the limit that tax law permits, or what's sometimes called additional deposit options (ADOs), given the long-term nature of this plan.

My corporation's planned contribution over 10 years is $25,000 per year. This plan allows for significant future payments if I choose, without further medical examinations. I like this structure as it gives me the flexibility to invest for up to 20 years, without having to initially commit beyond the initial 10-year plan.

Funding the Plan

Given that the small business corporate tax rate on active business income is 12.2%, I will only need to make $28,474 in income to fund a $25,000 payment. A non-incorporated individual would potentially need to make up to $52,665 to make this $25,000 payment outside of a corporation.

The Growth of Funds in the Plan

The growth on this permanent insurance investment will be tax-free and circumvents the new rules on passive income. Considering I am right on the cusp of the rule changes, this will likely save me approximately $75,000 in corporate taxes over 10 years. Most importantly, I avoid paying the 50.17% passive income tax on gains.

The investment in the insurance plan itself is broken down into two components: a guaranteed component and a dividend value. Since this is a long-term retirement and estate planning investment, at age 67, the new retirement government-push age, the guaranteed component is $270,375 and the dividend cash value at current low rates is projected to be $380,270, for a total of $650,645. The death benefit is projected to be $1,722,557 (see Table 4.1).

Assumptions in the Projections

This is a good time to discuss assumptions. By year 30 of the plan, 42% of investment and estate return are guarantees. Regardless of what happens in markets or to interest rates, I can't botch this.

Table 4.1   My Real-World Example: Projected Death Benefit

$25,000 × 10 Payments, 5.5% Dividend

	Cash Value	Death Benefit
Year 10	$ 183,313	$1,456,334
Year 20	$ 352,966	$1,316,645
Year 30	$ 650,645	$1,722,557
Year 40	$1,116,280	$2,193,943
Year 50	$1,817,188	$2,732,122

*Prepared from updated illustration of Canada Life Estate Achiever participating whole life, dated January 19, 2019—Ref #3.7.0.0190119213339.

The dividend value is a projection, but one important point is that it could never be negative. The worst return it has paid historically in the past 70 years is still above 5%. An important element here is that when the cash value or death benefit increases, those values are now the floor upon which next year's values are built.

Rates of Return Assumptions

The current dividend scale interest rate is 5.5%. While it is not the actual rate of return on the cash value of the policy, the dividend scale interest rate is used to calculate the investment component of participating policyowner dividends and is based on the smoothed investment performance of the assets backing the participating account.

It's important to note that in determining the dividend scale interest rate, Canada Life doesn't use calendar-year returns and the returns are smoothed over a number of years. Smoothing is used as one of the methods to help maintain the stability of the dividend scale interest rate. Smoothing works by bringing gains and losses into the dividend scale interest rate over a period of time. The actual cash value growth in a policy varies based on several factors, such as type of product, product features, premium-paying period, issue age, rating, and dividend option.

The 30-year average of the dividend scale interest rate is 8.7% as of December 31, 2017 (Canada Life Participating Account Details, as of September 30, 2018), though there has been a recent downward trend, and I would plan for a lower long-term rate than this average of 8.7%.

If dividends go up and average 6.5%, then at year 30, the cash value is projected to be $850,650 and the death benefit $2,221,291. If the Canadian market enters a very troubled 30-year period, with interest rates entering new lows, and we receive a lower average dividend rate of 4.5%, the cash value could be as low as $495,738 and the death benefit $1,326,377.

Table 4.2   My Real-World Example: Projected Death
Benefit with Dividend Payments in Years 11–20

$25,000 × 20 Payments, 5.5% Dividend

	Cash Value	Death Benefit
Year 10	$ 183,313	$1,456,334
Year 20	$ 669,944	$2,424,963
Year 30	$1,168,912	$3,048,048
Year 40	$1,949,095	$3,795,510
Year 50	$3,123,587	$4,670,400

*Prepared from updated illustration dated January 19, 2019—Ref
#3.7.0.0190119221721.

Beyond the First 10 Years

If I chose to continue making the $25,000 per year payments for the following 10 years, in years 11–20, a total of $500,000 of payments would look like Table 4.2. Keep in mind that with my plan I can make this election in year 11, and payments do not have to continue to be a full $25,000 per year.

Let's fast-forward 30 years and assume I am retired, though it is unlikely, as I really enjoy what I do. If I need funds from the plan, I could:

- Cash in and end the plan, with the consequence of my children losing the death benefit.
- My corporation could pledge the policy as collateral for a loan, borrowing up to 90% of my cash value to help with cash flow.
- Alternatively, I could direct my corporation to simply withdraw $89,514 per year for 20 years, accomplishing my goal of creating an income stream in retirement.

The Plan as an Investment

So, to wrap up, let's examine the math of the rates of return on the cash surrender value, the investment component of the policy.

Table 4.3   My Real-World Example: Rate of Return on Cash Surrender Value

	Pre-Tax CSV ROR	Required Equivalent Return on Investment
Year 10	−5.76%	−5.76%
Year 20	2.70%	5.42%
Year 30	4.09%	8.21%
Year 40	4.45%	8.93%
Year 50	4.54%	9.11%

What is the rate of return pre-tax on my investment and death benefit, and, most importantly, what would be the required rate of return to equal my projected investment and estate?

Let's assume I pay into the policy $25,000 per year for 20 years and take no withdrawals. Table 4.3 illustrates the rate of return on my investment and Table 4.4 illustrates the rate of return to my estate.

In summary, my plan invests $25,000 per year over 10 years with the option of paying in for a longer period:

- Growing my funds tax-free, avoiding the 50.17% passive income tax in corporations.
- At least delaying the loss of my small business deduction, given the new passive income rules.

Table 4.4   My Real-World Example: Rate of Return on Estate Value

Death Benefit: Required Equivalent

	Death Benefit ROR	Return on Investment
Year 10	31.62%	63.45%
Year 20	13.46%	27.01%
Year 30	8.62%	17.30%
Year 40	6.63%	13.31%
Year 50	5.54%	11.13%

*Prepared from updated illustration dated January 19, 2019—Ref #3.7.0.0190119221721.

- Creating options for income streams in retirement (likely $89.5,000/year).
- Meanwhile providing an estate for my children.

Understanding the Criticisms of Corporate-Held Permanent Life Insurance

Thus far, we have outlined the potential benefits of a tax-minimization, wealth-building, and estate planning strategy using corporate-held permanent life insurance, and we have illustrated these features using a specific case study.

Now let's turn to the criticisms levied against this strategy, which can be bundled into concerns about the risk and overall appropriateness of this strategy.

Risk Review: Economic and Tax Considerations

Critics of the strategy we have outlined in this chapter often point to the underlying economic and tax considerations that underpin it. These include questions about what happens to the strategy if tax laws change, dividends decrease, or interest rates increase. Will the strategy still perform as well?

At the outset, we note that any strategy contingent on economic conditions remaining static will almost certainly fail, as many moving parts of the overall economic and financial environment— particularly tax and interest rates, as well as tax policy—will change over time. Tax laws will be altered, interest rates will not remain constant, and dividends can and will fluctuate. These maxims hold true whether you are considering this strategy or any other.

Of course, these changes can and will impact many different strategies an incorporated professional might deploy, not just the use of corporate-owned permanent life insurance.

Tax Policy Risk: "What if tax rates change?"

Given that tax rates can and will change, your financial plans must be based on this reality. What this means in practical terms is adopting a strategy of tax diversification or diversifying your approaches, so you aren't overly reliant on one strategy or another.

Following this approach, the use of corporate-owned life insurance will ideally be just one of many strategies you implement, based on your personal financial plan.

One saving grace in the insurance world: when the tax legislation is changed, typically the changes leave intact existing arrangements, and only impact new plans on a go-forward basis. (Otherwise, insurance contracts would be toothless.)

The advice in respect of potential tax changes is thus straightforward: plan for change, diversify your approaches, and actively seek advice from those who will carefully watch where the tax winds are blowing.

Economic Risk: "What if dividend rates or interest rates change?"

Just like tax policy, dividends can and do change—and they can decrease. While a negative dividend can never be paid, a plan could fail to pay dividends any given year, and dividend rates have decreased since the 1980s and 1990s (just as interest rates have decreased and the overall economic environment has shifted).

An appropriate approach to the risk of dividends decreasing is, first, to adopt relatively conservative assumptions about dividend rates going forward, and second, to model varying scenarios—for example, how does the strategy fare if dividends continue to trend downward?

As with changes in dividend payout rates, interest rates cannot be assumed to remain static over the expected holding period of a corporate-held permanent insurance policy. However, dividends and interest rates are loosely correlated, in that rising long-term interest rates are usually linked to dividend rate increases— meaning that viewed from the perspective of the value of dividends, interest rate increases are to be welcomed. From the point of view of the borrower, however, when interest rates go up, so does the cost of borrowing.

In practical terms, this means that depending on how you are using a policy in the financial plan that supports your personal situation and financial goals, you may welcome or bemoan changes in interest rates—but the bottom line is that your personalized financial plan should be built and tested on the assumption that both dividends and interest rates can and will change. Are you getting appropriate professional planning support to help you through these calculations?

Appropriateness Review: Concerns about the Sales Process

"This strategy is designed to maximize advisor sales commissions—if it's so good, why do so many people oppose it?"

One of the important aspects of insurance is, of course, the transfer of risk from your personal balance sheet to the insurance company's books. Unlike the world of investments, which operates much more like "you pay your money, and you take your chances," the world of insurance is characterized by contracts, guarantees, and the doctrine of "utmost good faith."

Because of the ways that insurance differs from investing, the process of purchasing insurance is inherently not (and cannot be) a DIY process, and a salesperson—who is paid a commission—will necessarily be involved in the transaction. While a permanent insurance policy can include an investment component, fundamentally investments and insurance are significantly different. Reaping the tax and risk-transfer benefits associated with life insurance will require the use of a licensed insurance agent as an intermediary.

Now is a good time to note that how the plan is structured can have a huge impact on the results. Take my plan, for example—had I used a different insurance company, with a different structure, my estate benefit (projecting out 50 years) could be almost 40% lower than my current plan will provide, by my estimates. Not all plans are created equal!

That said, your personal financial situation should be diversified to include multiple financial strategies and options, all in the context of a comprehensive financial plan that is directly keyed to your situation, preferences, risk tolerance, and objectives. When you work with a professional advisor, make sure you get appropriate professional advice and support that goes beyond a sales transaction to meet your needs over time.

"Shouldn't I help my kids today, instead of building an estate?"

Given the meteoric run-up in real estate prices in many parts of Canada, many of our clients have expressed concerns about ensuring that they will be able to help their children financially without requiring them to wait for an eventual estate.

On this question, there is no right answer—nor is there a need to choose just one option. As with many other elements of a personal financial plan, the optimal path for any one individual will depend on their preferences, resources, and goals. Certainly, the attainment of one goal (to endow children during your lifetime) doesn't mean ruling out the other (to build a financial legacy upon your passing).

This strategy is "an expensive way to buy insurance, and I can get higher investment returns elsewhere"—shouldn't I just "buy term and invest the difference?"

Compared to buying term insurance, permanent insurance is a more expensive way to hedge against the risk of premature death—especially in the early years of the policy.

While the strategy of using permanent insurance will generally always lose when compared to the cheap and effective hedge of term life insurance, when you are using your corporation to buy permanent life insurance, you are not only protecting the value of your future earnings; you are accessing the tax, investment, and overall financial planning benefits of this strategy.

The True Cost of Term Insurance

Take my situation: if I were to purchase a Term-65 policy for $1,500,000, it would cost me $2,218/year for a total of $62,104, as opposed to $250,000. Keep in mind that, after age 65, I would have no insurance—and no cash value from the $62,104 of payments.

That said, no one should use permanent insurance strictly for income protection in their working years. It may accomplish that goal but it is an expensive way to do so. On a side note, I do not have any term insurance on my life. I do believe many policies are sold inappropriately with misleading purposes.

The use of corporate-owned permanent life insurance is not primarily meant to protect against the loss of your human capital while working: It is used to transfer wealth tax efficiently and provide access to a tax-preferred investment vehicle and other benefits outlined earlier in this chapter. That said, investors who pursue this strategy will also want investments outside the permanent insurance policy, and many will require additional term insurance.

A well-constructed financial plan will allow you to build wealth, protect your investments and your assets—including the value of your human capital, and minimize the effects of tax.

Meeting this diverse array of goals typically takes various products and strategies, working together in accordance with the parameters of your personal financial plan.

Buying Term and Investing the Difference: A Review of the Facts and Assumptions

First, I think many people should do both: buy term and invest the difference and explore a corporate-owned permanent policy. To make the comparison between permanent insurance and buying term and investing the difference, we have to make a series of simplifying assumptions. But are these assumptions fair?

- Is it fair to assume everyone, without knowing his or her risk tolerance, should be aggressive and keep 100% in equities? Is it reasonable to assume an 85-year-old investor will stick with a 100% equity allocation?
- Is it fair to assume the Canadian index, for instance, will average about 8%—given the TSX is lower than it was in 2007 at the

time of this writing? (Consider that the index for the Japanese Nikkei, the world's third-largest market, just recently overcame its previous high from 30 years ago.)

- Is it fair to ignore the sequence or order of returns? What if one retires or passes away at the end of 2018 with the TSX down 11.6%—or down 11.1% in 2011 and 2015—or 35.5% in 2008?
- Is it fair to assume that behavioural finance does not come into play, ignoring the work of Nobel Laureate Richard H. Thaler on why and how the average investor underperforms the index— even with index funds?
- Is it fair to assume ETFs are structured to be safe in downturns? (Look specifically at XFN, Canada's largest bank ETF, and the "flash crash" on August 24, 2015, during which it dropped 30% in one hour, with the underlying holdings only losing 5%!)

Ignoring all those lingering questions, the projected rates of return in Tables 4.3 and 4.4 speak for themselves (though keep in mind, it's all about how one structures these plans): the dividend scale interest rate assumes 5.5% but has a 30-year average of 8.7% and a 60-year average of 8.9%.

The last time dividends were this low was in the 1950s (a similar low-interest-rate environment), and the 60-year average ended up being greater than 8%.

In designing my own plan, I asked myself this question: Is it more likely that dividends will perform higher than the current projection or that equities will have a magnificent bull run? The truth is, I don't know, so let's invest in both.

Critics may also point to the fact that the returns are being compared to a fixed-income, interest-bearing investment, and not a capital-gains-generating investment for which 50% of gains are tax-free (for now, let's ignore what happened in 1988–2001 with a higher tax rate on capital gains).

In year 40, in your projected estate, you would need a 10%-plus capital gain versus a 13% return, but this would require an aggressive and outperforming portfolio. Ask yourself: Which scenario is more likely? Which poses the most risk? And which are you most comfortable with?

"What if something changes and I can't afford the premiums?"

Just like tax and interest rates, your own personal financial situation can and will change over time. As a result, you may face the risk that a plan you commit to becomes unsuitable because you become unable to make the required premium payments.

As with other risks to the achievement of your overall financial plan, you should evaluate and plan for this possibility, just as you evaluate and plan for other risks ranging from the risk of disability to the risk of divorce, job loss, and more. Other life changes, too—such as the decision to pursue employment or retire to a country outside Canada—will impact the fulfillment of your financial plan.

Over the short term, the expected return on this strategy is abysmal—but over the long term, the expected return is (in a word) fantastic. As a result, before deciding to pursue this strategy, a thorough risk analysis should be undertaken, modelling and planning for your expected cash flow, and risks to your cash flow, to the myriad of other risks and changes to your life circumstances and your financial future over the long term. (To date, my business partner and I have set up approximately 200 of these plans, and I am proud to say that not one of our clients has collapsed their plan—which speaks, I hope, to the strength of the planning that underpins the use of this strategy for our clients.)

Comparing U.S. and Canadian Scenarios

Sometimes, prospective clients will ask about U.S. insurance plans, perhaps because of reading websites such as The White Coat Investor.

I was asked recently by a good friend of mine living in Boston about whether he should purchase a U.S. insurance policy. My friend is a Boston Celtics fan, but despite this, I told him that the benefits are not nearly as great for him as they are with our Ontario corporations.

Let's start by addressing some of the differences between U.S. and Canadian policyholders: In the United States, most professionals are not incorporated, and therefore buy their policies with after-tax personal dollars, with tax rates ranging from 35% to 50%. Ontario professionals, by comparison, receive similar benefits with after-tax corporate dollars, with rates of 12.2% applying to active business income.

In the United States, the tax rate on investment income is much lower, as low as 15% in some states. Compare this to the tax rate on passive income in Ontario, which is 50.2%. Tax-free growth on investments in Ontario corporations is much more attractive than tax-free growth on investments held personally in the United States.

Lastly, while the United States has an estate tax, which comes into play (as of 2019) at over $11.4 million individually and $22.8 million for couples, the United States actually has very low taxes when one passes away. In Canada, with a corporation, one's estate can be subject to rates as high as 48%—and this has been increasing dramatically over the years.

The concept of the capital dividend account does not exist in the United States, meaning we have an enormous advantage in Canada with tax-free payouts from the corporation.

Finally, the structure of plans is different in Canada versus the United States, which comes into play when factoring how much of your investments can grow tax-free.

All these factors come into play when looking at rate of return. In summary, it's safe to say that insurance is definitely a much less attractive investment in the United States.

In closing: I believe the biggest risk investors face when considering the question of whether or not to invest in a corporate-owned life insurance policy is the risk of being impressionable.

At the time of this writing, there are 17 very vocal celebrities who are still questioning the science of vaccines. While I am no medical expert, I have faith in science and the physician community—and while I believe these celebrities have well-meaning intentions, I also think their actions have potentially serious unintended consequences.

The same can be said for many of the criticisms of the strategy outlined in this chapter. The risk here is not to anyone's health;

nevertheless, if someone were to enter into an appropriate plan but exit early for the wrong reasons, they may place elements of their lifestyle at risk.

Today, with the rise of social media, there are some very vocal critics with a tendency to lump all plans together, or shout "foul" due to their own bad experiences. Comments suggesting no one should have permanent life insurance or should cancel within 10 years is not helpful in improving financial awareness. Skepticism and caution can be helpful when navigating financial decisions, but not blanket exaggerations.

The bottom line? Find a qualified advisor whom you trust and explore solutions that are custom-fit to your specific situation, and then make an informed decision.

Key Takeaways from This Chapter

Criticisms of corporate-held permanent life insurance often focus on how changes in tax policy and economic conditions might impact the success of using permanent insurance over the long term, the cost of the life insurance component of the policy relative to term insurance, or concerns about the sales process.

What all of these criticisms overlook, however, is the benefits of using corporate-held permanent life insurance for the incorporated professional—which include lower-cost premiums (paid with lightly taxed corporate dollars), a means to avoid new passive income tax rules, a way to create cash flow including in retirement, and providing a tax-efficient financial legacy.

A careful review of the facts and assumptions—which we provide in this chapter—can help uncover whether this strategy may be right for you. Due to the size and range of the potential benefits from this strategy, dismissing this option outright, without getting a qualified advisor to weigh in, might mean you miss out on ways to optimize your financial and tax situation.

Top Questions to Ask Your Advisor

1. Are you familiar with corporate-owned life insurance for incorporated professionals? Have you used or recommended this strategy to other incorporated professionals? If not, why not?
2. Do you think corporate-owned life insurance might be a good strategy for me? Could we run some numbers to evaluate scenarios?
3. If you think that corporate-owned life insurance isn't the right strategy for me now, what might make your views change over time? Will you review my situation over time to review whether your views have changed?

Chapter 5
Risk Management

A Careful Examination

O ften in the financial sales world, a focus tends to get placed on buying (or being sold) a product over examining the roles, benefits, and trade-offs of insurance in an individual's overall financial picture.

Insurance and risk management conversations with clients often are limited to: *here are all the insurance products on the product shelf, and here is why you need all of them.*

What companies often teach their insurance agents is all that people are left with: scare them, tell a story, and offer a product-based solution. A singular focus that is not broadened by a bigger context easily strays into the realm of "when the only tool you have is a hammer, everything looks like a nail." Yet, clearly, insurance products are not a solution for every problem.

In this chapter, we provide a detailed examination of the roles and trade-offs that insurance provides, which are often missing from the discussion. We hope you find this section informative as it is sometimes omitted from countless financial planning books, advice books written by financial advisors, and even from the training materials from insurance-based financial designations, including the Chartered Life Underwriter (CLU).

What You'll Get Out of This Chapter

As a professional, you have probably had many conversations about insurance—but unfortunately, many of those conversations have been focused on insurance products rather than the underlying rationale for those or any insurance products.

In this chapter, we take a different tack: What are the two fundamental types of insurance any professional should consider, and what are the types of insurance you can safely ignore if you choose?

We distinguish between wealth insurance (protecting money or creating a financial benefit) and risk insurance (protecting you, when you need it, from the financial implications of death or disability).

By the end of this chapter, you should have a good understanding of how to think about the needs that can be met by different types of insurance, what types of insurance you might want and need, and how to assess your changing insurance needs over time.

The Way We Think About Insurance

Certainly the risk management and insurance chapters of financial books can be the boring ones that most of us skip. We hope to bring a different lens to the topic that keeps you reading, one that's relevant to you.

As a starting point, our view is that any insurance product you have needs to fall into one of the following two categories:

1. Wealth insurance

    Chapter 4 was all about accessing permanent insurance on the balance sheet. The first two examples examined here show how insurance can be used to insure your wealth.

2. Risk insurance

It is mandatory to have car insurance because many Canadians could not afford the potential damage created from a car crash. High potential risk costs are the guide; if you have dependents or debts, you should have life insurance. If you are starting out in your career, then you likely need disability insurance to protect an enormous asset: the potential loss of future income.

Surprisingly, I would suggest that much of what is out there in the insurance marketplace does not fall into either of these categories, and instead falls into what I consider luxury insurance. I believe most of us could safely avoid luxury insurance.

Wealth Insurance

Let's start off with what I believe to be one of the best, yet most controversial, investment ideas I know. It's so controversial that we have only implemented this plan with 10% or so of the clients we serve.

The reason is that it's very difficult to bring up given the implied payout one receives in such a tragic time. Perhaps, as this idea is buried halfway through this book, the discussion is softened.

So what is this idea? It's the concept of having wealth insurance on your parents; that is, ensuring that your parents have a permanent life insurance policy in place to pay out a guaranteed death benefit upon their passing.

Wealth Insurance on Parents

There are a few efficient methods of structuring this.

When You Pay the Premiums

The first is where you, the child and eventual heir, pay the insurance premiums for either an individual plan on one parent or joint plan on both parents. A good reason for the insurance may be to pay taxes in the parents' estate, or keep the parents' cottage within the family, and so forth.

We recommend structuring the permanent insurance plan as an increasing death benefit. That way, the longer your parents live, the larger the payout—in terms of ethos and karma, we are on the side of longevity. If the death benefit were static then the rate of return would be dramatically higher in the earlier years, an uneasy situation.

Now the question arises of how to pay these premiums. Ideally, it's cheaper to pay the premium from after-tax corporate dollars, given that you are likely to save up to 40% on the premiums. The controversial insurance element here is that when you apply for insurance, you have to indicate an insurable need to be approved.

For instance, someone with an income of $100,000 and little net worth would likely not be approved for a $10,000,000 death benefit without creating a reason for it. While every person's situation is unique, it may be easier to justify a personal insurable need (i.e., paying your parents' final tax bill) rather than a corporate insurance need. A lot of this is dependent on the discretion of the underwriter.

However, it should be noted that once an insurance plan is put into place, a change of ownership could always be enacted. As of January 1, 2017, there are some new rules regarding the transfer of personally owned plans to corporately owned plans that affect the tax-free element aspect of insurance through the capital dividend account. A proper analysis would need to be done here involving an insurance specialist.

Example

Let's take a look at a real-life example (see Table 5.1):

- A 35-year-old doctor deposits $40,000 per year over 10 years into a permanent structured insurance plan on his parents, each aged 65.
- The policy was structured corporately so that the premiums came from after-corporate-taxed dollars.
- By using the joint-last-to-die structure the insurance age cost is reduced to age 58, meaning you would be paying the same premium as an individual who is 58 years old.

Table 5.1 Cash Value and Death Benefit

$40,000 × 10 Payments, 6.25% Dividend

	Cash Value	Death Benefit
Year 10	$ 339,599	$ 564,466
Year 20	$ 642,737	$ 895,036
Year 30	$1,180,432	$1,389,206
Year 40	$1,809,626	$1,901,687

- The plan is structured to be 100% paid up in 10 years to avoid any additional payments.
- The plan is focused on the death benefit; thus no additional deposits or overfunding structures are needed—very different from the plan discussed in Chapter 4.
- The death benefit starts at $418,720 and grows throughout the years; that way the longer the doctor's parents live, the higher the death benefit's value.
- The long-term internal rate of return (IRR) on the death benefit paid to the corporation hovers around 4.5% to 6%.
- But remember, a 4.5% rate of return is the equivalent of a 9% interest-required equivalent.
- The more conservative an investor you are, the more attractive these returns become, as they are as close to risk-free as one can have in terms of investing.

A few things to take note of here:

- First, within limits, the growth of the policy is tax-sheltered. Second, the death benefit will pay out tax-free to the corporation.
- Finally, usually the majority, if not all, of the death benefit proceeds will credit the capital dividend account, allowing for tax-free dividends to be paid to the shareholders.
- Depending on when one passes, and the structure of the plan, a large percentage of the death benefit will become personal assets.

The IRR noted here does not factor in this element, which, when compared to alternative investments, could add another 40% to the return over the years, and may be a huge benefit for entering into this plan. In the end, it becomes a way to get funds out of the corporation without having to pay a significant amount of personal taxes.

It should be noted that in case of a need for a cash inflow, you can access the cash values or dividends on the policy. Also, keep in mind that corporate-owned insurance does not create passive income given the new passive income measures introduced in 2018.

The purpose of insurance is not supposed to be for a high rate of return, and especially not for the removal of funds from a corporation tax-free. The purpose is to be for practical reasons such as paying a final tax bill or taking care of dependents. Where this is important to note is that when applying for this plan there should be a good reason to justify entering this plan, and a "good rate of return" will not be responded to well by an underwriter.

When an Estate Bond Pays the Premiums

Another strategic insurance plan would be where parents structure an estate investment, sometimes referred to as an estate bond. While there are a myriad of ways to structure these types of investments, one of the ideas I bring up with clients is where the parents pay the premiums either in the earlier years and have the children eventually take over the payments, or simply split the premiums with the children from the start.

The rationale behind these plans is to accomplish a few goals:

- First, the rate of return for the children will end up being very high, very safe and tax-efficient. From the children's perspective, it would be the equivalent of having a massively enhanced tax-free savings account.
- Second, it hopefully creates behavioural discipline. Did you know that a third of lottery winners go bankrupt, and are more likely to do so than the average citizen, within three to five years? By having the children commit to the payments, whether

fully or partially, they are more likely to view this strategy as an investment that they have earned as opposed to a lottery inheritance that they have been gifted.

I typically suggest that for these plans the structure be simple, a level payment every year with a simply rounded flat death benefit payout.

Example
- For instance, let's look at a plan I set up for clients in 2011, where they are paying $480/month.
- For this structure, there were no additional costs to pay monthly (many plans do have extra costs for monthly premiums).
- The payments were $5,760 per year for a death benefit of $400,000.
- The parents at the time were 65 and 63.
- The payments will never increase, and are split; the parents are paying $280 per month and each child is paying $100 per month.
- This way, the children are paying $100 per month for an eventual payout of $200,000 tax-free.

From a strictly returns point of view, the children would be crazy not to be engaged in this investment. From their perspective, they need to ask: How many investments out there generate 9.55% per year tax-free over 30 years, with zero market risk? In this specific client example, this death benefit would conveniently pay for the taxes on the cottage that the clients wanted to keep within the family for legacy purposes.

The most important part of this is to make sure the payments are made, otherwise this is a colossal waste of funds. Hence, it is very important to bring children into these conversations, and even better to have them involved financially if possible.

A tragic case I know of is a 90-year-old physician who had a level universal life insurance plan that would have paid out over $1,000,000. The problem was that he never had a conversation with his heirs about the purpose of this plan. The physician was very sick and ended up cancelling his plan simply because he did not want the headache. I had to think that had that advisor planned with the children on board as well, the plan could still have been in place, ultimately producing a much better financial outcome than foregone premiums with no ultimate death benefit payable.

I do wonder what would happen if more Canadians had these open conversations about finances with their children. Imagine how much better off many Canadians would be if children were using some of their non-registered funds to pay for an insurance policy on their parents. It would dramatically reduce risk in portfolios and provide us with better risk-adjusted rates of return.

Risk Insurance (Life and Disability Insurance)

Risk Insurance

The second type of insurance we believe in is what we refer to as risk insurance, which should also be viewed as necessary or necessity insurance.

Protecting income in the early stages of wealth building or providing for dependents falls into this type of insurance. Before we go any further, a goal you should have when looking at necessity insurance is to have enough wealth accumulated that you're in a position to be self-insurable from your assets. That is, you should buy this necessity insurance with the specific view that it will become unnecessary over time.

But if that's our starting point, why have this extra cost in insurance?

Example

I remember a conversation I had with my father, a cardiac surgeon at University Health Network in Toronto, years ago when he was in his 60s, in terms of paying for his disability insurance (DI).

His debts were paid off, both his children were self-sufficient, his assets were enough to cover his lifestyle. Although disability insurance would have been necessity insurance for him when he had young children, debt, and fewer assets, at this point in his life there really was no need for this unnecessary cost. The necessity had become unnecessary. I told him to cancel his plan, which was to his benefit.

Life Insurance

How much does one really need and do we go with an association plan or an individual plan?

How much life insurance do we need?

My general rule is that you need term life insurance when you have dependents or have debts.

The textbook definition tells us you need 10× to 20× your annual income in terms of life insurance.

Based on this, if you have $300,000 of income you should have $3,000,000 to $6,000,000 in coverage.

I have also seen advisors use a formula:

Your income × 2 +

Your total debts outstanding +

$15,000 per year per child prior to 18

For instance, if you have an income of $500,000 with $800,000 in debt and a 2- and a 4-year-old, you should have, based on this formula, $2,250,000 in life insurance.

I have issues with this textbook definition, as other factors apply (savings, earning level of spouse, spending habits/lifestyle, need to save for retirement ...).

Bottom line, everyone's situation is completely different as you have to factor in not only all the financial elements including age and cost, but also your preferences and wishes.

Example

Should you consider how much you have saved up? The more you have, the less insurance you likely need. How much are you saving from the income you currently have? Let's be realistic for a second.

- If you are saving $100,000 or $200,000 per year in your corporation, while possibly very noble of you to want to protect your family, do you still need the same coverage, or do you still want the same coverage?
- How much does your partner make? The more your partner makes, the less need for insurance.
- How much of that debt is tied to your student loans and principal residence and how much is tied to rental properties? The latter arguably might not need to be insured.
- On the higher side, if you want to send your children to private school, you may want to add another $25,000 per child per year to that formula (and sometimes upwards of $40,000 per year at certain private schools).

My biggest issue with these formulas is that if all this holds true (whether we are speaking of the textbook definition of insurance or a more catered solution to your specific need), should we not eventually decrease the insurance coverage every year?

Ask how many of your colleagues perform this kind of analysis. I believe the answer would likely be none. It appears to me that an insurance needs analysis is completed when the insurance plan is put into place, but often forgotten about when all the factors change.

For instance, ceteris paribus—my high school economics teacher's favorite Latin term meaning "other things equal," for holding all other variables constant—if you have saved $100,000 this year, would it not be safe to say you need $100,000 less insurance next year? All plans discussed will give you the option to reduce the death benefit each year—the only caveat is someone needs to take the initiative to do so. However, the other caveat is that if you are making more money each year, then you might want to keep that insurance at that level or even increase it. (No spouse ever said they didn't want the extra life insurance proceeds when their spouse died.)

It's good to point out that term life insurance should almost always be paid by the corporation, where you are paying with after-lightly-taxed corporate dollars as opposed to heavily-taxed personal dollars. The death benefit will essentially be the same as with corporate life insurance. The corporation has a capital dividend account that allows for proceeds to be credited to your estate tax-free.

However, the reason I say "almost" here is that a benefit of owning insurance personally is that it is protected from creditors upon your estate. For instance, in the event you lose your life in a car crash, and in the act of doing so hurt someone such that they sue your estate, they could technically go after corporate insurance payouts but not personal insurance payouts. While this is rare, some feel comfortable owning insurance personally for that reason alone.

Some may also point out that insurance payouts from the corporation are subject to probate in some provinces; however, this can simply be avoided by having a secondary will for your corporation (more on that later).

Association Plan or Individual Plan Life Insurance?

Once an amount is determined, the question becomes whether we go with an association plan, also known as group coverage, or an individual plan.

Before we dive into this, I should point out that I have an insurance license and I am compensated on individual plans but not compensated on association plans. With that said, I usually recommend association plans for physicians under 50 but individual plans if there is an insurable need over 50. However, in both situations a combination of the two can very well make sense.

Association Plans 101
- Priced based on a group, not individually, usually broken down by age, gender, smoking status, preferred, or regular.

- You are accepted or rejected.
- Plans are usually much cheaper in the earlier years, and often have step-rate premiums, where premiums increase at various age bands every five years.
- There are often high annual premium refunds (i.e., OMA life insurance rebates were 60%, 58%, and 40% in 2016, 2017, and 2018, respectively). It should be noted these refunds have been dropping with very low interest rates that are prevailing right now. The association plans may need to keep more in reserves and will therefore potentially have less for refunding.
- Some association plans need to be paid with after-tax personal dollars.
- Plans can be altered by the association.

Individual Plans 101

- Priced based on an evaluation of your health by an underwriter with possible modifications/exclusions that can vary company to company.
- Can be structured as 1-, 5-, 10-, 20-, or 30-year or until-age-65 plans.
- Once in place, plans can only be altered by you.

So why do I like association plans earlier on? Simply put, they are cheaper when cost matters.

Ultimately, they can become more expensive, but the goal is to reach financial independence before that time comes. Every year that goes by, assuming you are saving money, your children are one year closer to being self-sufficient, you are paying off debts, and so on. Ideally your insurable needs are decreasing.

One of the most common financial goals for a high-income professional is to be self-insured. I am often told by clients that they want to be in a position to work if they want to, but not because they have to.

Any insurance broker can show you a chart that illustrates the savings an individual carrier will have with an association plan over a 30-year period. However, what is missing from this analysis is why we are positioning ourselves to have the same insurable need 30 years from now. By following this missing analysis, it's as if we are setting up our financial plans for failure! Most importantly, you should view this as what you could do as an alternative with those savings in the earlier years.

That is not to say that individual plans never make sense. Here are examples of where they are preferred:

- If one is looking to possibly switch careers, individual plans are portable, unlike most group coverage (rare for physicians but more common with other professionals).
- If one is age 50 or older a cost analysis should be done, as many individual plans may be cheaper around this age, assuming they are approved with underwriting. For instance, many group plans reduce coverage at age 60 while the premiums remain the same.
- If one is looking to eventually convert to permanent insurance, this is sometimes available up to age 70 with individual term insurance.

Disability Insurance

Disability 101: As a start, I always tell clients that I wish they would rename this *financial protection against permanent disability insurance*, as that's a more appropriate title. For most of us, we are told to pay tens of thousands of dollars in premiums throughout our career for coverage of a potential disability that pays out a monthly figure, likely after 90 days (though this could be 14, 30, or 60 for higher costs or 120, 180, 365, or 730 for lower costs).

I think the name sounds as if it really eases our financial burden if we are disabled for a few months. The reality is that it really only benefits us if we are disabled for a very long time or permanently cannot do our jobs.

The undisclosed kicker is that while the premiums stay the same or even increase with every year that goes by, the potential long-term payout is less, as many plans pay out only until age 65 or less.

As a case in point, imagine a 63-year-old with disability insurance paying thousands in premiums for a potential two-year payout. There may be a good reason Warren Buffett loves investing in insurance companies as investments.

Disability Insurance: Do We Need the Ferrari Disability Package?

In terms of hierarchy in the importance of insurance rankings, especially in the earlier years, disability insurance is arguably the most important type for you (term life insurance is for your beneficiary).

However, let's not confuse the need for disability insurance with the need for what I like to call the Ferrari disability package. What do I mean by the Ferrari package? The disability insurance with all the bells and whistles, that is, all the extra cost riders. Buyer beware: the higher the premiums, the higher the likely payout to insurance agents, including me.

The Good Insurance Rider

Let's start off with the rider that arguably is the most important rider decision: the **own-occupation rider**. Own-occupation ensures that you collect your disability benefit if you are unable to perform the main duties and tasks of your regular job. The downside is that the cost of this rider can be in the range of 35–45% more than a basic plan that covers "any occupation."

If you are a surgeon and injure your hands, this rider would be the lynchpin between being paid or having the insurance company reject your claim based on the grounds you can still practice medicine in another capacity. For most of us, I would say that it is safe to have this rider.

The exception to this rule would be if you determine that the purpose of having disability insurance is not for disabilities that prevent you from doing your current job, but more for financial accommodation in the event of a catastrophic disability.

For instance, if you are a family doctor and concerned that an insurance company would conclude that although you cannot do your own job, you can do medical consulting, then you should have the own-occupation rider.

If the need for disability insurance is only for financial accommodation in the event of a debilitating permanent illness, such as multiple sclerosis, then while I would still suggest that the own-occupation rider is preferred, it's not a requisite.

The Situational/Dynamic Insurance Riders

The next two riders are situational riders that require a dynamic approach. At some point in our careers they may make sense, but at some point, they may not.

1. The first is the **cost of living adjustment (COLA)**, which increases your benefit each year you are on claim, ranging from 2% to a maximum of 8%, with the latter option being more expensive. Overall, this rider will cost 15–25% more in premiums in the earlier years.

   In the earlier years, we should view this as a valuable option given the longer time horizon potential payout in the event of a permanent disability, but the closer we are to 65, the lesser the value given the shorter time horizon potential payout.

   However, if one applies for this rider in the later years, the annual cost is higher, even though the value is less. Go figure!

   I would make the case that at some point in our careers, after a proper needs analysis is complete, we may want to drop this extra cost by removing this rider.

2. The second is the **future insurability option** (FIO), commonly referred to as the **future earnings protection option (FEPO)**—or FIG, FNR, MIR, GIR depending on the company.

   This rider allows you to increase your coverage up to 25% or a fixed-dollar amount without having to go through the underwriting process.

   While I understand certain scenarios where this makes sense, such as a resident with very little approved coverage planning to increase their coverage every year, for a lot of us this ends up being a waste of money.

I have sat down with many doctors who have no intention of ever increasing their disability—if anything, they will likely be decreasing their coverage—yet they are paying an extra premium for this option. I see this as paying a premium for an insurance plan on an insurance plan. If you have no need to increase your coverage and yet still have this option, then save yourself some money by removing this rider.

The Don't Always Recommend Riders

Retirement protection rider: Redirects a specified amount toward a retirement account, for a cost. I have never seen a single case where this was a valued benefit. However, if one absolutely needs a forced savings plan, then adding this rider would perhaps be worth a discussion.

Catch-up rider: If you are disabled for at least six months, then you can be paid for the first 90 days after the fact. If this is truly a need, you are living paycheque to paycheque. In this scenario, looking at a disability payout date sooner than 90 days likely makes more sense.

Return of premium rider: Returns 50–100% of the premiums at predetermined dates if you have not become disabled or sometimes, based on the plan, if you've made only minimal claims. For example, for 55% more costs, you can have 50% of your premiums refunded in year 8, 15, 22, or 29. On the surface, this rider looks appealing. However, let's look at scenarios:

Scenario 1—You become disabled.

In this event, it would have been preferable to pay less in premiums for this coverage; therefore no rider is preferable.

Scenario 2—Your disability insurance needs to be reduced.

With the return of premium rider, you are essentially locked in to keeping your plan until that eight-year interval to recoup those extra costs. Without the rider you can adjust when applicable.

Scenario 3—Seven years pass with no changes.

With no rider, let's say your cost was $1,643 for seven years, and you are "out" $11,501.

With a rider, let's say your cost was $2,547 for seven years, where you are refunded $8,914 tax-free (the tax-free element is something that is currently being reviewed in terms of rule changes) and the cost ended up being $8,914 instead of $11,501 ($2,587 less).

In the no-rider scenario, let's assume you invest that $904 differential for seven years and in the eighth year you take those funds back. If you average approximately 8% in returns, you would have that same amount.

When evaluating whether this rider makes sense, you should assign a probability of the likelihood of these three scenarios, using probability theory to do the calculations.

Example

- For instance, if you believe that Scenario 1 is 10% likely and Scenario 2 is 30% likely, then you should assign a 60% probability of Scenario 3.
- Given that, your required rate of return is not 8% but 4.8% (60% of 8%), as probability theory can tell us what's likely to happen.
- Now you know how to price stock options!

Looking at these three scenarios, I would suggest that if you were a conservative investor, then there is an argument for a return of premium rider, especially if you think Scenario 2 is very unlikely. However, if you are a moderate or aggressive investor, I think it's safe to stay away from this rider.

Other Common Questions

Should we own insurance corporately?

Our financial industry says no, because although there is a saving on the premium payments by paying with after-tax corporate dollars, the payout is tax-free to the corporation, meaning we still could pay taxes on the way out.

However, if your disability coverage is $5,000 per month or less, then a strong case could be made to own the plan through the corporation. Why? Because even though payouts of tax-free personal dollars are preferable to tax-free corporate dollars, given that dividends are taxed at extremely low rates in the lower brackets, you may be in a position to be able to take out that payment with very little in taxes anyway.

I'm young and invincible; should I have disability insurance?
Yes.

Should I get a lump-sum payout instead?
In the unfortunate event you are paid claims that look to continue indefinitely, it may be wise to negotiate with your insurance carrier to have a lump-sum payout instead. I have been involved in negotiations with clients where we discounted cash flows at a required return to build a case for a higher amount. In the end, it paid off well for the clients to have received the lump sum upfront.

Critical Illness Insurance

Critical illness (CI) insurance pays a tax-free lump-sum benefit if you are diagnosed with a serious medical condition, based on the carrier's definition, that persists for 30 days.

The "big three" conditions are cancer, heart attack, and stroke, with another 20 or so illnesses also included. If you have the financial resources and if you have the want and need for it, it is definitely an insurance protection to at least consider.

Earlier in this chapter and in Chapter 4, we discussed how insurance can be a great wealth asset. As discussed disability and life insurance in many people's lives are necessities. CI insurance is not; it's luxury insurance. That's not necessarily a bad thing, but I would start by making sure your life and disability needs are covered before addressing this need.

In fact, this is the one issue that my business partner and I disagree on—he even has his own CI plan.

Sometimes the probability of a claim works against you. For example, you would need to suffer a heart attack, based on the insurance company's definition of a heart attack, then live for 30 days, and only then can you make a claim. If you pass away, no benefit for you. In our experience, we have seen more claims rejected then accepted.

There is recourse if the insurer denies your claim, and, unfortunately, we have had to refer clients to appropriate lawyers to fight for their claim. In the end, settlements were made in many cases so there was a good final outcome.

The expected rate of return probability is poor. In terms of cost per coverage, the premium percentage is much higher than other insurance plans.

- A 28-year-old male buys a simple $100,000 CI plan with level payments of $755 per year.
- If that same person invests $755 per year at approximately 6%, he would have $100,000 in an investment by the time he is 65.
- It's a fair question to ask: Which path do you feel more comfortable with?

If you thought there were unnecessary riders with disability insurance, you are in for a treat with CI insurance. In addition to the return of premium riders that are often promoted, you can have costly riders such as: return of premium on death (also known as life insurance), waiver of premiums if you are disabled, and even a rider that allows for $500 charitable contributions.

With all this being said, there are some exceptions:

- If you are denied DI coverage but can obtain CI coverage (I have seen this), then the coverage becomes more of a necessity than a luxury.
- If you might leave your work for another profession, the portability of an individual plan may be beneficial.
- If you are not saving or investing, then the value of CI in the risk management conversation increases.
- If you're okay with paying a high premium to hedge against a critical illness, then I see absolutely no issue in having this protection.

Long-Term Care Insurance

Long-term care insurance can help pay for care or services if you can't perform two of the following six activities of daily living: bathing, eating, dressing, toileting, transferring, and continence.

We usually set these plans in place when someone is retired or close to retirement and is single/widowed or divorced and has the financial risk of facing long-term care costs. In contrast to this approach, we worked with a young radiologist whose insurance advisor recommended this plan to him in his 30s. Safe to say there was zero need for this product in this instance. This is what we refer to as selling the entire product shelf.

For practical purposes, we won't cover many of the other insurance plans out there, as they are separate topics of their own:

- **Practice insurance:** Office contents, practice interruption and general liability, office overhead expense insurance, and buy/sell insurance.
- **Liability and legal insurance:** Malpractice insurance, personal umbrella liability insurance, and legal expense insurance.
- **Staff insurance:** Group benefits.

Key Takeaways from This Chapter

When you're fulfilling your insurance needs, keep in mind that a product sales focus may mean that insurance proposed for you can easily be inappropriate: the wrong insurance, the wrong amounts, or too expensive for your actual needs.

Two truly useful categories of individual insurance can be distinguished as *wealth insurance* and *risk insurance*:

1. *Wealth insurance* as a category cements the transfer of wealth between generations.
2. *Risk insurance* as a category demands an appraisal of your key risks: life insurance, disability insurance, and critical illness insurance. Not all products are suitable for all people at all stages of life.

Insurance riders can be very valuable, or they can be next to useless. A critical eye can help determine the best value for you. No matter what insurance you're considering or putting into place, a careful analysis of your specific situation is necessary. Don't get sold the whole product shelf!

Top Questions to Ask Your Financial Planner

1. What's the underlying rationale for any of the insurance products I'm currently holding? Do I need more protection, or less?
2. Have we reviewed my insurance needs since I first entered into the policies I hold now? Should my existing coverage be adjusted in light of changes to my overall situation?
3. Are we taking full advantage of the benefits that insurance could offer?
4. Am I overspending on unnecessary luxury insurance coverage?
5. What plans do you have to review my insurance coverage over time? When and how frequently should we review and potentially adjust my policies?

Chapter 6
Borrowing to Invest

What Is Leverage?

The majority of the wealthiest people in the world have, at some point in their lives, relied on borrowed money to create their wealth. This is why leveraging, or borrowing to invest, deserves a chapter of its own.

In a nutshell, borrowing money to invest is like doing what banks do. Banks take the money we deposit, pay us an interest rate, and then go off and invest in something else, generating a potentially higher rate of return. It's known as the concept of using other people's money (OPM).

The most important aspect of leverage is that it is a blade that cuts both ways: it can offer massive financial benefits or become a major financial burden. The key is to use leverage prudently, investing wisely in the appropriate investment accounts within disciplined and certain time frames, and to make sure that it is suitable for your specific risk tolerance.

Leveraging can be used to improve your long-term effective rate of return within your corporation assets, or help build your non-registered assets.

In this chapter, we explore how leverage can enhance returns in the corporation, assist in removing funds outside of the corporation with offsetting deductions, and make your mortgage tax deductible—but we'll also look at the downside of leveraging.

What You'll Get Out of This Chapter

In this chapter, we review the ins and outs of borrowing to invest, also known as the use of leverage.

We review who is a suitable candidate for the use of leverage, and what products and strategies may allow you to benefit from leverage—and importantly, we also review when and for whom leverage is not appropriate, including some cautionary tales from real-life examples we've seen.

You will leave this chapter with a good overview of how to use leverage to your advantage, and when to steer clear.

First, let's review the pros and cons of leveraging.

Pros of Leveraging

- It may increase your effective returns.
- Your investments start working for you right away, as opposed to waiting the time it takes to save the same amounts.
- Borrowing money to invest allows you to create a tax deduction for interest costs.
- Behavioural finance principle: Leverage creates a forced savings plan, which forces you to be disciplined in your saving, perhaps resulting in less impulsive spending.

Cons of Leveraging

- It may decrease your effective returns.
- If interest rates rise, your breakeven benefit rate will rise while your costs go up.
- It becomes a cash-flow constraint.
- Some loans allow for margin calls, where you may be forced to come up with more assets or sell investments to allow for the loan to continue.

- It can affect future borrowing capacity: the more leverage you have, the harder it is to be approved for future borrowing (such as a mortgage).
- Behavioural finance principle: If you are likely to sell when (not if) the investments lose value, or you lose sleep at night worrying over investment returns, leveraging your investments could really backfire on you.

To show the effect of leveraging on returns, let's look at Table 6.1, which shows a one-year time frame, assuming the return breakdown is 65% in the form of capital gains and 35% in the form of

Table 6.1 How Leverage Impacts Effective Returns

Ontario Scenario: 53.53% marginal tax rate, 65% capital gains, 35% dividends, 4% interest on debt

	Scenario 1 8% Gain	Scenario 2 Leveraged 8% Gain	Scenario 3 8% Loss	Scenario 4 Leveraged 8% Loss
Non-borrowed investment	$1,000,000	$500,000	$1,000,000	$ 500,000
Borrowed money		$500,000		$ 500,000
Return on investment	$ 80,000	$ 80,000	$ (80,000)	$ (80,000)
Less: Interest cost		$ (20,000)	–	$ (20,000)
Add: Tax savings from interest deduction		$ 10,706	–	$ 10,706
Less: Tax on investments	$ (24,928)	$ (24,928)	$ (11,015)	$ (11,015)
After-tax return	$ 55,072	$ 45,778	$ (91,015)	$(100,309)
Effective after-tax return (%)	5.51%	9.16%	–9.10%	–20.06%

dividends, and using a portfolio that is made up of $500,000 of your own funds and $500,000 of borrowed funds.

- Under the +8% scenario with 50% leverage, you end up with an effective rate of return of 9.16% after taxes, compared to 5.51% with no leverage.
- Under the –8% scenario with 50% leverage, you end up with an effective rate of return of –20.16% compared to –10.20% with no leverage.
- **Note:** What is not included is the tax benefit of having a capital loss to be claimed in the previous three years or carried forward into future years indefinitely, applicable in Scenarios 3 and 4.

Looking at this example, it's good to address some of the rules I recommend:

Rule 1: *Leverage only for the long term—more than 10 years.* The shorter the time horizon, the higher the probability that Scenario 4 will occur. The longer the time horizon, the higher the probability that Scenario 2 will occur. This is because you have a much higher probability of averaging 6%, 7%, or 8% returns over the course of 10 years as opposed to in one year.

Rule 2: *The higher your tax rate, the lower your required break-even when looking at tax savings from the interest rate.* These examples assume the highest tax bracket, but the numbers would look different if your tax savings was at the 29.65% rate ($47,631 to $77,317 in income in Ontario) as opposed to 53.53%. However, this is partially offset by the taxes paid each year on the investment returns.

Rule 3: *The after-tax gains are more important than the pre-tax gains.* The more your returns are in the form of tax-deferred capital gains, the higher your effective rate of return. The more your returns are in the form of interest and dividends, the less your effective rate of return will be.

Rule 4: *Choose an appropriate loan structure.* Interest-only debt in a positive-return environment works best mathematically in your favour, whereas principal and interest debt reduces your leverage exposure—and ultimately risk—over time. Avoid margin loans where more capital is needed; for example, you don't want to sell and lock in losses in a Scenario 4 situation. Also, the higher the interest rate the higher the required break-even rate. One needs to be very cognisant of the current interest-rate environment.

Rule 5: *Do not invest in riskier stocks with leverage.* Given that leverage has the potential to enhance effective after-tax returns by the leverage structure itself, this also means that we don't have to have a riskier portfolio based on composition of stocks to achieve positive results.

Rule 6: *The higher the percentage of leverage in your account, the higher the differential between your leveraged effective after-tax return compared to non-leveraged effective after-tax return.* These scenarios assume 50% leverage. In real-life terms, I usually recommend no more than 15%.

Who Are Good Candidates for Using Leverage?

Good candidates are high-income earners in high tax brackets (who receive more benefit from deductible interest), with a minimum of a 10-year time horizon, adequate and consistent cash flow, whose risk tolerance is in the moderately aggressive to aggressive category, and who have both the ability and willingness to take on risk. It is important to consult an advisor before using leverage to determine whether it's a suitable strategy for you.

Conversely, if you are a low-income earner, have a shorter time horizon, or are a conservative investor, leveraging is just not suitable for you.

Enhancing Returns in the Corporation with Leverage

Some people believe we are in the glory days of corporations, due both to the fact that the tax rate on active income—the small business deduction (SBD)—is at an all-time low and that we have great mechanisms such as the capital dividend account (CDA) to pull money out efficiently.

If you follow this line of thinking, you might also argue that we should position ourselves to save up as much as possible, and as quickly as possible. Leveraging can assist us in this effort.

Given that these boon times may pass by, we could liken it to a race for savings.

To model approaches to this race, let us compare two hypothetical scenarios, one leveraged and one not (see Table 6.2). We'll assume a 6% return (keeping things simple, using tax-deferred capital gains but also factoring in CDA and RDTOH accounts) with a 6% interest rate on borrowed money and assuming the top personal tax rate.

Scenario 1: Dollar Cost Averaging Inside Your Corporation

- Let's assume you can save $5,000 per month in an investment plan.
- Fast-forward 10 years later, you would have $816,321 pre-tax with a cost base of $600,000.
- Assuming you sold your investment then and there, factoring in CDA/RDTOH, you would end up with $795,229 in the corporation.
- If you took out all your corporate funds, assuming the top tax bracket for ineligible dividends, you would have *$467,223 personally*.

Scenario 2: Using Leverage Inside Your Corporation

- Let's assume you borrow $1,000,000 at a 6% interest rate (prime is currently at 2.45%), which would cost you $5,000/month.
- The $1,000,000 portfolio at 6% would grow to $1,790,848.
- Additionally, your interest is tax deductible. If you happen to have interest income, it would be deductible at the passive income rate at 50.2% (in Ontario).
- If all your investment income is tax-deferred capital gains, then it would be deductible at the 12.2% rate (in Ontario). Let's be conservative and assume 12.2%. Over the course of 10 years you would have an additional $73,200 from tax deductions ($301,200 at most).

Table 6.2   Enhancing Returns in the Corporation with Leverage: Two Scenarios

Corporation:	Scenario 1—Dollar Cost Averaging	Scenario 2—Leverage
Capital gain after 10 years	$216,321 (816,321 – 600,000)	$790,848 (1,790,848 – 1,000,000)
Taxable portion at 50%	$108,161	$395,424
Tax @50.17%	$ 54,261	$198,384
RDTOH	$ 33,172	$121,277
CDA	$ 108,161	$395,424
Benefit from interest deduction		$ 73,200* (600,000 deducted at 12.2%)
Cash available in corporation	$795,230 (600,000 + 216,321 – 54,264 + 33,172)	$786,940 (1,790,848 – 1,000,000 – 198,384 +121,277 + 73,200)
Individual:		
Non-taxable capital div.	$108,161	$395,424
Taxable dividend to S/H	$687,068 (795,229 – 108,161)	$391,516
Tax (non-eligible) @ 47.74%	$328,007	$186,910
Net after-tax cash retained	$467,223	$600,030

*Interest paid on money borrowed to purchase income-producing property is generally deductible. In *Swirsky* 2014 FCA 36, a deduction was denied because the company shares had no history of paying dividends, so there was no subjective "reasonable expectation of income." The position of the Canada Revenue Agency, however, appears to be to not challenge the deduction on funds used to buy shares of a company with no history of paying dividends; however, if the company (whose shares were purchased) has a stated policy of not paying dividends, then the deduction may be denied.

- Assuming you sold your investment then and paid off your loan, factoring in CDA/RDTOH, you would end up $786,940 in the corporation. The likelihood is that you would have some interest and dividends, so that number is going to fall somewhere in the middle.

- Now for the most important factor, remember that $1 non-registered is worth more than $1 inside our corporation. If you took the $786,940 out of the corporation, assuming the top bracket for ineligible dividends, you would have *$600,030 personally.*

Comparing the two scenarios, at the exact same rate of return of 6%, Scenario 2 with leverage gives you 28% more money, or $132,807 more.

- Remember, this is a scenario in which you are making 6% and paying 6% in debt payments.
- In fact, working backward, you would need almost a 10% return in Scenario 1 to outperform Scenario 2's leveraged scenario of the same 6% returns.
- With that said, Scenario 2 carries much more risk given a potential market crash.

Sensitivity factors on these scenarios are as follows:

1. Assuming no other income, the interest expense would create a non-capital loss, not a refund. The loss may be carried back up to three years for a potential refund of income. This tax benefit in Scenario 2 would likely be invested, creating a larger spread. This assumes 0% on the $75,000.
2. Given our current interest rate environment, the interest rate likely wouldn't be 6% over the next 10 years, therefore creating a larger spread.
3. The tax deduction wouldn't likely be only 12.2% over the 10-year time frame, given that there likely is at least a percentage of your portfolio generating interest, rental income, or foreign non-business income (no deduction is available for income subject to Part IV tax, i.e., Canadian dividends), therefore creating a larger spread. However, if some of this were to reduce the CDA benefit from your capital gains, the spread would be smaller.

4. The characteristic of the returns is a consideration; i.e., the more interest and dividends, the closer the spread becomes between the two scenarios.
5. The rates of return should also be considered. The higher the rate of return, the larger the spread. The lower the rate of return, the lower the spread.
6. The new passive income rules should be examined. If a large capital gain is triggered, this could reduce the small business deduction rate in the following year, something we would want to especially be careful of in Scenario 2.

Strategic Prudent Leverage: Timing

While the previous hypothetical scenario holds true, in a real-life example we also have to look at the market timing factor in leveraging your investing.

What if you leveraged on October 11, 2007, right before the start of the financial crisis?

- With a dollar cost averaging strategy, we buy the lows and the highs, reducing our risk of potentially being bad market timers—which most investors (and advisors) are.
- With that in mind, we subscribe to the view that both strategies should be examined and could work together.

Let's look at a way to use prudent leverage to enhance your returns.

Some Basic Assumptions

A moderately aggressive investor who plans to work for more than 10 years and has consistent income may want to consider leveraging up to a maximum of 5–15% of their corporate portfolio.

For a start, we would set up a line of credit, using our investments as collateral, of up to 50% of our portfolio.

(We recommend 50% collateral as you never know when you may need the balance for liquidity, i.e., for capitalizing on a market downturn, using proceeds for a rental property, etc.)

In this scenario, let's say we have $1,000,000 to start, with additional investments of $5,000 per month.

Step 1: Let's now slice off $625 per month of that savings and use it toward paying off the interest on a $150,000 line of credit (15% of your corporate assets).

The $625 per month or $7,500 per year will likely give you a tax reduction of $938 (and potentially up to $3,765) on your investment income.

Given the size of your portfolio you would likely have at least an offsetting $7,500 in a combination of foreign dividends and interest income.

Step 2: Every year we would want to re-evaluate our risk tolerance and current state of affairs.

We should not only look to rebalance the portfolio, getting us back to our original allocation, but also evaluate whether we want to pay down some of the line of credit, reducing the leveraged exposure, or increase our line of credit, getting us back to 15% leverage.

There will be certain times where we want 15% exposure to leverage but also certain times where we may want 10%, 5%, or even 0%. The point is that there is an opportunity to be strategic in our exposure to enhance returns but in a disciplined way.

Building a Non-Registered Portfolio

One of the concerns of many incorporated professionals is having too much of their wealth concentrated in one spot: the corporation.

While I don't necessarily agree with planning for hypothetical rule changes that could punitively affect corporations, I do believe that (usually after mortgage debts are paid off) it's good to diversify your asset allocation between account types and not just asset types—which includes building up a non-registered portfolio. The issue, if one is in the top personal tax bracket, is that it is not tax-efficient to withdraw funds directly and pay a lot in taxes to do this.

Let's start off by talking about the advantages of having non-registered assets, especially in retirement. Ultimately, the more flexibility one has in choosing where to withdraw funds from, the greater the likelihood that taxes can be reduced.

Example

- Assuming you want $100,000 per year in cash flow and your only asset is a registered retirement savings plan (RRSP), you would have to withdraw upward of $200,000 from the RRSP, assuming over 50% personal tax, as RRSP withdrawals are fully taxed as income.
- However, if you happened to have different accounts, you can choose to withdraw $10,000 from your RRSP and the rest from a combination of corporate savings, nonregistered, and tax-free savings accounts (TFSAs), reducing the tax payable compared to RRSP-only withdrawals.

A general guideline:

If you wish to minimize your current tax payable in the current year, generally withdraw from your investment accounts and the Canada Pension Plan (CPP) in this order:

1. TFSA
2. Personal nonregistered
3. Corporation
4. CPP
5. RRSP/RRIF

However, if you want to preserve your estate, withdraw in this order:

1. RRSP/RRIF
2. CPP

3. Corporation
4. Personal nonregistered
5. TFSA

Migrating Efficiently to a Non-Registered Portfolio

One tax-efficient way to move funds out of the corporation would be to use leverage.

In this specific strategy it may be prudent to use a principal amount and interest debt repayment.

- For instance, if one were to take out a principal amount and interest leverage loan of $300,000 at a 6% interest rate amortized over 25 years, the payment would be $23,033 per year (or $1,919 per month).
- The interest in the first year would be $17,628.
- In the highest tax bracket, this would generate a tax refund of $9,436 in the first year.
- To pay for this $23,033, let's assume we are taking out dividends from the corporation.
- If the dividends are eligible (from your general rate income pool dividend account), the additional tax rate on taking out a $23,033 dividend is $9,061 in the first year, where you come out slightly ahead ($375).
- As you might have noticed, because dividends offer tax credits the tax increase on $1 of dividends is less than the tax deduction on $1 of interest on a loan.
- If the dividends are ineligible, the additional tax rate on taking out $23,033 is $10,996, where you come out slightly behind ($1,560).

In this situation, what we are essentially doing is transferring the growth on your portfolio inside your corporation to be outside of your corporation. Now if you fast-forward some years out, we ultimately will have more funds non-registered, and less funds in the corporation, putting you in a better position for retirement, or simply to have more funds available to pay for personal items.

Of course the same risks apply with all leverage accounts. I would only look at this option in situations where we have 10-plus years, we have adequate cash flow, and we are moderately aggressive to aggressive investors.

Withdrawing from the RRSP with the Use of an Offsetting Deduction

The same strategy of using corporate funds can be employed in a similar fashion when withdrawing from an RRSP.

Depositing money into your RRSP is great, as you receive a tax refund on the contribution.

However, while the gains are tax-deferred inside the RRSP, withdrawing from the RRSP/RRIF is taxed in the worst possible way: as 100% taxable income. Ultimately, the RRSP becomes a tax-inefficient vehicle on the way out, and especially for your estate.

The financial industry, for many good reasons, has moved away from representing this strategy (sometimes referred to as the "RRIF meltdown") in recent years given the previously aggressive methods promoting the plan, which were sometimes inappropriately advised.

While it can be beneficial for some, in transitioning your registered assets to non-registered assets, all the same rules apply as earlier: a 10-plus-year time horizon, adequate cash flow, moderately aggressive or aggressive investor, and prudent use of leverage.

However, given that this is a strategy you would likely look at a later stage in your career, generally speaking this may also mean your portfolio is likely to be more conservative, there is a shorter time horizon, and the rules around borrowing are much stricter over 60.

This particular strategy requires a lot of attention to detail to make sure it is executed to your benefit.

Make Your Mortgage Interest Tax-Deductible

Before we describe how to make your mortgage interest tax-deductible, we need to review three kinds of debt: bad, normal, and best.

1. Bad debt is financing a depreciating asset or paying a high-interest-rate credit card.
2. Normal debt is financing an appreciating asset, such as a home.
3. Best debt is tax-deductible debt financing of an appreciating asset.

In many countries, mortgage interest on your principal residence is tax-deductible. For example, in the United States, interest on your principal residence is deductible up to a specified amount, $1,000,000 in mortgage debt (the limit is $500,000 if married and filing separately).

In Canada, your mortgage interest is not deductible, unless you are claiming a percentage as an office expense (subject to the tax rules), which usually is in the 5–15% range at most.[1] Due to this rule, we have to get creative if we want our normal debt to be the best sort of debt in Canada.

Debt Swap Scenario 1: Making Your Mortgage Interest Tax-Deductible

If you look at your assets and liabilities, you may find that you have a non-registered investment portfolio (outside your corporation and outside your RRSP) and also a home mortgage that is not tax-deductible.

The common rationale we hear from clients is that their investments are performing better than the interest rate on their mortgage, therefore they want to keep both. Almost always I would suggest cashing in your investments and using the money to pay off your mortgage. Then you can borrow new funds secured by a new mortgage to purchase new investments.

While it appears that the final outcome is the same, it's not. The new interest that you will be paying is now considered 100%

tax-deductible as it is for the purpose of investing, not for the purpose of paying off the mortgage on your principal residence.

Example

We did this recently with a client who had a $1,000,000 mortgage amortized over 15 years. Assuming a 4% interest rate and a top marginal tax rate (53.53%), over the course of 15 years she will have paid $349,116 in interest. By having this rate be tax-deductible, she is saving a total of $186,882, or 53.53% of the cost.

Some key notes:

- Ideally you would want to sell investments without triggering significant gains. If all your investments have significant gains, then a proper analysis should be done on whether the benefit of deductible interest is greater than the loss of compounded growth on the taxes paid on the gains today.
- Mortgages typically have lump sum repayment options of only 10%, 12%, or 15% per year on the original amount (unless it's an open mortgage), after which penalties kick in. However, most good mortgage brokers can do a debt swap without triggering this penalty.
- You need to do this properly to ensure that the interest deduction will be allowed. Specifically, there needs to be a clear connection between the borrowed funds and the eligible property acquired. For example, you want to ensure that you do not comingle your debt acquired for other purposes with the debt for investment (i.e., 80% of the debt is for investments and 20% for home renovations). It should be crystal clear for Canada Revenue Agency purposes that 100% of the debt was for investments and nothing else.

Debt Swap Scenario 2: Parents Helping Kids Help Themselves

Given the meteoric rise in real estate prices in many cities across Canada, many of us want to be able to help out our kids with their future home purchases and mortgage payments, but at the same time may not want to lose control over our assets.

Example

Let's take a look at an example in which you have $250,000 in guaranteed investment certificates (GICs) paying 4%. In a 50% tax bracket, this would net you $5,000 per year in after-tax profits. If you are over 65, this income may even claw back some government income-tested benefits. Fast-forward 10 years, you would have a total of $50,000 in after-tax income from this plan.

Let's say your child's mortgage (or a portion of it) is $250,000 at a fixed rate of 4%, amortized over 25 years, where your child is paying $1,334 per month.

- First, you cash in those GICs and then pay off $250,000 of your child's mortgage.
- That same day we go to the bank and take out a $250,000 line of credit in your child's name, returning the share certificates to you as well as a form declaring your ownership of the $250,000.
- The reason for this is that if your child splits up with his or her partner, we can come to them and demand $250,000 in cash.

Given that the debt is tied to an investment loan, the interest is tax-deductible in your child's hands.

- Assuming that same 4% interest rate and that your child is in a 50% tax bracket, this would now cost your child $833 per month or $10,000 per year in interest, which would be a deduction in their taxable income, for a savings of $5,000 of tax otherwise payable.
- With this refund your child can either pay an interest payment to you or, better yet, give it to you as a gift. (Note that in the case of loans between parties not operating at arm's length, such as parents and children, attribution rules may apply. Professional advice can help here.)

- Gifts between parents and children, as long as everyone is over 18, have no attribution rules and therefore no tax implications or taxes due.
- The end result to you is that you receive that same $5,000 per year in payments with the potential benefit of lowering your income tax bracket, given that this income is tax-free.

The benefit for the child is several-fold:

- First, they are now only paying $10,000 per year as opposed to $16,000 per year.
  - This extra $6,000 can go toward any other mortgage debt that is not tax-deductible, or be used toward an investment vehicle such as a TFSA (or possibly catch up from previous years).
  - At a 6% return rate, in 10 years that TFSA would be worth $79,085.
- Second, the $250,000 is now invested in an investment generating returns.
  - If you structured your investments to predominantly pay capital gains, at a 6% rate of return the $250,000 would return you $394,794 after-tax.
  - The net result is that in a little over 11 years, as opposed to 25 years, at a 6% return your child would have enough after-tax funds to pay off the $250,000 mortgage.
  - This would save them 14 years of mortgage payments.
  - Even at a 4% return, your child would have enough after-tax funds to pay off the $250,000 mortgage in a little less than 15 years, saving them 10 years of payments.

Some sensitivity analysis would need to be made on these assumptions in terms of rate of return, characteristic of return (interest, dividends, or capital gains), whether your child is already contributing to TFSAs (we would want to avoid possible over-contribution here), their tax bracket, and yours and any other contributing factors.

Overall, if you have liquid assets, especially those paying a conservative rate of return, these could be better off used to help your kids with their payments while making you no worse off financially. It is very important that this strategy be reviewed with a qualified tax advisor.

Investments That Use Leverage

We have covered:

- Leveraging to enhance returns in your corporate portfolio.
- Leveraging to effectively withdraw money from your corporation with an offsetting deduction.
- Leveraging to turn your debt into tax-deductible debt.

While many times these strategies make sense, owning investments with built-in leverage characteristics is a whole different ball game.

Leveraged and Inverse ETFs

Leveraged exchange-traded funds (ETFs) include both inverse and non-inverse ETFs that attempt to achieve performance of an index by a multiple. While they are typically designed to achieve their stated performance objectives on a daily basis, some investors may invest in these funds with the wrongful expectation that these funds may meet their stated daily objectives over the long term as well. This is due to the effect of compounding, fees, and daily resets.

With these products, in the long run, you are guaranteed to lose. In the United States, the Financial Industry Regulatory Authority (FINRA) and the Securities and Exchange Commission (SEC) have jointly issued an Investor Alert on these specialized products. Unfortunately, I have sat down with do-it-yourself investors who had no idea this would occur.

Example

Here's a hypothetical example over a two-trading-day period for a 2× leveraged fund assuming no operating expenses (see Table 6.3):

Table 6.3   How Do Leveraged ETFs Work?

	Index	2× Leveraged ETF
Start	1,000	$1,000
End Day 1	900	$ 800
End Day 2	1,000	$ 978

- Day 1, the index decreases 10%.
- Day 2, the index increases 11.11%, taking you back to the original starting point.
- With the leveraged ETF, Day 1, your 2× exposure to the index decreases your investment by 20% to bring your $1,000 to $800.
- Day 2, your 2× exposure to the index increases your investment 22.22% but only takes you back to $978, whereas the index you are tracking is back to par.

In Canada, Horizons is a large provider of these types of products. Unless you are trading these daily, I would suggest staying away from them.

Risk Parity Funds

In recent years many investment companies have begun offering "risk parity" funds, mainly due to an increase in attention since the 2008 financial crisis, as the risk parity approach fared better than traditionally constructed portfolios (60% stocks, 40% bonds).

The risk parity approach attempts to equalize that same risk by allocating funds to a wider range of categories such as stocks, government bonds, credit-related securities, and inflation hedges, while maximizing gains through financial leverage.

The risk parity approach asserts that when asset allocations are adjusted (leveraged or de-leveraged) to the same risk level, the risk parity portfolio can achieve a higher risk-adjusted return (otherwise called a higher Sharpe ratio, for those who may have learned about the principle in studying for their CFA) and can be more resistant to market downturns than a traditional approach.

Given that this is not a CFA-level book, we feel that these are really only suitable for accredited investors, as they are very complex investments. Nor would we recommend these products inside the corporation generally, given their very high distribution rates, making them tax-inefficient for the most part.

I will say that I do use risk parity for my own RRSP and TFSA and for clients who are comfortable with this approach.

When Does Leveraging Go Bad?

At the time of this writing, the average Canadian is now using 14.9% of their income for debt payments (Statistics Canada)—almost matching a 2007 high. You only need to look at one of the catalysts for the financial crisis—excess leverage—to see that leveraging has the potential to create some very big financial problems. Every client's situation is unique. While some of the previous scenarios may seem appealing, you should absolutely do your homework on whether leveraging makes sense for you.

Some Built-In Conflicts of Interest

It should be pointed out that many advisors are paid from an assets under administration (AUM) model, meaning the more money invested for a client, the more they are compensated. The reason we make mention of this is that a lot of bad sales practices exist out there, with the end result that people may have more money invested in the market and more exposure to debt than they should.

Examples

A sad example of this is a couple I know whose previous advisor not only recommended a RRIF meltdown (discussed earlier), but also had a formula where whatever the value of your RRSP was (i.e., $200,000 in this case), you would be advised to take a leverage loan equal to double this ($400,000).

- For that advisor a $200,000 client became a $600,000 client.
- Regardless of the client, this was the formula.

The supposed strategy was that over a 10-year period your RRSP essentially dwindles down to close to $0, and hopefully your non-registered account will perform well.

Then the 2008 financial crisis occurred, both their investments dropped 40%. These clients had no other assets. They were lower-income earners, were not aggressive investors, and had no other non-registered accounts. They were simply wowed by the concept.

This was a game changer for their financial situation in the very worst way.

However, a scarier story is the following one.

I was recently asked to sit down with a 91-year-old lady whose only asset was a $900,000 leveraged portfolio, tied to a $500,000 interest-only debt.

- The $900,000 served two purposes:
  1. To help fund her lifestyle ($20,000 per year).
  2. For the loan to fund itself, meaning that the interest on the $500,000 debt was paid from the gains on the asset.
- Thankfully for her, her rate of return averaged 12% per year for 10 years, as it was 70% invested in U.S. technology mutual funds.
- However, if she had averaged 7% per year, she would have had approximately $485,000 in assets tied to a $500,000 debt, ultimately meaning she would have been broke.

She got lucky here. This investment was not suitable for her circumstances. I told her, contrary to what she wanted to hear, that she should be thankful how well this worked out—the bad advice worked out in her favour—but to get out immediately while she was ahead.

The sad truth is that for every case like this, there are another four families that lose everything from leveraging. The problem is that we typically only hear of people telling us about their winning investments rather than losing ones. In behavioural finance, this is known as survivor bias.

The reason I believe that this is even scarier is that I imagine these clients recommend this advisor to all their friends given how well their portfolio performed.

With the first story, the bad advice was likely contained, as it was not a happy story to retell. With the second, the bad advice approach could spread because of a positive survivor story.

Key Takeaways from This Chapter

Leveraging is borrowing money to invest, which may allow you to increase your effective returns.

It's important to note, however, that using leverage is only appropriate for some: high-income earners in high tax brackets with a minimum of a 10-year time horizon, adequate and consistent cash flow, and whose risk appetite is in the moderately aggressive to aggressive investment risk tolerance category.

Especially since leverage builds in certain risks, we do not advise investing in riskier vehicles than you might otherwise: maintaining discipline is key to effective leveraged investing.

Leveraging investments inside a corporation can be a productive strategy, but the regulatory environment must be considered, particularly the passive income rules.

Evaluating on a regular basis is prudent for all leveraged investments, as market conditions and risk appetite are major factors in determining whether adjusting the plan is required.

Tax-efficient means that withdrawing funds from either the corporation or RRSP can make use of offsetting deductions for tax-deductible interest payments. Debt swaps are a strategy that may make Canadian mortgage interest tax deductible.

Caution is advised when selecting investments that incorporate leverage. We have some strong "do not recommends" in this area, such as leveraged ETFs. Risk parity portfolios, on the other hand, may hold value for accredited investors.

Last, leverage can attract conflicts of interest when financial advice is based simply on sales or assets under management. We have some cautionary tales to share.

Top Questions to Ask Your Financial Planner

1. Am I a suitable candidate for leveraged investing? Why or why not?
2. How have you successfully used leveraged strategies with your other clients?
3. Where have you cautioned against using leverage, and why?
4. Could I benefit from using leverage to get funds out of my corporation, make my mortgage tax-deductible, or to help my kids? What specific strategies should I consider, and when?

Note

1. Note that in the Income Tax Act, section 8(13) (for individuals, not corporations) requires the space to be where your duties of office or employment
are *principally* carried out, or used on a regular and continuous basis for
meeting clients or customers. Further, section 18(12) limits the deduction
to the extent that income is earned (that is, the expenses cannot create a
loss) and any amounts not used may be carried forward.

Chapter 7

Investing: Active or Passive?

I f you've invested even a single dollar over the past decade, and likely even if you haven't, you've heard about the "active versus passive" investing debate. And before we dive into this topic, let's clarify something—the debate has a point!

Consider the ads you may have seen from discount brokerage firm Questrade: while those ads only tell one side of the story and are exaggerated in many ways and misleading in others, they are nevertheless hitting on something. And the reason that negative campaigns such as the Questrade ads work is that speaking generally, there is much need for improvement!

With that preamble in hand, we're now ready for this chapter, which covers the debate between passive and active management. Indeed, the debate that began several decades ago over the merits and shortcomings of active versus passive investment management is ongoing—and seems to be one of the investment world's most popular literary pursuits.

What You'll Get Out of This Chapter

In this chapter, we take on the hottest debate in investing: the "active versus passive management" debate. This issue probably inspires the most passionate commentary in the entire investment world, with each side amassing evidence to support their argument and points of view.

In contrast to that passionate, "winner take all" debate, however, in this chapter we present a different view: first, it's possible that both approaches have a place in your portfolio—but more importantly, understanding the debate is likely more important for your finances (and your peace of mind) than choosing a winning side.

What Is Active Investing and What Is Passive Investing?

Before we start, let's review some basic definitions.

The investor who practices *active management* selects individual securities for purchase or sale, usually making their decisions based on fundamental research and/or utilizing a broad array of quantitative methods.

In contrast, the *passive investor* buys an index fund or exchange-traded fund (ETF) that tracks an entire index such as the Standard & Poor's 500 (S&P 500) in order to match its performance in their own accounts.

However, the choice between passive and active is not, in contrast to what you might have heard, synonymous with ETFs versus managed products (e.g., pooled accounts, mutual funds, etc.). Instead, both active and passive strategies may be found packaged as ETFs, and both active and passive strategies may be packaged as managed products.

Today, the subject of active versus passive investing inspires a lot of debate. Most people who advocate for passive investing focus on the cost advantage of passive products, and the active manager's performance relative to their benchmarks. However, a majority of the financial industry will point to the underperformance of do-it-yourself investors using passive portfolios, along with the greater range of tools for risk management with active portfolios, and the ability of active management to meet objectives that go beyond the simpler lens of risk versus return.

In our opinion, *there is room for both active and passive products in a financial plan.* Most importantly, this constant ongoing debate is only beneficial to you! However, there are some investment arrangements that we would recommend being cautious of, which we explore here.

Understanding Investment Trends

There has been an increasing trend toward passive investing through low-cost ETFs. One of the reasons for this has been the full implementation of what's called the Client Relationship Model—Phase 2, or CRM2, on July 31, 2017. CRM2 is an initiative by the Canadian Securities Administrators (CSA)—a body representing securities regulators in Canada's 10 provinces and three territories—to improve the porting of investment costs and performance.

As a result of CRM2 reforms, all investors now receive an annual fee/compensation report, detailing in dollars the amount paid for products and services, including operating charges, transaction charges, payments from third parties, and trailing commissions.

A recent study by BlackRock estimates that less than 18% of all global equities are passively managed, and if we focus on the universe of delegated or external management, only 38% is passive.[1] In September 2019, Morningstar reported that Canada-listed ETF assets are about one-tenth of the size of mutual fund assets, and that retail investors are estimated to hold 60% of ETF assets, according to data from *Investor Economics*.[2]

Let's start by taking a look at what people are saying out there ...

A Deep Dive into Passive Management

Academic studies and literature typically support passive management, especially in the highly efficient large-cap indexes. Simply stated, studies have sought to prove that active investment managers are incapable of beating the market over the long term, amassing empirical evidence to support that position.

By investing passively, the argument goes, the investor gains exposure to broadly diversified sets of stocks or bonds that target specific investment styles in a tax-efficient manner. Over long periods of time, the performance advantages are, in no small part, the result of low fees and expenses. The passive investor also has the luxury of avoiding the challenges and costs associated with selecting successful active managers.

Fees—Passive Management

Let's start off with the bad news first: Canada has a long history of high mutual fund fees.

- Canadians have some of the highest mutual fund fees in the world.[3]
- The 2015 Global Fund Investor Experience Study by Morningstar ranked Canada as the absolute worst among 25 countries in terms of mutual fund fees and expenses.[4]

In more recent years, things have become a little better but still need much improvement—we went from "very high" to merely "high."

- On September 17, 2019, Morningstar released a report: Canada's fund industry has crawled out of the basement in Morningstar, Inc.'s global rankings of fund investor costs but remains "below average" due to the impact of high ongoing fees, although this represents an improvement from past years. According to the report, Canada's improvement in the study reflects the increased availability of fund share classes without deferred sales charges, reduced trailers, and relatively low upfront sales charges. "When purchasing funds without advice, investors have found it increasingly possible to invest without paying loads or trailing commissions, or at least a much smaller trailing commission," it notes.[5]

- However, the Canadian industry still rates poorly because asset-weighted median expenses are relatively high. In particular, Canada has the highest median expenses for asset allocation funds at 1.94% and is third-highest in the equity category at 1.98%. Fixed-income funds rate slightly better with median expenses of 0.99%. However, those numbers are factoring in fee-based advice (22% of the market share) and do-it-yourself (3% of the market share). Excluding those two distribution channels and only using commission-based advice (75%), the asset-weighted median equity category is 2.28%, fixed income is 1.49%, and asset allocation is 2.04%. Note: *It's worth pointing out that because this fee assessment considers only retail funds, it doesn't include pooled, institutional, or high-net-worth share classes, of which many might have negotiable fees.*

The Impact of Fees

Fees are important, especially if they don't represent added value.

Let's compare two investments: the first has a 0.5% annual fee, while the second has a 2.0% annual fee. Let's assume both investments have the same gross return of 6% before fees. Table 7.1 shows

Table 7.1   The Impact of Fees

After 25 years	Investment 1 0.5% fee	Investment 2 2.0% fee
Total Contributions	$100,000	$100,000
Actual value after fees:	$381,339	$266,584

how the two investments look after 25 years. Investment 2 represents 43% more value.

Performance

So, we discussed the fee impact, but who cares if we pay a high fee as long as we outperform (the benchmark), right?

Well ...

The S&P Indices versus Active Funds Scorecard, or SPIVA, releases semiannual scorecards on active managers.[6] The SPIVA Canada Scorecard shows the performance of actively managed Canadian mutual funds compared with indices in their respective categories. Although many such reports are available, the SPIVA Canada Scorecard is unique in that it offers the following characteristics:

- **Survivorship Bias Correction:** Many funds might be liquidated or merged during a period of study. However, for a market participant making a decision at the beginning of the period, these funds are part of the opportunity set. Unlike other commonly available comparison reports, SPIVA Canada Scorecards remove this survivorship bias.
- **Apple-to-Apples Comparison:** A fund's returns are often compared with a popular benchmark regardless of its investment category. SPIVA Canada Scorecards make an appropriate comparison by measuring a fund's returns against the returns of a benchmark that reflects the fund's investment category.
- **Asset-Weighted Returns:** Average returns for a fund group are often calculated using only equal weighting, which results in the returns of a CAD 10 billion fund affecting the average in the same manner as the returns of a CAD 10 million fund. The SPIVA Canada Scorecard shows both equal- and asset-weighted averages. Equal-weighted returns are a measure of average fund performance. Asset-weighted returns are a measure of the performance of the average invested Canadian dollar.

Overall, the results for Canada don't look good. Granted, there has been no deduction of index returns to account for fund investment expenses—after all, an ETF will always underperform the underlying index given the bid–ask spread, commission to buy and sell, and total annual fees.

Over a 10-year period, Table 7.2 shows that 91% of S&P/TSX funds underperformed the S&P/TSX index.

Over a 10-year period using equal-weighted returns, Table 7.3 shows that the average rate of return on Canadian Equity Funds was 6.77% per year over 10 years, versus the S&P/TSX Composite 7.92% per year average (a 1.15% differential). With the exception of the Small-/Mid-Cap space, every other group seems to have lagged.

Table 7.4 shows that once again, over a 10-year period using asset-weighted returns, the average rate of return on Canadian

Table 7.2 SPIVA: Percentage of Funds Underperforming the Index

Fund Category	Comparison Index	1-Year (%)	3-Year (%)	5-Year (%)	10-Year (%)
Canadian Equity	S&P/TSX Composite	76.92	94.37	90.28	91.01
Canadian Small-/Mid-Cap Equity	S&P/TSX Completion	80.00	95.24	80.49	76.36
Canadian Dividend & Income Equity	S&P/TSX Canadian Dividend Aristocrats	65.22	79.59	71.74	100.00
U.S. Equity	S&P 500 (CAD)	78.57	91.92	96.00	97.41
International Equity	S&P EPAC LargeMidCap (CAD)	55.56	85.96	91.53	95.24
Global Equity	S&P Developed LargeMidCap (CAD)	77.52	93.24	95.07	93.83
Canadian Focused Equity	50% S&P/TSX Composite + 25% S&P 500 (CAD) + 25% S&P EPAC LargeMidCap	83.12	90.24	96.55	95.05

SOURCE: S&P Dow Jones Indices LLC, Fundata. Data as of December 31, 2018. CFSC categorizations are used. Financial information provided by Fundata Canada Inc. Past performance is no guarantee of future results. Table is provided for illustrative purposes.

Table 7.3   SPIVA: Equal-Weighted Fund Returns

Category	1-Year (Annualized, %)	3-Year (Annualized, %)	5-Year (Annualized, %)	10-Year (Annualized, %)
Canadian Equity	−7.02	4.91	3.03	6.77
S&P/TSX Composite	−8.89	6.37	4.06	7.92
Canadian Small-/ Mid-Cap Equity	−13.60	1.16	−0.11	8.62
S&P/TSX Completion	−12.85	3.97	1.35	8.35
Canadian Dividend & Income Equity	−7.95	3.55	2.31	7.14
S&P/TSX Canadian Dividend Aristocrats	−8.29	5.76	3.74	11.39
U.S. Equity	−0.16	5.48	9.37	11.21
S&P 500 (CAD)	4.23	8.64	14.08	14.27
International Equity	−3.14	2.31	4.77	6.55
S&P EPAC LargeMidCap (CAD)	−5.60	3.14	6.40	8.16
Global Equity	−2.66	3.48	6.10	8.51
S&P Developed LargeMidCap (CAD)	−0.16	6.35	10.51	11.45
Canadian Focused Equity	−5.39	4.15	3.84	7.24
50% S&P/TSX Composite + 25% S&P 500 (CAD) + 25% S&P EPAC LargeMidCap	−4.83	6.25	7.23	9.71

>SOURCE: S&P Dow Jones Indices LLC, Fundata. Data as of December 31, 2018. CFSC categorizations are used. Financial information provided by Fundata Canada Inc. Past performance is no guarantee of future results. Table is provided for illustrative purposes.

Table 7.4 SPIVA: Asset-Weighted Fund Returns

Category	1-Year (Annualized, %)	3-Year (Annualized, %)	5-Year (Annualized, %)	10-Year (Annualized, %)
Canadian Equity	-10.06	4.47	3.01	6.73
S&P/TSX Composite	-8.89	6.37	4.06	7.92
Canadian Small-/ Mid-Cap Equity	-16.39	-0.01	-0.62	8.03
S&P/TSX Completion	-12.85	3.97	1.35	8.35
Canadian Dividend & Income Equity	-7.87	5.63	4.17	8.00
S&P/TSX Canadian Dividend Aristocrats	-8.29	5.76	3.74	11.39
U.S. Equity	1.83	6.79	9.92	11.25
S&P 500 (CAD)	4.23	8.64	14.08	14.27
International Equity	-8.82	0.32	3.76	5.59
S&P EPAC LargeMidCap (CAD)	-5.60	3.14	6.40	8.16
Global Equity	-4.74	2.98	6.17	8.36
S&P Developed LargeMidCap (CAD)	-0.16	6.35	10.51	11.45
Canadian Focused Equity	-9.22	2.16	2.60	6.38
50% S&P/TSX Composite + 25% S&P 500 (CAD) + 25% S&P EPAC LargeMidCap	-4.83	6.25	7.23	9.71

SOURCE: S&P Dow Jones Indices LLC, Fundata. Data as of December 31, 2018. CFSC categorizations are used. Financial information provided by Fundata Canada Inc. Past performance is no guarantee of future results. Table is provided for illustrative purposes.

Equity Funds was 6.73% per year over 10 years versus the S&P/TSX Composite 7.92% per year average (a 1.19% differential).

What about Outside Canada?

An analysis by Bank of America Merrill Lynch showed that in the 12 years studied, in only two years did more than 50% of U.S.-based active large-cap stock fund managers beat their benchmarks.[7] The truth is that after the financial crisis of 2008, U.S. active large-cap managers fell short of their benchmarks for fully nine years in a row (after fees). That news, however, is followed by the reality that in eight of the following 13 years, more than 50% of the managers beat their benchmarks (before fees). Additionally, some research in the United States has shown that passive investing has outperformed active investing in this decade, but active investing had outperformed passive investing in the prior decade.

Nobel Laureate William Sharpe, in his 1991 paper "The Arithmetic of Active Management," concluded that "properly measured, the average actively managed dollar must underperform the average passively managed dollar, net of costs. Empirical analyses that appear to refute this principle are guilty of improper measurement."[8]

To hammer home a point, the following are key highlights on fees and performance from two recent books on this subject.

Key Takeaways from Larry Bates's *Beat the Bank*[9]

- On behalf of Tangerine Bank, 36% of Canadian investors surveyed (July 2016) claimed they don't pay any fees, and another 11% were unsure if they pay fees. The point Bates makes is that the "old Bay Street" charges high fees unbeknownst to the consumer.
- T-REX Scores (Bates's measure of what he calls the Total Return Efficiency Index, which shows the impact of fees on a hypothetical investment portfolio) will tell you how fees affect long-term performance, fully capturing the ever-growing compounding loss. For example, a 2% extra cost in fees will cost you over 50% of your returns over a 30-year period.

- Bates really doesn't like the CIBC Canadian Bond Fund (which I have never recommended or personally owned)—an example of a fund where he does not believe the fund justifies the cost, citing a yield to maturity of 2.02% with fees of 1.43% (the 10-year return is 4% per year and the 5-year performance is 2.9% per year). It gets a 29% T-REX Score—which is really bad—and a true fee, by Bates's calculations, of 71%. More on this later.

Key Takeaways from Rob Carrick's *Guide to What's Good, Bad, and Downright Awful in Canadian Investments Today*[10]

- There's a lot of propaganda out there, such as the idea that performance, not fees, is what matters.
- Carrick is not a fan of money market funds, bond funds, or, especially, balanced funds—and calls out the RBC Balanced Fund for charging a higher rate on their balanced fund than their equity fund and fixed-income fund.

So, does that mean we sell everything and buy passive ETFs? Well . . . wait. Let's hear from the active managers, and then look at the big picture.

Diving into Active Management

The Behavioral Gap

A study by Boston-based DALBAR Inc. showed that even when passive investments outperformed active investments, the *average investor* in the active funds outperformed the average investor in passive funds.[11]

The study concluded that active investors knew that professional advisors were guiding their product choices, and the investors were less likely, as a result, to make ill-informed or hasty investment decisions. Passive investors, in contrast, were much more likely to make rash decisions without the advisor oversight.

The takeaway is that *investment results are more dependent on investor behavior than on fund performance.* Investor behavior can be more important to overall investment outcomes than the actual performance of investment portfolios, and active management may provide advantages in guiding that behavior.

Morningstar's May 2017 "Mind the Gap" research report shows that the typical Canadian stock mutual fund investor's return over the past 10 years was reduced by an annual average of 1.38% percent due to "buying high and selling low."[12]

Better Risk Management

What is the role of active managers? Simply put, it is to manage risk—whether that is by protecting against losses, reducing volatility, or some other mechanism. Viewed from this perspective, the passive investor is not, in fact, protected against risk. In fact, the more an investor's strategy is passive, the more they are exposed to investment losses when markets tumble.

Active managers have multiple techniques they can use to reduce risk and minimize losses. They can avoid securities from poorly performing companies, and by ensuring that portfolios are not over-concentrated in particular sectors or regions. Active management can also include strategies such as hedging against currency fluctuations, using put options to protect against any future losses, or allocating part of a portfolio to cash to protect against the impact of withdrawals.

The use of cash buffers is particularly important, for several reasons: the manager is not forced to sell when conditions are not favourable in response to investor requests—and the manager can take advantage of any opportunities that arise when securities are mispriced, due to sell-offs.

Fees—Active Management

According to the Investment Company Institute, since the 2007–2009 financial crisis, the average expense ratio for an equity fund has fallen by fully 20% or more.[13]

Our industry also points to the fact that passively managed products are bought and sold in a similar manner to individual stocks, with the per-unit commissions paid by investors on top of the cost of the fund shares themselves. The comparisons between active and passive strategies that regularly make the rounds of the mainstream media often fall short, however, of a full accounting of the costs of acquiring and disposing of securities in order to correctly describe the net returns to investors.

Flexibility to Manage After-Tax Returns

In addition to having more risk-management tools at their disposal, active managers can also more completely manage the tax consequences of their investment choices. An active manager can use tax-loss harvesting, for example, to maximize an investor's after-tax returns.

Allowing Pursuit of Expressive Objectives

Increasingly, investors are looking at their investment strategies as a reflection of their values and belief systems. This might look like choosing to invest in specific companies that have particular environmental practices and workplace diversity and inclusion programs. Similarly, it might mean avoiding certain companies with questionable workplace practices.

Selecting companies to invest in based on their practices is the basis of the ESG (environmental, social, and governance) investment movement, and of responsible investing.

While passively managed products can follow ESG and responsible investing practices, they rely on ESG scores or other sorting mechanisms to identify the products that the funds will invest in. An active approach, however, allows managers to exercise discretion over the securities in a fund.

Market Return Does Not Equal Average Investor Return

A very common point of view is that because all of the investors in a given market comprise "the market" by definition, then the average investor's return must be the market return. Thus, this argument continues, if an investor has higher-than-average investment costs, they must have a lower-than-average investment return.

This argument, while compelling, is nevertheless flawed. If you have, for example, a market made up of just two investors, each with a very different investment thesis, and each investing different amounts, it is virtually impossible for their average returns to be equal to the market return.

If one looks at the actual ownership of corporate equities (in the United States, the world's largest market), they are spread among traditional mutual funds, ETFs, individual households, foreign investors, public sector retirement plans, private pension funds, insurance companies, and more. It cannot be true that the average investment return of any one of these subgroups is equal to the market return! Instead, it is clear that active managers have, in fact, the capacity to outperform (or underperform) both market averages and market benchmarks.

Performance

According to Morningstar data, since 1980, the average performance of the actively managed Canadian equities group has outperformed the benchmark S&P/TSX 59% of the time—and funds in the top 25% outperformed the index 80% of the time. Viewed over this longer time frame, the relative performance of active managers as a group appears to wax and wane over multi-year periods.

In the United States, between 2003 and 2010, a majority of the universe of domestic equity funds outperformed the benchmark S&P 500 in five of those eight years.

Is Your Fund "Truly Active"?

A study in 2009 by Martijn Cremers and Antti Petajisto found that investment funds that were truly active, taking positions that significantly deviated from their benchmarks, were able to outperform those benchmark indices both before and after expenses.[14]

The Growth of Passive Investments May Sow the Seeds of Their Underperformance

When a company is added to an index, there is typically a spike in demand as passive investors now need to acquire stock in that company. However, research from Amherst College and the Board of Governors of the Federal Reserve System discovered that the largest spike in price, around 7%, actually takes place between the time the addition is announced and when the stock is actually added to the index. That's because speculators, not investors, drive up the prices in anticipation of the increased demand from passive investors![15]

The study's authors also note that the excess return on the newly added stock mostly reversed once the stock was actually in the index. Their conclusion, along with others such as Professor Jeremy Siegel of the Wharton School, is that passive investing can result in companies entering benchmarks at inflated prices, thus—contrary to expectations—lowering potential future returns for all passive investors. What this means for active discretionary managers is that as flows into passive strategies increase, there are more arbitrage opportunities. In addition, as more and more dollars are passively managed, the number of active investors will likely decline. One possible outcome is increased opportunity for active managers who are making discretionary decisions.

Access to IPOs May Become More of a Differentiating Factor

Early investors who jump on securities sold via initial public offerings (IPOs) can often enjoy a price advantage, as IPOs frequently are sold at a discount relative to their price when public trading begins. But once again, here is another opportunity the passive investor forgoes, as most passive investors will wait to purchase a security until it forms part of a benchmark index upon which their strategy is based. Usually, adherence to this practice will rule out securities that have recently been offered via an IPO.

The upshot? The more investors use passive strategies, the more inefficiencies in markets, and thus opportunities for active managers are likely to arise.

Wrapping Up the Debate

Because this has been constantly framed as a crossfire debate, it's a fallacy to think that because one side is wrong, then the other must be right.

If we are truly looking at this from an evidence-based approach, then the evidence is showing that both sides work in certain situations.

I think one of the consequences is arranging your affairs in what may be the worst of both worlds. Some advisors have hammered down the point of why one needs the passive approach. Reading the comments on SPIVA and fees, one can see how effective that can be. However, the solution tends to be to therefore invest in passive ETFs and charge a fee of 0.75%–1.5%.

Just so we are clear on what this means, you are now getting a passive approach paying all the ETF fees—plus an advisory fee! If the whole argument is that active managers underperform due to fees, then why capitulate—surrender to a passive approach—and then pay a fee? If you truly believe this is the best option, would it not make more sense to buy those passive indexes on your own?

Overall, we believe active and passive investing can both play a role in a financial plan. Let's address the issues covered with some conclusions.

Fees

Showing a fee drag for a high-fee mutual fund versus no fees can be quite impactful. Bottom line, we all want to pay less for the same thing. The good news is that the fee trend has been heading lower. Additionally, many institutions allow fee negotiations at certain thresholds, giving the advisor the ability to lower fees.

It's also important to note the tax implications of fees. For instance, a tax-deductible 1% advisory fee in a corporation off-setting some taxable passive income in many cases is lower than a 0.5% non-deductible fee. This also is important to note when comparing returns (e.g., a 6% posted annual ETF return would be lower than a 6% after-fee managed product return, assuming the fees are tax-deductible). Rates of return do not display the net savings from deductible fees. Also, when fees are quoted, they may not show the total annual expense of the investment; for example, Vanguard All-Equity ETF Portfolio (VEQT) has a posted MER of 0.25%, but also has a foreign withholding tax (FWT) of 0.25%, for a total annual expense of 0.5%.

Overall, fees are always important in all types of accounts, that is, RRSP, TFSA, non-regulated, and corporations. However, fees are more important in RRSP and TFSA accounts given the inability to deduct fees. Therefore, among other reasons including characteristics of return, if you were to want a mixture of low-cost passive investing and active investing, it may be best to place the passive investments in the RRSP and TFSAs and active investments inside the corporation. There is nothing wrong with having both approaches work for you.

Performance

Advocates of passive investing point to evidence such as the SPIVA results. Let's dissect these a little more:

1. While beating benchmarks is important, what's even more important is asset allocation—the breakdown of the portfolio. An academic study called "Determinants of Portfolio Performance" illustrates how asset allocation carries a larger weight than security selection and marketing timing for risk and returns.[16]

   For instance, the best returns in the past 10 years came from the United States. I think we could all agree that having a below-average investment in the United States over the past 10 years would be better than an investment in the Canadian index.

   However, rewinding another 10 years shows that it was the Canadian index that outperformed the U.S. space. The decision on how much to have in Canada, U.S., international, emerging markets, and fixed income is more important than the benchmark comparisons. Make no mistake, both are important, but one just happens to be more important than the other.

2. Let's go back to the SPIVA results: a 1.15% differential of index versus the average Canadian equity fund over the past 10 years. Using corporate investments, let's factor in a few more variables:

   (a) CDN Equity fund fees have declined 20% since the financial crisis—an approximate 0.4% savings.

   (b) When purchasing index funds, you have to account for bid-ask spreads, trade commissions on both the buy and sell side, and the MER of the ETF—a wide range, but let's say a 0.1–0.5% savings (which the index is not accounting for).

   (c) Tax-deductible fees not reported in returns: For a corporation, these can be as high as a 50.2% deduction to offset other passive income—let's say a 0.5–1% savings given the range in your fee.

   (d) Fee negotiations: If the average fee now is 2.28% (10 years was higher), how much lower (or higher) are your fees from this?—let's say a 0–1.5% savings.

   (e) Tax characteristic of returns: What percentage breakdown of the portfolio is interest, Canadian dividends, foreign dividends, capital gains, and tax-deferred capital gains? This can be significant but is more a function of rate of return—let's say 0–3%.

   As one might note, looking at these five variables—especially when looking at corporate and non-registered funds—one could position themselves to be in a much better situation to have an active portfolio with those variables working in their favour.

Another way of looking at this was best illustrated in John J. De Gooey's 2019 *STANDUP to the Financial Services Industry*,[17] where he divided advisors into four categories (which resulted in him later calling for a firing of 20% of advisors):

1. Those who add over 2% in value: 25%
2. Those who add between 1% and 2% in value: 25%
3. Those who add between 0% and 1% in value: 25%
4. Those who actually subtract value: 25%

I would ask: Which category does my advisor fall into, if he or she is using an active approach, factoring in the five components above?

Behavior

As Nobel laureate Richard Thaler concluded, investor behavior ends up being the biggest cost to investors.[18] Of course, fees and performance are important, and so are taxes. However, selling and buying at the worst of times is the biggest drag on a portfolio's return.

This brings me to my knee-jerk feeling when I read advocates for do-it-yourself passive investing. I wish they heard the conversations I had in March of 2009, when clients were calling wanting to sell everything, only to have the portfolio skyrocket over the next few years. Or when I was taking those phone calls on December 24, 2018, convincing numerous clients to stay invested after the S&P 500 dropped 19.8% in three months, but then rebounded 25% the following four months. I wish they could be in those meetings, the countless times we met with doctors who had watched their do-it-yourself portfolios go from over $1,000,000 down to $100,000—and yes, they were just buying boring blue-chip companies.

Let's also revisit those do-it-yourself books I mentioned earlier, which, on a side note, I truly enjoyed.

For instance, in Larry Bates's book, the author points out the rewards that would have been reaped had you just owned TD stock over the past 25 years. As the argument goes: It's simple, it's safe, it's obvious.

Given this, would the same thought process hold true if that concentrated position had been in two of America's biggest banks? Citigroup lost 47.1% in 2007, lost 77.2% in 2008, and then lost 50.6% in 2009. For every dollar put in, you would have been left with 6 cents (and it's not even close to recovered). Bank of America lost 22.7% in 2007, 65.9% in 2008, made up 7% in 2009, but then saw a 11.4% loss in 2010 and a 58% drop in 2011.

Maybe the thinking is that Canadian banks are different—so is there no artificial intelligence risk? Are there no transformational technology solutions out there in lending? Are there no disruptors in the industry? Is there no compression on fee income given lower interest rate margins? Could technology limit the ability of banks in growing their compounded annual growth rate (CAGR) in fees?

The problem is, neither of us knows. But what I do know is that by the time we find out, it will be a year or two after it's already been reflected in the stock price. The point is that this would have been an absolutely catastrophic situation. If a planner ever recommended this concentrated approach, they would have likely lost their license by now.

When many publications display annual fees, they are posting the highest fee possible for the selected mutual funds—most of those mutual funds have many lower fee structures. As mentioned earlier, CIBC Canadian Fund is an example of a fund where Larry Bates does not believe that the fund justifies the cost, citing a yield to maturity of 2.02% with fees of 1.43% (the 10-year return is 4% per year and the 5-year performance is 2.9% per year). The VSB ETF (promoted alternative) has a 5-year performance of 1.79% per year and 1.89% since inception (August 2019).

In Rob Carrick's book, he recommends CPD, iShares Canadian Preferred Shares Index, as a bond ETF. As of August 2019, the five-year return has been –2.08% per year and a year-to-date rate of –14.12%.

Many Canadian preferred shares have rate resets. A rate-reset preferred share offers a fixed dividend payment where the rate of that payment is reset upon a specific date, typically every five years. This financial innovation is for the most part a Canadian innovation.

However, rate resets have worked out poorly—trying to predict interest rates is very difficult. In 2016, everyone was suggesting rates would not go lower, but they did and the whole preferred share market performed very poorly. Owning all preferred shares as an index has not turned out to be a good move. On the next page of Rob Carrick's book, the recommendation was to own XEG, iShares Canadian Energy Sector Index Fund, with a –15.41%/year five-year performance. When looking at 12 good stocks, SNC-Lavalin Group was a good dividend grower—but it has since declined 65% in less than two years. (Hopefully there was an exit strategy.)

However, my knee-jerk reaction is to point out the flaws, perhaps subconsciously, because I am in the financial industry. This is wrong-headed of me. There are good reasons these books resonate with many Canadians. The above comments are not really the point of the authors. The point is that the authors are calling out bad practices regardless of their recommendations. While they have their holes, so do we in the financial industry.

As a financial advisor, your mission is to serve clients. You are to fight for them, go to bat for them, and do your best for them, as well as to keep up with the times and adapt. I have come to realize that simply pointing out the flaws makes me no different than the critics who say we as advisors have commission breadth. The takeaway here is to strive to be better and I hope that resonates on both sides. Overall, active managers are not a dying breed, but the competitive pressures from passive investing require that they keep raising their game and/or lowering their fees—a healthy development for investors.

Key Takeaways from This Chapter

While the "active versus passive" debate rages on, it's unlikely to come to a definitive end anytime soon. Even if it were possible to definitively conclude the debate at a given point, that conclusion would quickly become obsolete as changes over time affect the conclusions.

Rather than selecting only one approach for your personal portfolio, it's worthwhile to evaluate the pros and cons of each approach and then potentially to employ both to help you meet your goals. Keep in mind that much of what you are reading is focused on investors with registered (TFSA, RRSP) accounts only, and not investors—like you—with corporate accounts as well.

(continued)

(*continued*)

No matter where you or your advisor come down on this debate—that is, if you pick a side or not—the continued debate actually serves to help investors over time, as it advances the conversation about how best to provide value for investors like you and me.

Top Questions to Ask Your Financial Planner

1. What is your personal view on the active versus passive debate, and how have you incorporated (or not incorporated) your personal views into your professional practice?
2. How are you keeping up-to-date on the "active versus passive" debate so that your practice evolves to keep abreast of changes and help your clients take advantage of developments?
3. If I was a new client and a DIY investor, what would you tell me about why I should invest with you, and why should I believe it?

Notes

1. Trevor Hunnicut, "Less Than 18 Percent of Global Stocks Owned by Index Investors: BlackRock," *Reuters Business News*, October 3, 2017. Available at https://www.reuters.com/article/us-funds-blackrock-passive/less-than-18-percent-of-global-stocks-owned-by-index-investors-blackrock-idUSKCN1C82TE.
2. Ruth Saldanha, "Canadian Investors Get a 'Below Average' Fee Experience: Morningstar's sixth Global Investor Experience Study on fees

and expenses sees Canada rise from dead last," Morningstar, Inc., September 17, 2019. Available at https://www.morningstar.ca/ca/news/195738/canadian-investors-get-a-%E2%80%98below-average-fee-experience.aspx.

3. Ajay Khorana, Henri Servaes, and Peter Tufano, "Mutual Fund Fees around the World," HBS Finance Working Paper 901023, May 8, 2006. Available at https://papers.ssrn.com/sol3/papers.cfm?abstract_id=901023.

4. Morningstar, "Morningstar Announces Findings from Fourth Global Fund Investor Experience Report; Korea and United States Score the Best," June 15, 2015. Available at https://newsroom.morningstar.com/newsroom/news-archive/press-release-details/2015/Morningstar-Announces-Findings-from-Fourth-Global-Fund-Investor-Experience-Report-Korea-and-United-States-Score-the-Best06092015/default.aspx.

5. Morningstar, "Morningstar's Sixth Global Investor Experience Study Finds Investors Are Paying Less to Own Funds Worldwide But Disparity Among Markets Persists," September 17, 2019. Available at https://shareholders.morningstar.com/newsroom/news-archive/press-release-details/2019/Morningstars-Sixth-Global-Investor-Experience-Study-Finds-Investors-are-Paying-Less-to-Own-Funds-Worldwide-But-Disparity-Among-Markets-Persists/default.aspx.

6. Available at https://us.spindices.com/spiva/#/.

7. As cited in Stephen Rogers, "The Advantages of Actively Managed Funds: Why the Playing Field Is Tipping in Favour of Active Management," Investment Strategy Group whitepaper, 2018. Available at https://www.investorsgroup.com/content/dam/investorsgroup/more/wp-content/themes/ig_magazine/pdf/Whitepaper-The-Actively-Managed-Fund-Advantage.pdf.

8. William F. Sharpe, "The Arithmetic of Active Management," *Financial Analysts' Journal* 47, no. 1 (January/February 1991): 7–9. Available at https://web.stanford.edu/~wfsharpe/art/active/active.htm.

9. Larry Bates, *Beat the Bank: The Canadian Guide to Simply Successful Investing* (Audey Press, September 16, 2018).

10. Rob Carrick, *Rob Carrick's Guide to What's Good, Bad and Downright Awful in Canadian Investments Today* (Doubleday Canada, December 29, 2009).

11. DALBAR Inc., "Active versus Passive Investor Returns," March 2017. Available at https://www.dalbar.com/Home/Index.

12. Ben Johnson, "Mind the Gap: Active Versus Passive Edition," *Morningstar ETF Investor*, April 2016. Available at https://www.morningstar.com/articles/755644/mind-the-gap-active-versus-passive-edition.

13. Investment Company Institute, Inc., "Trends in the Expenses and Fees of Funds, 2018," *ICI Research Perspective* 25, no. 1 (March 2019). Available at https://www.ici.org/pdf/per25-01.pdf.

14. K.J. Martijn Cremers and Antti Petajisto, "How Active Is Your Fund Manager? A New Measure That Predicts Performance," March 31, 2009, *Review of Financial Studies* 22 (March 31, 2009): 3329–3365. Available at https://papers.ssrn.com/sol3/papers.cfm?abstract_id=891719.

15. Daniel Cooper and Geoffrey Woglom, "The S&P 500 Effect: Not Such Good News in the Long Run," FEDS Working Paper No. 2002-48, October 2002. Available at https://papers.ssrn.com/sol3/papers.cfm?abstract_id=347380.

16. Gary P. Brinson, L. Randolph Hood, and Gilbert L. Beebower, "Determinants of Portfolio Performance," *Financial Analysts Journal* 42, no. 4 (1986). Available at https://www.tandfonline.com/doi/abs/10.2469/faj.v42.n.4.39.

17. John J. de Gooey, *STANDUP to the Financial Services Industry: Protecting Yourself From Well-Intended But Oblivious Advisors* (Page Two Books, May 7, 2019).

18. See, for example, Eshe Nelson, "The Flaws a Nobel Prize-winning Economist Wants You to Know about Yourself," *Quartz*, October 9, 2017. Available at https://qz.com/1098078/behavioral-economics-the-flaws-that-economics-nobel-prize-winner-richard-thaler-wants-you-to-know-about-yourself.

Chapter 8

The Role of Trusts in Your Financial Plan

T he concept of trusts reminds me of Warren Buffett's saying, "Give your children enough so they can do anything, but not so much they can do nothing."

This is a real dilemma for many professionals, as most of them do not come from "lucky womb syndrome," where you are born into wealth and happen to have a last name like Buffett or Rockefeller—or, in Canada, Irving, Thomson, or even some high-profile politicians.

Instead, most professionals in Canada studied and ground it out and continue to grind it out for every last dollar. As a result, they can expect to leave their children a much larger estate than what they received, and with that financial legacy comes a lot more responsibility.

In the financial world, trusts have been around for hundreds of years, and there are many types of trusts out there—immigration trust, health and welfare trust, charitable remainder trust, bare trust, age 40 trust, life insurance trust, blind trust, Henson trust, family trust, spendthrift trust, real estate investment trust, joint survivor trust, alter ego trust, spousal trust, and more. In and among those you can have an inter vivos (living) trust or a testamentary

163

trust (upon instructions in your last will and testament after your death); and within those categories you can have discretionary, non-discretionary, revocable, and irrevocable trusts.

For the purposes of this chapter we will look at how trusts can be part of a plan to achieve an objective: minimize taxes or protect and deal with a family need—with a focus on the types of trusts that get recommended the most by professionals.

What You'll Get Out of This Chapter

Although you've probably heard of the concept of financial trusts, you may not understand what they are and how they can help you and your family achieve financial objectives over time.

In this chapter, we review the different types of trusts with a focus on the specific kinds of trusts that are most relevant and helpful for the professional planning their finances—and we explain what a trust is, how a trust can lose its trust status, and the tax planning benefits (with examples) of using trusts in your overall financial plan.

Speaking the Language of Trusts

First, let's review the basics. There are three basic vocabulary words you will need to understand the language of trusts: the settlor, the trustee, and the beneficiary.

Settlor: The person who creates or establishes the trust in life or in death under the terms of a will (i.e., places assets in trust, sets up rules for operating and winding up trust).

Trustee: The person or people who are the legal owner of the trust, and administers the assets in accordance with the terms of the trust document (i.e., manages assets, files income tax, abides by trust agreement).

Beneficiary: The person or people for whom the trust is established to benefit (i.e., income beneficiary, capital beneficiary, or both).

Trust Concepts

In order to function as a valid trust, the trust must meet what are called the "three certainties":

1. Certainty of intention
2. Certainty of subject matter
3. Certainty of objects

If these three certainties are not in place, the trust is not validly established. The point here is that the correct legal wording is extremely important and can help you avoid tax and legal problems down the road.

Residency of Trusts

Trust assets can be held anywhere in Canada, from the small town of Gander, Newfoundland to Zenith Point, Nunavut. The beneficiaries of the trust could live in Cape Saint Charles, Labrador or Toronto, Ontario.

However, what truly matters for tax purposes in determining the residency of a trust is the location of the trustee (or, if you have multiple trustees, the majority of them). As a result of its residency, the trust will be subject to both local trust laws and tax rates in that province.

This is important to know when picking a trustee: many of the benefits identified in this chapter are eliminated if, for instance, your trustee is living in the United States.

Taxation of Trusts

Inter vivos or living trusts are taxed as if the trust is at the highest marginal tax rate. As a result, you would prefer to pay out the income to a beneficiary. The issues we have to deal with here are the tax rules around income attribution, where income may be attributed back to the person who gave the funds to the trust in the first place.

The structure of the trust is absolutely crucial here, resulting in potentially very polar opposite outcomes.

Previously, testamentary trusts (those established upon death) were taxed in a similar manner as individuals (excluding the basic personal exemption on the first approximately $12,000 of income) indefinitely.

In 2016, that changed as a result of that year's federal budget, which changed this benefit to only occur for a 36-month settlement period, known as graduated rate estates (GRE). Compared with a top tax bracket, this could save you $35,000 per year in taxes (in Ontario), albeit now for only three years.

However, we have seen far too often that because of this new GRE concept, many have wrongly written off the utility of testamentary trusts. Trust income can be taxed in the hands of the trust or, potentially more advantageous, paid out to beneficiaries of the trust—where we can likely choose how much to pay out every year. This discretion gives us the chance to save a lot in taxes, by having your future grandchildren pay taxes on the investment income being generated.

Another way of looking at this is for every child with no income, your family may be in a position to save up to approximately $37,500 per year in taxes (compared to the top tax Ontario tax bracket), which we review later.

The 21-Year Rule

After 21 years, many trusts have a deemed disposition of assets at their fair market value—also known as triggering of capital gains. In this event, it is helpful if the trustee can make sure there is enough cash to pay the tax bill without having to sell assets at this time.

Sometimes it may make sense to avoid this rule by having assets distributed at their adjusted cost base to one or more of the capital beneficiaries. Lastly, alter ego and spousal trusts do not require the 21-year rule.

Probate

Having assets in a trust can eliminate or significantly reduce probate or estate administration taxes by keeping assets away from the estate.

However, what you need to be cautious of is whether the benefit is dwarfed by the potential cost of this strategy.

Example: We have seen an unfortunate situation where someone moved their principal residence into a trust. They saved 1.5% (when the value of the estate exceeds $50,000 in Ontario) but at the cost of losing the tax-free benefit of the capital appreciation on the home.

Privacy

The terms of the trust offer privacy, as they are not made public to anyone other than the trustees and beneficiaries (and lawyer) in contrast to wills, which become public information. If your family dynamic is sensitive in nature or perhaps you would prefer to allocate your estate "unevenly," a trust may be a tool that comes in handy to satisfy your wishes without providing insult or injury to some.

Inter Vivos Trusts

One example of an inter vivos trust is an educational trust, sometimes using what is called an "age 40 trust" structure, which allows the trustee control over everything (principal and income) until the beneficiaries reach age 40. One of the purposes of this structure is to have the income generated in the trust to fund educational costs such as daycares or private schools.

Given the new rules that apply for dividends to children starting in the year they turn 18, and the new passive income rules, many professionals have been looking at alternative strategies that happen to use children's income tax brackets. One of the more recently favoured plans is to use inter vivos trusts to have children pay taxes on the investment income.

Before we dive into this, there are a few big issues to consider here:

- *First, where does the money come from?* The use of this trust requires non-registered funds, meaning either you happen to have them available, your parents happen to have them available, or you are using alternative strategies, such as leverage (Chapter 6) or a capital gains strip (Chapter 9), to have them become available.
- *Second, how are we investing the proceeds?* If the investments generate a high percentage of interest income and dividends, we may require a different loan arrangement than if we are able to generate capital gains from our investments.

This brings me to the loan arrangement. There are two common structures we see, each with their own strengths and weaknesses:

1. If your loan is at the prescribed rate of interest (currently 2%), the funds will need to be invested to cover the prescribed interest rate payment to the settlor (likely where the funds came from). The prescribed rate loan can be locked in at the current rate without having to fear future interest rate hikes. Here, while there is no attribution of income or gains to the settlor, he or she must report the 2% prescribed interest rate.

    Note that if a prescribed rate loan is used, the interest must be paid within 30 days of year-end every year or attributions apply and the structure will have to be unwound and started again at the prevailing prescribed rate.

2. If the loan does not bear interest, capital gains can be realized and taxable gains distributed to pay for services for the beneficiaries, making the taxable gains reportable by the beneficiaries.

    It's important to note here that no "kiddie tax" will apply—the tax rule that prevents the transfer of income from the settlor to children ("kiddies") under the age of 18. Using investments that reduce the potential for dividends and interest would be preferred here, as those types of income would be attributed back to the settlor.

A cost–benefit analysis should be completed when comparing which route makes the most sense.

Example

A settlor in the highest tax bracket, with a $1,000,000 investment at a 2% prescribed rate, incurs a $20,000 income inclusion, giving rise to $10,706 in taxes.

The question becomes, how much in dividends and interest are your investments projected to pay out, factoring in your children's tax rates compared to yours?

- For instance, if the investment pays out 3% interest, or $30,000, of interest income, you are better off setting up the structure with a prescribed loan.
- If your investments are in tax-deferred capital-gain-generating vehicles, then you are better off with no prescribed rate loan arrangement.

Remember, though, that here you want to trigger the capital gains every year, given the opportunity with the children's low tax brackets. Those low tax brackets may not be available forever.

Example

- A trust was enacted before March 31, 2018, where the client decided to use the prescribed loan approach, which at the time allowed us to lock in their 1% rate indefinitely.
- The purpose of this trust was to have the trust's income be used to pay for private school for the grandchildren, using tax laws to our advantage.

Discretionary Investment Trust for Grandchildren

Out of his personal investment assets, Grandpa should consider funding a discretionary investment trust for his grandchildren. The strategy would be structured as follows:

- Grandpa would have a relative or friend (perhaps his sister) settle a discretionary trust for the benefit of his grandchildren.
- Child 1 and Child 2 can be trustees of the trust.

  Grandpa would loan the money to be invested to the trust:

- If the loan is at the prescribed rate of interest, the funds will need to cover the interest rate payment to Grandpa.
- There is no attribution of income or gains to Grandpa, but he must report the 1% for tax purposes.
- If the loan does not bear interest, funds should be invested in corporate-class ETFs to reduce the potential for attribution of income (there is no attribution of capital gains).
- Capital gains can be realized and taxable gains distributed to pay for services for the grandchildren, making the taxable gains reportable by the grandchildren.
- If using a no-interest loan, we would recommend a small annual principal payment on loan owing to Grandpa to maintain its enforceability.
- This avoids the need for regular loan renewal to deal with statute of limitations on the enforcement of contracts.
- Investment assets can be transferred to the grandchildren prior to the 21-year anniversary at the adjusted cost base to avoid a deemed disposition.
- Distribution of trust property to beneficiaries can be paid conditional on assignment of loan owing to Grandpa.
- Grandpa should never forgive the loan in his lifetime, as debt forgiveness rules would grind down the cost base of investment by the amount of debt forgiven, converting tax paid capital into capital gains.

It should be noted that childcare expenses that are otherwise deductible by the parents are likely not the best use of trust income.

Example

If the trust directly pays the childcare expenses, the trust would not be able to claim the deduction (as the trust is not a supporting parent) and the supporting parent would not be able to deduct the expenses as he or she (the lower-income spouse) did not actually pay the expense.

In the scenario where one absolutely requires the trust income to pay childcare expenses, it is recommended that Grandpa could make a no-strings-attached gift to the supporting parent, who then in turn makes the payment, allowing the deduction to be claimed.

Last, if you are looking at using this strategy it is very important to have the right people involved. Many firms will require an opinion, especially when using a loan that does not bear interest. Any small misstep could put these trusts offside the tax rules, losing many of the benefits we have discussed.

Bearer Trusts

The previous example with Grandpa should not be confused with bearer trusts for children under age 18. You might even have one already, normally registered as (for example) "Andrew Feindel in trust for Sophie Feindel." This is not a formal trust and therefore does not have many of the financial benefits discussed earlier.

However, there are some funding mechanisms that allow for income and capital gains to be taxed in the child's hands, such as childcare benefit (CCB) funds which can be paid to the respective child, and are not subject to attribution back to the parent. These funds should be clearly documented as such.

It should also be noted that there is a loss of control as investments in the bearer trust eventually pass to the child when they reach the age of majority.

Inter Vivos Cottage Trust

Cottages are often one of the most difficult assets to deal with when exploring your estate plan. There are many variables at play that would completely alter the advice on how to pass them on to the next generation. They can carry different special attachments with many family members, they may have historically skyrocketed in price, and, unlike monetary assets, they are not divisible.

The best advice here is to speak to your children about whether they would like to receive the vacation property, or perhaps something else instead.

One alternative to the other methods out there (e.g., rearranging terms of ownership or using insurance to pay the final tax bill) would be to leave it in a discretionary inter vivos trust (though you can also use a testamentary cottage trust established in your will).

The trustees of the trust could be one or more individuals who would have the power to make certain decisions and the beneficiaries could include not only children, but potentially grandchildren or other relatives.

Advantages of a Cottage Trust
- None of the beneficiaries have any vested right to the property—they will only be entitled to use the property when you allow for it. This protects from adverse financial scenarios if, for example, a beneficiary suffers a marriage breakdown, experiences creditor issues, or even passes away.
- While there would be a tax hit upfront on the current capital gains (unless you are using a joint partnership trust if you and your spouse are over 65—but you do not pass on the gains to the beneficiaries moving forward), moving forward for any gains from the transfer we would be deferring the capital gains taxes.
- Tax deferral savings if the cottage is transferred to beneficiaries prior to the 21st anniversary, then capital gains will only be realized at the time of sale or death of owner (assuming beneficiaries are residents of Canada).
- A cottage trust avoids probate taxes.

Disadvantages of a Cottage Trust

- Capital gains taxes need to be paid upfront (opportunity cost of these funds).
- A cottage trust adds another level of administration (higher cost).
- Complex family dynamics are involved—who will be entitled to use the cottage, especially if the trustees do not agree?
- Capital gains will be taxed every 21 years (this deemed disposition may occur before trustees pass away, making the tax bill come sooner rather than later).
- If one of the beneficiaries decides to use the principal residence exemption on the cottage, it will force the others to forgo those years of exemption.

Testamentary Trusts

A testamentary trust is a formal trust created as a result of the death of a settlor, in contrast to an inter vivos trust.

Establishment of Testamentary Trusts

The trust is not formed until after you pass away and all debts and taxes are paid. Assets are then transferred from your estate into the testamentary trust.

There are two major benefits—and then some minor benefits—of using testamentary trusts in your estate plans:

1. Asset protection
2. Tax savings

Asset Protection

According to Statistics Canada, roughly 43% of marriages end in divorce, with the average length of marriage being around 14 years. Take note: Yukon has the highest divorce rate, followed by BC and

Ontario. Nunavut, North West Territories, and Newfoundland have the lowest divorce rates.

The reality, for anyone with children, is that there is a high risk that either your or one of your children's marriages will end in divorce (unless they live in Nunavut, of course!).

Why is this relevant? Anyone with a normal will has what's called a net family property exclusion. The Family Law Act allows for inheritances (other than a matrimonial home) to be excluded under the equalization process of a divorce.

In theory that makes sense, but in practical terms it often doesn't play out that way. Inheritances used to pay expenses or used to purchase family assets (e.g., a TV) will not be excluded. Any inheritance used to improve a home is lost. Parties rarely keep inheritances in a separate, sole account. That is just not the way life, or families, work.

Ontario courts have historically applied a variety of tracing methods, such as the "first in, first out" and "pro rata" approaches, and more recently the courts seem to favor a tracing method.

Bottom line, there is a good chance our hard-earned money will be up for grabs if our children inherit it and then end up in a divorce.

However, with the use of a testamentary trust, as long as the assets stay within the trust, they are protected. Here, the trust gives that extra layer of protection from potential marriage breakdowns, as well as from future creditors. If one ever needs a lump sum from the trust temporarily, with the appropriate legal consultation, they may want to consider a loan from the trust at a prescribed rate of interest. This way those funds may still be viewed as assets within the trust.

Tax Savings

To illustrate the tax savings, let's look at a hypothetical scenario if my wife and I were to pass away 30 years from now with no trust structure versus with a trust structure in place.

Example Assumptions

- $6,000,000 after-tax estate (this number could be any number, but we are using this arbitrary number to show the effects of taxation)
- Two children (aged 32 and 34, each with two children of their own); both are professionals taxed at the highest marginal rate
- Inheritance invested at 6% interest
- Trustee fees are nil (administered by a family member)
- Trust tax returns cost $500 annually

Table 8.1 shows that the tax savings would be $58,450 per year per child for the first three years in existence.

- In the first column, the income is taxed at my son and daughter's highest personal tax rate at 53.53%.
- In the second column, the income is split $65,000 to each of my grandchildren and $50,000 (allocated less given there is no personal exemption) in the graduated rates of the trust.

As discussed earlier, after three years, we no longer have the advantage of income-splitting with the trust.

Table 8.2 shows that the tax savings would be $53,940 per year per child until the trust is dissolved or converted, or the grandchildren start to have other income.

- The first column is the same as before.
- In the second column, the income is split $90,000 to each of my grandchildren.

Table 8.1 Estate Trust Tax Savings: The first three years

	Inheritance Transferred to Adult Child	Inheritance Transferred to Testamentary Trust
Value of estate per child	$3,000,000	$3,000,000
Taxable income	$ 180,000	$ 180,000
Taxes payable	$ 96,350	$ 37,400
Trust tax return fees	—	$ (500)
Net income	$ 83,650	$ 142,100

Table 8.2   Estate Trust Tax Savings: After three years

	Inheritance Transferred to Adult Child	Inheritance Transferred to Testamentary Trust
Value of estate per child	$3,000,000	$ 3,000,000
Taxable income	$ 180,000	$ 180,000
Taxes payable	$ 96,350	$ 41,910
Trust tax return fees	—	$ (500)
Net income	$ 83,650	$ 137,590

Here's my sensitivity analysis on the after-three-year scenario:

- The tax rates for the beneficiaries:
  - Assume no other income for the grandchild.
  - The higher the beneficiaries' income, the lower the benefit.
- If our children ultimately have three children each, then the savings would be $60,970.
- If our children have one child each, then the savings would be $35,221.
- Bottom line, the more children there are, the more the potential savings!
- The larger the estate, the greater the savings (up to a certain point, before everyone is in the highest tax bracket).
- The higher the return, the higher the savings.
- However, if the income is in the form of dividends and capital gains, the lower the savings.
- The higher the future tax rates, the higher the savings.

This scenario makes certain assumptions about tax rates, the basic personal exemptions, and so on.

Overall, if done properly there could be a significant savings when splitting income.

- Using these scenario numbers, over a 20-year period there would be a potential savings of a total of $1,092,330 in tax.

When you factor in the protection elements discussed earlier, you can see how in most scenarios we recommend the use of testamentary trusts in estate plans.

Other Factors to Consider

Probate

Another benefit of a trust is avoiding a second round of probate (i.e., if you pass away, your assets may be subject to probate fees).

- With no trust, if your beneficiaries receive your assets and then eventually pass away, probate fees could be payable again.
- With a trust, this second round of probate process and fees is avoided.

However, it should also be noted that transferring assets to a testamentary trust could result in upfront probate taxes on the death of a parent; i.e., a joint non-registered account held in joint tenancy with right of survivorship for a child would not be subject to probate, unless it passed through the estate to form part of the trust assets.

The exception to this rule is with insurance policies, as it is possible to transfer a death benefit payable from an insurance policy to a testamentary trust without the benefit forming part of your estate, meaning no probate taxes are paid.

Costs

The initial cost of documenting a testamentary trust is included in the lawyer's fee for preparing the will. The terms can then be changed with updates to the will, such as with a new will or codicil.

Once the trust is set up, there will also likely be bookkeeping and administrative fees, annual tax returns, and final distribution fees. There could also be professional trustee fees, though if you use a family member, the trustee fee could be waived.

While generally the tax savings on assets of less than $250,000 might not be large enough to offset the costs of the trust structure, it still may be worthwhile for the children to keep if they are currently married.

Minor Children

If there is no will or trust set up, your estate may be administered by a government-appointed public trustee until the age at which your children can legally own assets (18 in Ontario), when they can receive the entire estate all at once.

However, even if your child is entitled to receiving your hard-earned money, do we really want them to have everything outright—is a 19-year-old more likely to invest all the proceeds or spend them on a luxury car?

While every situation is different, we believe that often it's best to have these payments staggered.

Example

Instructions noted in the will:

1. Income earned by the trust is to be paid to the child annually, but the capital is held until a specific age, with or without discretion for special needs—or the "training wheels" scenario, where the child can receive one third of the capital at age 25, one third at age 30, and one third at age 35.
2. All trust capital can be paid out at any time as long as it's used for education.

For spendthrifts (children who enjoy spending the rewards of your thriftiness): If you have a child or children who happen to not be the most savvy with their investments, structuring your testamentary trust as a protective trust may help with money management. For instance, you could set up the trust so that your child receives regular income on a monthly or yearly basis as opposed to receiving it all at once.

For Family Members with Special Needs

If you have a child with special needs, you will probably want to ensure that they are taken care of financially after you are gone. If a potential beneficiary qualifies for the federal disability tax credit, you may want to consider a qualified disability trust—a trust that jointly elects, together with one or more beneficiaries under the trust, in its T3 return of income for the year to be a qualified disability trust for a year (renewed on an annual basis).

It should be noted that qualified disability trusts have graduated rates of tax, and are not taxed at the top marginal rates in the province of trust residency, unlike most testamentary trusts.

In most provinces you may be able to leave assets in a testamentary Henson trust that allows your disabled beneficiary to qualify for provincial disability support.

Without a trust, many of these support benefits could be clawed back if a certain amount of income is generated.

Spousal Trust

While many point to the benefits of having a testamentary spousal trust as benefiting your spouse, much of the benefit is more so for protection and legacy planning.

For tax purposes, there is a roll-over provision that allows your assets to be paid to your spouse on a tax-deferred basis, though this is innately already the case if the assets were going to your spouse regardless of the trust.

This is why many people may rearrange their joint non-registered accounts to become individual non-registered accounts, allowing their assets to roll over to a spousal trust (unlike joint accounts).

Section 73(1.01) of the Income Tax Act frames the rollover into a spousal trust in terms of looking at the individual who created the trust, and property transferred by that individual (as opposed to their spouse). Therefore, the rollover may fail if jointly held assets are transferred into the trust given that a portion of those jointly held assets are owned by the spouse.

Use of Spousal Trust

If you pass away and your spouse remarries, your assets are protected as long as they stay within that trust. As of now, we are not aware of any case law declaring assets in a spousal trust to be divisible.

However, if the assets are removed from the trust, then they are outside the control of the trust and trustee. The settlor of the trust can dictate the distribution of trust assets (i.e., a percentage of income and capital to be distributed per year) and ultimately allow for the residual value to be divided amongst your children.

This certainly does give the ability to plan for more control, protection, and assurance that one's estate will ultimately provide for a desired outcome—though I have also seen it being interpreted as managing your spouse's financial affairs from the grave.

Three different trust arrangement plans might be:

1. **First spousal trust:** Any capital remaining would be distributed among children—which may result in not enough desired estate value for children.
2. **Second spousal trust:** A spouse is entitled to receive income, not capital—which may result in not enough income for his or her lifestyle.
3. **Third Spousal trust:** This gives the trustee full discretionary authority to pay the spouse any combination of income or capital—which could result in all kinds of scenarios.

Trustees have to act impartially and in the best interests of all beneficiaries, which can create very different decisions. Outcomes can vary significantly depending on the powers and instructions given to the trustee.

When a Testamentary Trust Loses Its Status

A testamentary trust can sometimes become an inter vivos trust, but an inter vivos trust can never become a testamentary trust. The following are two examples of a testamentary trust losing its status:

1. *New contributions are made by anybody other than the settlor.* However, the trust may reinvest its income or borrow money without losing its status.
2. *The trustee fails to distribute its assets as required by the trust document.* If it's required, for example, to distribute all property to the beneficiary once the beneficiary reaches age 18, it would be considered an *inter vivos* trust from that point forward.

Key Takeaways from This Chapter

- There are multiple forms of trust that can be created to help meet financial objectives over time.
- In order to be a valid trust, a trust must be set up correctly and meet certain legal tests. A trust can lose its validity if any of these tests are not met or are no longer met.
- Some of the most common uses of trusts are to pass wealth between generations, to help meet educational or childcare costs, and to provide for a spouse or a dependent child (including a child with a disability) upon your passing.
- Because there is such a wide variety of trusts, and a similarly wide variety of objectives for a trust, there are many different decisions that must be made in establishing a trust. Careful, professional guidance that is aligned with your goals is a must.

Questions to Ask Your Financial Planner

1. How have we considered and incorporated trusts in my financial plans?
2. If I don't have any trusts established now, why not? Is there a plan in place to establish trusts at some point in the future? How will we know when that point has been reached?
3. If we do have trusts in place as part of my plan, how have we confirmed that they are still valid and appropriate for my current situation and goals?

Chapter 9

Alternative Investment Strategies

I n the previous chapters, we've looked at what we could call mainstream financial strategies. Mainstream investment strategies look for ways to use the corporation to shield income from taxes, distribute earnings to gain advantage, or create structures that allow virtually everyone to play within the system to find ways to maximize and improve outcomes.

Alternative investment strategies, on the other hand, look outside the mainstream to find strategies that sometimes involve more than the usual risk or volatility, and often demand different qualifications such as greater wealth, longer time horizons, or elaborate structures that truly require experienced professional advice.

In this chapter we explore some of those alternative investment strategies that are either most effective or, in some cases, simply widely spoken about but, in our experience, are of dubious outcome—all so you can be fully informed.

What You'll Get Out of This Chapter

Thus far in this book, we've reviewed what I think of as mainstream strategies to help ensure financial success for the incorporated professional or business owner. This chapter, in contrast, covers strategies outside the mainstream. These include more complex strategies or strategies that have a more narrow application as their benefits are dependent on a specific set of circumstances.

It's important to realize that some of these strategies are exactly the ones that may be pitched to high-income individuals. You may have heard, from colleagues or from financial advisors, about the benefits of individual pension plans, retirement compensation arrangements, or of making investments in luxury items such as watches, fine art, or the like. One risk you can face as a high-income earner is being sold on the apparent benefits of a financial strategy or mechanism without a full review of the specific application to your situation.

This chapter is designed to help you understand the basics of some alternative strategies by removing the sales context. In that way, if and when you encounter these proposals—or even if you decide you'd like to pursue some or all of them yourself, independent of a sales conversation—you'll have some basic background to help you evaluate the benefits and drawbacks for yourself.

Capital Gains Strip

A *capital gains strip* refers to the process of extracting money from a corporation, through a series of transactions, as part capital gains, part taxable dividends. This could lead to a lower overall effective rate instead of taking the equivalent amount entirely as a taxable dividend. By the time you are reading this, this strategy may be off limits. This type of planning is under pressure as the government has indicated it is not in favor of it.

In fact, on July 18, 2017, under the new "tax fairness" proposal, this plan was on the chopping block, until the government discovered it would have affected farmers (and may have also affected inter-generational succession planning) and thus the attempt to do away with the plan was subsequently dropped on October 19, 2017.

Therefore, at any time we may see legislation that shuts this planning down. In fact, it's typically been the best practice for accountants who implement this strategy to ensure there is documentation of the business purpose of the transaction/series of transactions. (This planning and documentation is often coupled with other planning, such as an estate freeze.) That's because if a capital gains strip is implemented, it's important that it be seen as a business transaction rather than a tax avoidance transaction.

There are many ways to undertake a capital gains strip, and each firm will have their preferred method. Most that we have seen mimic a pipeline strategy typically undertaken to mitigate double tax on death. (A *pipeline* is a common term in the world of Canadian taxation, referring to a strategy of minimizing income taxes after someone has died when the deceased person owned shares of a company at the time of death.)

Some plans involve the individual shareholder triggering personal capital gains, while others involve a holding company triggering gains internally, allowing the capital dividend account to flow up to a shareholder.

Most methods involve some type of holding company, which typically results in this planning to be limited for many professional corporations whose governing bodies refuse to allow operating company shares to be held by a holding company.

Some of the reasons for the recent uptick in attention for these types of plans:

- The government unintentionally just did promote this plan, obscure until now, by mentioning it in the first place.

- An available strategy to remove funds from the corporation to avoid or delay the new $50,000 passive income rule, especially considering this passive income grind is on an associated group basis.
- Loss of income-splitting opportunities with children or spouse, resulting in a higher personal tax bill.
- The fear of the government changing the rules in future budgets.

Often, these plans are tied into additional planning, such as using the proceeds to fund a trust, possibly having children pay taxes on the gains.

Overall Outcomes

- The plan generally is to exchange what would have been a taxable dividend to the shareholder into a capital gain, only 50% of which is taxable. If you look back at the table of personal tax rates in Chapter 2, you will see capital gains are always lower than dividends.
- Other plans trigger corporate capital gains, thus triggering an addition to CDA, which can be paid to a shareholder tax-free upon filing an election in prescribed form.

Suitability for Capital Gains Strip

When is a capital gains strip suitable? We've identified the factors you will want to consider:

- You should already be taking large amounts of dividends or salary as income or will have a high cash need in the future. A lot of the versions of this plan will include triggering an immediate capital gain that is taxable in the year in which the plan is implemented. The immediate tax bill can be off-putting for some people, and one would need to look at the opportunity cost of using these funds elsewhere. This is more palatable if you were going to see high taxation in the immediate future and using the plan would reduce the tax bill. Solvency and liquidity in the corporation are areas of concern when contemplating these plans.

- A capital gains strip will be more beneficial if you are not able to receive eligible dividends, as the spread of applicable tax rates will be higher. This justifies potentially paying tax sooner than necessary as well as the implementation costs.
- You must be willing to accept CRA scrutiny and be willing to challenge the plan in court—there is risk associated with this plan and that needs to be clearly outlined to anyone considering this type of planning.
- You must be willing to pay the fees necessary to do the work correctly, as any misstep can throw the plan off and cause unintended consequences (keeping your corporate minute book up to date will reduce the amount of pre-work required).
- You should engage a competent team of advisors who can match their expertise to the complexity of this strategy.
- I wouldn't ever recommend engaging in this alternative strategy for anything less than $1 million strip as the fees (in the $15,000 to $50,000 range) start to outweigh any tax savings.

Overall Bottom Line

If you need less than $200,000/year in ineligible dividends or $300,000/year in eligible dividends paid personally to you over the next five years, then we would rule out the capital gains strip strategy completely.

The logic for this exclusion is that any value less than these amounts would likely result in a lower average tax rate than the capital gains strip provides.

If you need more than the above values or have an immediate cash flow need (or have a significant shareholder debit balance), then we would encourage a look at all the other financial planning ideas on the table first. Are there any income splitting opportunities with your spouse, even factoring in the new rules with spousal dividends? Is there anything available in the CDA? Is there anything we can transfer into the corporation for cash flow savings?

If you are presented with this plan, it's best to review the pros and cons with a financial planner familiar with this strategy. It is sometimes best to have a sober second look!

Individual Pension Plans (IPP and PPP)

An individual pension plan (IPP) can be thought of as an RRSP on steroids. If you dislike RRSPs, then you will dislike IPPs even more.

However, if you have read our comments on salary versus dividends (Chapter 2) and investing inside the corporation (Chapter 3) and still would like an RRSP or RRSP-like structure, then an IPP is an option worth exploring. An IPP is a pension arrangement similar to an RRSP that offers tax deductions and tax deferral on your investments. It's usually a one-person defined benefit pension plan that is available to incorporated individuals taking salary from their corporations.

Why an IPP?

An IPP allows an individual to place the maximum amount allowable into a registered pension plan under the Income Tax Act, meaning likely more than an RRSP would.

- *Greater funding:* If contributing to an RRSP, then a client is subject to the limit of 18% of earnings (to a maximum of $27,230 in 2020).
- Once the client is over 40 years of age and making in excess of approximately $125,000, the amount required to fund the maximum benefit of the IPP will exceed the RRSP contribution limit.
- Therefore, effectively you are able to place more funds into a tax-deferred account (in the case of an IPP, a registered pension plan) than you otherwise could have with an RRSP.
- See the latest IPP contribution numbers in Table 9.1.
- In addition, *past service benefits* can be provided, which would result in greater contributions into the plan from the corporation as well as enhanced benefits.

Table 9.1 Tax-Advantaged Contributions: IPP versus RRSP

Age	IPP Contribution (vs. $26,500 RRSP)
40	$27,731.00
45	$30,461.00
50	$33,460.00
55	$36,754.00
60	$40,372.00
65	$42,309.00

- You may have to transfer assets from your RRSP into the IPP to fund some of the past service benefit so you are not considered to be double dipping on tax deductions with both an RRSP and pension plan.
- There may be the ability to *terminally fund* the IPP when you retire once certain restrictions are lifted, providing a further avenue to shift funds from the corporation into the pension plan.
- Terminal funding only typically makes sense the longer the assets remain in the IPP and the more conservative an investor you are—i.e., a weighting to more interest-bearing investments.
- An example of this scenario that gets promoted is: if you retired in 2009, right after the 2008 financial crash, you would have been given the option of topping up your plan, as opposed to RRSPs where your losses cannot be topped up.

As a defined-benefit pension plan, these benefits will appeal to you if you are looking for a guaranteed source of income outside of the corporation. IPPs can also assist in removing investment assets from the corporation, to mitigate the effect on the small business deduction resulting from the new passive income rules. There's flexibility with the IPP to have survivor benefits, guarantee periods, bridging, and indexation, and payments out of the IPP are eligible for pension-income-splitting (similar to RRSPs and like most corporate scenarios with dividends when age 65). Similar to an RRSP, an IPP provides a level of creditor protection.

Considerations

- IPPs are costly to administer. They require the services of an actuary, and there are regulatory filing fees. These requirements add additional costs (which are deductible to the corporation) and complexity.
- Typical costs, in addition to managing the investment, could look like:

Set-up and registration:	$1,500 to $5,000
Triennial (every three years) valuations:	$1,500 to $3,000
Annual administration:	$600 to $1,200
Consulting fees:	Fee-for-service

- Note that these fees are tax-deductible expenses to the corporation. As an alternative, these fees can be built in to the annual corporate funding levels, so that the fees can be paid from the IPP.
- There will be loss of RRSP room. This will limit your ability to use RRSPs (including spousal RRSPs). It should be noted that the corporation takes the deduction instead of the individual.
- Funds are in a pension plan, therefore amounts to be received are restricted by pension legislation. At retirement you can receive an income stream from the pension, or purchase a life annuity, or commute to a locked-in plan with any excess being fully taxable to the extent RRSP room is not available.
- The corporation has to be able to fund the IPP (thus, the importance of solvency and liquidity). Therefore, the cash flow and financial situation of the corporation must be sufficient to meet its obligations in this regard. If not, then additional service will not be credited if the corporation cannot fund the pension; alternatively, the IPP may have to be wound up. If these situations occur, this could become a big financial burden.
- The IPP can be funded such that the pension is paid for your lifetime, and your surviving spouse receives a pension equal to

two-thirds of the amount that was being paid to the plan member prior to death.

- There will be a guarantee of at least 5 years of pension payments where there is a spouse, and 15 years of payments where there is no spouse. The pension must be provided as a lifetime benefit—a term-certain annuity is not a retirement option.

Suitability

The following are guidelines as to whether IPPs are a suitable strategy for you:

- You should be receiving a high salary (>$150,000) from your corporation (and high salary in past years helps here, too) and be over age 40 in order to maximize pension benefits. Benefits are based on your T4 earnings, so dividends do not qualify.
- There should be a desire to receive a guaranteed retirement income utilizing assets outside of the corporation—you are a conservative investor.
- Creditor protection of these assets is important to you.
- The corporation must have the ability to fund the IPP and fulfill its obligations.

Next Steps

- You should consult your financial planner and accountant to review both your personal and corporate situations. If it makes sense to proceed, then the IPP would be established by an actuarial firm (e.g., Westcoast Actuaries and Gordon B. Lang) and that firm would be responsible for all filings with the CRA in regard to registration and ongoing administration.
- Both Westcoast Actuaries and Gordon B. Lang have a free online quoting system if you wished to investigate further. Here are links to each of these:
  - https://www.westcoast-actuaries.com/individual-pension-plans/quote-request-form/
  - http://www.gblinc.ca/resource/ipp-questionnaire/

What's the Difference between an IPP and a PPP?

A personal pension plan (PPP)—usually from Integris—is a form of individual pension plan (IPP), which contains a provision that allows the employer, at any time, to designate a year of service as being ineligible under the defined benefit component of the plan, such that the employer can make a contribution to the IPP in respect to that year on a defined contribution (DC) basis.

Where contributions are being made on a DC basis, the employer can choose to contribute any amount between 1% of the plan member's T4 income and 18% of the plan member's T4 income (limited to a dollar amount, which is $27,230 in 2020). The amount of the benefits to be provided on a DC basis are dependent on the investment performance of the DC contributions.

Defined benefit (DB) is a type of pension plan in which an employer/sponsor promises a specified pension payment, lump sum, or combination thereof on retirement that is predetermined by a formula based on the employee's earnings history, tenure of service, and age.

Defined contribution (DC) is a type of pension plan in which employer/sponsor contributions are invested, for example in the stock market, and the returns on the investment (which may be positive or negative) are credited to the individual's account.

Thus, the PPP is nothing more than an IPP, a defined benefit (DB) plan, which has been modified to include a defined contribution (DC) component.

This modification allows you to switch between DB and DC plans in order to reduce the employer contribution requirements when you can't afford the DB contribution. For jurisdictions like BC, Alberta (which has plans for connected persons) and Manitoba, in which IPPs are exempt from a minimum funding requirement, this tactic is simply not required.

Even in other non-exempt jurisdictions, we believe this model is unnecessary for the following reasons:

- If the member's earnings fluctuate, the contribution under the DB program will fluctuate in the same manner as the DC contribution.
- CRA takes a dim view of mixing DB and DC benefits under one plan.
- Having to keep track separately of DC and DB account balances (which is a CRA requirement) complicates the administration and is subject to errors.

This arrangement makes the plan's administration requirements much more complex than is necessary.

In addition, it is commonly suggested that the PPP does not require actuarial, custodial, or investment management services and hence is cheaper to administer. This is not true, as contributions for any DB plan benefits have to be certified by an actuary before they can be approved by CRA as being deductible.

Pay careful attention to where PPP providers sub-contract this work, usually to a firm of actuarial consultants who presumably do not work for free. These extra costs are likely buried in the fund management fees.

Therefore, the most significant advantage the PPP would provide over a defined benefit IPP is the flexibility for you to reduce contributions if you do not have adequate cash flow.

However, if you have concerns in regard to cash flow and not being able to make the required contributions to the IPP, you are most likely not a good candidate for an IPP to begin with!

Overall Bottom Line

When corporate tax saving applicable to IPP contributions is at the small business rate (12.2% in Ontario in 2020), then in many cases having no IPP at all is probably the better route—unless you prefer investing in RRSP-type structures and lean toward conservative investing (e.g., interest-bearing GICs).

When corporate tax savings is at the higher corporate rate (26.5% in Ontario) and you are already taking a salary, you have consistent cash flow, and you prefer conservative interest-bearing investments, then IPPs are worth exploring—as long as you can justify the extra costs.

Retirement Compensation Arrangements

Retirement compensation arrangements (RCAs) are defined under subsection 248(1) of the Canadian Income Tax Act, which allows 100% tax-deductible corporate dollars to be deposited into an RCA, on behalf of the private business owner and/or key employee. No tax is paid (other than the 50% refundable tax required to be remitted to CRA) by the owner/employee until benefits are received at retirement.

RCAs were recently brought into the spotlight as one of the hypothetical tax pulls to keep Kawhi Leonard as a Toronto Raptor, before his ultimate heartbreaking decision to leave to go to the LA Clippers. Whatever was deposited into an RCA would eventually have equalized tax rates for Kawhi to effectively pay no more tax in Canada than he would have in the United States.

Example
- For instance, let's say Kawhi received $30,000,000 a year in the RCA, and years down the road he finds himself in Dallas and then collapses the investment.
- He would pay a Canadian withholding tax, but he is in the United States and Texas has no state tax. He would be subject to federal tax, but the United States will give him a tax credit on the Canadian withholding tax, so it works out that he will pay much less on his RCA holdings than if they were in Canada.
- While this strategy is commonly used for NHL players, the bad news is that the NBA's collective agreement outlaws RCAs altogether, believing they would give the Raptors a competitive advantage. The good news is they are not outlawed for us regular folks!

An RCA is the Canadian Income Tax Act's retirement solution for high-income-earning Canadians, but be forewarned, this is a very complicated investment structure. It is ideal for executives and professionals with professional corporations, and in particular appeals to the corporate owner who wishes to move or retire to another country.

The ability to deduct potentially large sums of money has made the RCA a powerful income tax and retirement planning tool.

An RCA is a super-sized pension plan. It allows for larger tax-deductible contributions, making it the highest tier of retirement product in Canada. It provides a way to increase retirement assets to the maximum level allowable.

Like most alternative strategies, a thorough cost–benefit analysis should be done to determine whether this is a suitable strategy for you and your family.

Steps to Implement an RCA

The corporation sets up an RCA to provide retirement benefits for its key employees and/or executives, which for most of us would simply mean just ourselves.

Deductible contributions are made from the corporation into the RCA and are held in trust for the beneficiaries, the owners of the corporation.

- Each year the company will make tax-deductible contributions on behalf of the employees named in the plan.
- 50% of all these contributions are made to an investment account (IA).
- The other 50% is remitted to a refundable tax account (RTA) with CRA (deposits with CRA are non-interest-bearing).
- The investment account (IA) is *self-directed* and is subject to yearly remittance to or from the RTA.

Advantages of the RCA

- You can defer tax to a time and place of your choosing. Contributions are 100% tax-deductible by the corporation, and are a non-taxable benefit in the hands of the corporate owner. Most taxes (excluding withholding taxes) do not apply until money is withdrawn during retirement.

- Employees/owners can also make contributions up to the amount of the corporate contribution. This personal contribution is 100% tax-deductible on the individual's personal taxes.
- There is the ability to withdraw at reduced tax rates (presumably because you are in a lower tax bracket when you are retired) if the corporate owner retires/resides outside Canada to a lower-tax-rate jurisdiction where they can pay as low as 0% tax on the proceeds from their RCA. (See the tax treaty tax rates shown in Table 9.2.)
- If you maintain Canadian residency, you can use income splitting with a joint RCA to effectively reduce tax.
- Owners of RCAs can arrange to borrow up to 90% of the amount of the RCA contribution and loan it back to their corporation to invest in the growth of the business, or simply use this leveraged money tax-free.
- Assets held in an RCA are creditor-proof and are separate from the sponsoring corporation's or practice's assets and are therefore protected from the corporation's or practice's creditors.
- Assets in an RCA investment account compound tax-free.
- Allowable contributions are substantially higher than in an individual pension plan.
- Contributions to an RCA can enable a company to get down to the small business tax level.

Table 9.2   Countries with Tax Treaties with Canada

Country of Residency	Tax Treaty Rate
United States	15%
Ireland	0–15%
Hong Kong	10–15%
England	0–15%
Australia	15%
France	25%
Italy	15%

- RCAs are exempt from payroll and healthcare taxes.
- RCAs are exempt from provincial pension regulators.
- Assets in an RCA are excluded from the holder's estate and are not subject to probate fees when a beneficiary is named.
- RCAs allow you to purify a company prior to selling the business in order to qualify for the capital gains exemption.
- Funds in an RCA are not locked in and are not regulated like a pension plan and can be withdrawn at the time and place of the owner's choosing.

Disadvantages of the RCA

- These are very complicated structures. If you like to keep things simple, this is not for you!
- Half of the contribution is remitted to a non-interest earning refundable tax account (RTA) and held by the CRA.
- This disadvantage is offset by the tax shelter and flexibility to lower taxes below the top marginal rate.
- Also, the use of life insurance can tax shelter the gains on the investment account (IA) so that 50% of the gains do not have to be paid to the RTA every year.

In addition, you will need to make sure your RCA is deemed *reasonable* for tax purposes.

As addressed in Section 248(1) of the Income Tax Act, as long as the contributions are reasonable, large tax-deductible contributions may be put into an RCA, resulting in substantial tax relief to the company. To ensure reasonableness it is recommended that every RCA be certified with an actuarial certificate. This calculation is based on the member's best three years' T4 earnings and period of service.

Investment Account

The investment account is managed by the trustees of the plan and directed by the company or the principal plan member. There are no investment rules or restrictions.

However, we recommend that the investments be of a non-distributing nature, as 50% of all dividends, realized capital gains, and interest income (less expenses) must be remitted by the trustees to the RTA annually, unless the funding vehicle is tax-exempt life insurance.

Withdrawals

Upon retirement the beneficiary will draw from the assets of both the RTA and the RCA trust. Withdrawals are flexible, and not subject to any restrictions on maximum or minimums. They are however, subject to tax at the applicable income tax rate.

Another benefit at withdrawal is that money contributed at today's tax rates may be withdrawn in the future at potentially lower rates. This will depend on the beneficiary moving to a lower-tax jurisdiction in Canada or outside Canada, such as the United States or Australia, where tax treaties result in lower rates.

The tax treaty rates shown in Table 9.2 are subject to change depending on international tax treaties and agreements.

Overall Bottom Line

If you want to keep things simple and plan on retiring in Canada, the RCA is an extremely complex structure that is not suitable for you. However, if you are saving a significant sum every year, enjoy complex structures, and plan on retiring in a lower-tax jurisdiction, then it's worth exploring an RCA.

Investing in Watches: Can I Buy My Rolex through the Corporation?

From a very high level perspective, there is nothing preventing you from purchasing a luxury watch through your corporation. If you can consider it a collector's item, like gold certificates, then yes. However, you need to be aware of the potential tax consequences.

- First, like, gold, if you sell anything with an increase in value, you will realize a taxable capital gain.
- Second, the risk is that if CRA audits you, and they deem there is a shareholder benefit by purchasing the watch, the result could be significant.

Under subsection 15(1) of the Income Tax Act, there is an income inclusion of the amount of value of the benefit when "if, at any time, a benefit is conferred by a corporation on a shareholder of the corporation." This is a fairly broad definition.

For example, if you wore this watch once to a function, then a benefit might be deemed to apply. It is up to you and your accountant, but we feel it comes down to your acceptance of any risk a shareholder benefit could be found to have occurred.

Now, is it a good investment? Almost always no, though most watch experts will point to Rolex, Patek Philippe, and Audemars Piguet as the exceptions (though you are going to need to form a relationship with the dealers to actually obtain them for retail prices), since the secondary market tends to sell above the retail price. Since 2003, Chrono24, a German marketing company, has tracked daily watch prices in a similar fashion to the stock market (see Table 9.3).

Table 9.3 Is Your Watch a Good Investment?

Watch	Retail Price	Market Price (September 1, 2019)	Gain (market price over retail price)
Rolex:			
Steel white-faced Daytona 2016 (nicknamed "The Panda")	$13,000	$32,841	253%
Patek Philippe:			
Nautilus 5711 blue-faced 2018	$31,000	$93,010	300%
Audemars Piguet:			
Royal Oak 15202 Jumbo 2014	$26,000	$55,964	215%

Overall Bottom Line

While these are all beautiful watches, unless you are in the know, have a great relationship with a retailer, are very patient in waiting for many years for these watches to become available, and will not wear it out in public, for most of us this is likely a depreciable asset and therefore not a good investment plan.

Art: Can I Buy My Pablo Picasso Painting through the Corporation?

Let's consider this question from three different angles:

1. Buying art
2. Transferring art
3. Selling or donating art

Buying Art

Yes, we can buy art through our corporations, but, as with buying watches, we have to be aware of the personal taxable benefits that may result. If you are buying art through the corporation, hopefully it is for display in the office and not at home. An important caveat is that non-Canadian art is not considered depreciable property.

Transferring Art

If one happens to have a material piece of art that's currently owned personally, we could transfer this to the corporation in exchange for the appraised marketable value of the piece. There likely would be taxes to be paid in terms of capital gains on the fair market value of the piece minus the adjusted cost basis (the ACB, or what you paid for it) plus freight and delivery. The value here is that this exchange could help out with personal cash flow in the near term as we are able to extract funds in this exchange. As stated earlier, we would have to avoid any personal-use benefit from the art piece.

Selling/Donating Art

Here's where it gets interesting. First, I have to thank my good friend Alexander Herman, assistant director at the Institute of Art and Law, for bringing this to my attention.

CRA's website, under the heading "Information for donors of certified cultural property," notes that the tax credit available from donating certified cultural property is "based on the fair market value of the property as determined by the Canadian Cultural Property Export Review Board, that may be claimed up to 100% of net income (any unclaimed portion may be carried forward over the following five years)." In comparison, charitable contributions allow for a claim of only 75% of net income. The United States caps the tax deduction for donated art at 30% of one's income. Canada has no such cap.

There are three special tax considerations:

1. The amount that can be claimed as a tax credit is *not* limited to a percentage of net income.
2. Capital gains from the disposition of the cultural property are not subject to tax. Capital losses are treated in the normal manner.
3. A gift of certified cultural property made by a graduated rate estate (GRE) will qualify for the 0% capital gains inclusion rate, provided that the donation is made by the estate within 36 months after the death of the individual.

With respect to donations made after February 10, 2014, of certified cultural property that was acquired as part of a tax-shelter arrangement, the exemption from the rule that deems "the value of the gift to be no greater than its cost to the donor" is removed.

Thus, the amount reported on the donation receipt as a gift cannot exceed the cost to the donor of acquiring the property under the tax shelter arrangement. To certify a gift, the institution or public authority that is to receive the gift must apply with the donor, or on the donor's behalf, to the Review Board to have the property certified.

As Alexander pointed out:

> The Cultural Property Export and Import Act was developed in the 1970s as a reaction to the recent sale of two great Canadian art collections in the United States. As a result, great works of art being permanently taken out of Canada would henceforth be metaphorically "held at the border" by the Review board for up to six months to see if a Canadian institution could afford to acquire them and keep them in the country.
>
> However, every year only seven or eight cultural objects are refused export permits on the basis of "national importance" by the Export Review Board. But this number is dwarfed in comparison to applications to the Board for tax certification. In a given year, the Board might deem 6,000 to 8,000 cultural objects or collections of national importance for tax certification, leading to credits that can reach over $100 million in total.
>
> As of June 2019, eligibility for tax certification has been made even easier. As a result of the Caillebotte[1] controversy, the federal government decided in its latest budget to remove the "national importance" standard for the Board to apply when assessing tax applications (but not, strangely, for export applications).
>
> This means that donors looking to avail themselves of the tax breaks now only have to show their works are of "outstanding significance" for reasons related to history or national life, aesthetic qualities or value for study, not necessarily that they are of great importance to the country.[2]

A couple of interesting takeaways from this:

- Because prices in the art market have been soaring for the past 30 years, you can easily get a fair market value determination

---

[1] *Iris bleus, jardin du Petit Gennevilliers* by French impressionist Gustave Caillebotte was originally purchased in 2016 by a foreign buyer, but deferred by the Canadian Cultural Property Export Review Board on the basis of "national importance." It ultimately was donated to the Art Gallery of Ontario.

[2] Alexander Herman, "Caillebotte Painting Shines Light on Woefully Out-of-Date Rules Governing Canada's Cultural Sector," *Financial Post*, September 17, 2019. Available at https://business.financialpost.com/opinion/caillebotte-painting-shines-light-on-woefully-out-of-date-rules-governing-canadas-cultural-sector?fbclid=IwAR2LD-XhD-DnDOnHj4YEWLa-INddiZnJ8QdfqSeqHyEJHG86AFNC3yZ8mqo.

for art that's way higher than what you bought it for. Since valuation of art is an art, not a science, there is much room for error/machination. We have to wonder: Why would the museums care if it isn't their money they are purchasing it with?

- Only 2% of cultural object exports get referred to the Board as "nationally important," whereas 96% of tax credit applications get approved by the Board as "nationally important."

Overall Bottom Line

For those of us who are interested in art, especially Canadian artists such as Alexander Colville or Christopher Pratt who have shown "outstanding significance," it is important to know the changing tax environment with art.

Private Health Services Plans

A Private Health Services Plan, or PHSP, is defined under subsection 248(1) of the Income Tax Act as a contract or plan of insurance in respect of hospital care or medical expenses, which includes dental expenses. A PHSP must meet all of the following three criteria:

1. It must be a contract or plan of insurance for hospital or medical expenses.
2. All or substantially all of the coverage must cover only medical expenses (note that nominal coverage for items such as supplements is allowable) covered under subsection 118.2(2) of the Income Tax Act (i.e., expenses eligible for the medical expense tax credit).
3. It must only reimburse the medical or hospital expenses of the employee, the employee's spouse, or the partner or a dependent of the employee.

The payments made by an employer to a plan that satisfies all of these conditions are a tax-deductible expense, while benefits paid to an employee from the plan are not subject to taxation. CPP and EI premiums do not apply to the PHSP premiums.

Following are the general rules for corporations that establish a PHSP:

- There is no limit under the Income Tax Act for the premiums paid to a PHSP.
- The PHSP can be established solely for shareholder employees if they represent all of the employees within a selected class.
- The payments to shareholders from the PHSP are tax-free to the shareholder only if the benefits were received in the person's capacity as an employee, not as a shareholder.
- In order to qualify, the shareholder must be an employee and be actively engaged in the company's business activities but does not need to be receiving a salary.
- The benefits must be reasonable, and be consistent with what would be provided to an arm's-length employee providing similar services.
- The plan can provide for different annual benefit limits for different employee groups.
- If the payment of shareholder medical expenses does not qualify as a PHSP benefit, this is a taxable benefit for the shareholder, and is not a deductible expense for the corporation.

There are a number of organizations (corporate administrators such as Medi-Direct, Olympia Trust, and Benecaid) that will establish and administer a PHSP, often on a "cost-plus" basis.

However, where an employment contract provides that the employer is required to reimburse the employee for qualifying medical expenses, the payments made to the employee may qualify as PHSP premiums.

Health Spending Accounts

Under *most* health spending account programs, the employer places a set amount into the employee's individual health spending account (the reasonable guidelines as outlined earlier for PHSPs must be followed).

The amounts are referred to as *credits*. The employee uses the credits to pay for medical expenses not covered under the basic group insurance plan, but which are eligible medical expenses under the Income Tax Act.

Another type of health spending account provides that there is no regular employer payment or premium. When an employee makes a claim for a medical expense, the employer pays the amount of the claim.

However, it is important that the program be considered a PHSP so that the benefit payments (reimbursement of qualified medical expenses) are not a taxable benefit for the employee, and thus a third-party administrator must adjudicate and process the claims. The third party is required, as there are privacy issues involved with respect to the employee's medical details.

To establish a contract of insurance under this type of HSA, the following must be satisfied:

- There is a contractual obligation for the employer to cover the eligible expenses.
- There is an undertaking between the employer and the administrator that the employer will cover the claims as adjudicated by the administrator.
- There is an undertaking between the employer and the administrator that the administrator will reimburse the claim to the employee upon receiving a payment from the employer equal to the amount of the approved claim expense plus the administrator's processing fee.

Key Takeaways from This Chapter

- The capital gains strip is one of those tax planning strategies that are under the scrutiny of government policymakers and the CRA, making it a volatile proposition. It involves moving money out of the corporation to estate

(continued)

(continued)

   distributions and is recommended only for those who have very high levels of capital and income needs.

- An individual pension plan (IPP) and its variant personal pension plan (PPP) attempt to mimic a pension plan to distribute guaranteed income based on a model of either defined benefits (DB) or defined contributions (DC) or a mix of the two. Funds invested in these plans enjoy tax deferral and tax deduction, in excess of any RRSP, through the use of annuities. You can build your own pension in a variety of ways, including past years' service, topping up, survivor benefits, and a host of other considerations.

- Retirement compensation arrangements (RCAs) are designed to equalize the tax treatment of income over a period of time for highly paid professionals who intend to operate in different tax jurisdictions. These are complex arrangements that allow considerable tax-deductible contributions to a pension-like arrangement, along with creditor protection, splitting options, and frankly a host of advantages.

- Watches, works of art, or valuable luxury items can be stores of value, but face some considerable hurdles to qualify as worthwhile investments. There can be no personal use, which immediately brings to bear the question of the intent in possessing such high-value items—which could well be depreciating assets.

- Selling and donating art is an interesting proposition. Some previous strategies have exposed clients to practices that were deemed improper by the CRA. Currently, new tax certification and valuation processes have made transactions more transparent, and may be worth examining as a tax-deduction strategy.

- Private health services plans (PHSPs) can provide tax benefits on premiums, which can be set with a great deal of latitude. Health spending accounts are quite close in nature, also providing for payments as tax-free benefits.

Questions to Ask Your Financial Planner

As we've said, most of the strategies in this chapter are alternatives to the mainstream strategies described in other chapters. As a result, the first question you should ask is not to your advisor, but to yourself: Are you sure you've taken advantage of or at least considered (and not ruled out) the strategies described in the other chapters?

If yes, you may want to ask your advisor about the strategies outlined in this book:

1. Are any of the deferred-compensation strategies described in this chapter—principally IPPs and RCAs—right for me? If not, why not? Do you foresee my situation changing so that I could benefit from any of these strategies? How can I read and understand the sales pitches I might encounter for RCAs, IPPs, and PPPs?
2. Have you evaluated the value of pursuing the other strategies described in this chapter in my situation? Specifically, is a capital gains strip, luxury-good investments, or a private health services plan and/or health spending account right for me?

Chapter 10

Pulling It All Together: Your Financial Plan

F or most Canadians, the idea of a financial planner is synonymous with having an investment portfolio. When considering using a financial planner to create a financial plan, questions are usually limited to: What's the rate of return you can provide, and what are your fees?

Now while it's true that generally speaking, the higher the rate of return, the better, and the lower the fee, the better, your conversations about your finances shouldn't start and end with your investment portfolio. Instead, your investment portfolio should really be viewed as a means to an end—*as a way to help you implement your overall financial plan*.

What You'll Get Out of This Chapter

This chapter brings all the chapters that precede it into focus, just like your personalized financial plan should

(continued)

(*continued*)

bring all of the elements of your personal situation—your resources, goals, plans, and strategies—into focus.

In this chapter, we review the specific questions that you should have in mind when approaching your own financial planning needs and your personalized financial plan. We also show you a sample financial plan prepared for a representative client, including the strategies we recommend to optimize their financial position over time.

By the end of this chapter, you should have a good idea of what a financial plan is and why you'd want one—as well as the limitations of a written financial plan (a plan is only as good as its implementation and execution!).

When Canadians think of a financial plan, the first question they have is almost always: How much do I need to retire?

To answer this question, there are a few considerations:

1. *How many years will the money last* if you are earning, let's say, 6% annually on your portfolio?
2. *How much money do you need* for a 30-year retirement?

So, in a vacuum, here's your answer to the two basic retirement questions.

How long will your money last?

Assuming a 3% real rate of return (or 6% minus a 3% increase in the cost of living), Table 10.1 will give you a rough idea.

- A portfolio of $4,000,000 with a 6% return would pay out $200,000 per year in cash flow and will last a little over 30 years.
- Not coincidentally, a $3,000,000 portfolio at 6% return would pay out $150,000 per year in cash flow and will last a little over 30 years.

Table 10.1   How Many Years Will the Money Last?

At Real Annual Spending Rate	Portfolio				
	$1,000,000	$2,000,000	$3,000,000	$4,000,000	$5,000,000
$100,000	11.9	30.5	76.8	–	–
$150,000	7.4	17	30.5	53.6	–
$200,000	5.4	11.9	19.9	30.5	46.2
$250,000	4.3	9.1	14.9	21.8	30.5
$300,000	3.5	7.4	11.9	17.0	23.1
$350,000	3.0	6.3	9.9	14.0	18.7
$400,000	2.6	5.4	8.5	11.9	15.7

- As you may be able to intuit, there's a simple rule about how long a portfolio will last. This simple rule is that with a return that's 3% above inflation, you can withdraw 5% of your total portfolio value to last 30 years.

How much money do you need for a 30-year retirement?

Real spending factors in inflation by increasing the withdrawals by 3% each year, as shown in Table 10.2.

Table 10.2   How Much Do I Need for a 30-Year Retirement?

Rate of Return	Real Spending				
	$100,000	$150,000	$200,000	$250,000	$300,000
4%	$2,591,818	$3,887,727	$5,183,636	$6,479,545	$7,775,454
5%	$2,255,812	$3,383,718	$4,511,624	$5,639,530	$6,767,436
6%	$1,978,101	$2,967,152	$3,956,202	$4,945,253	$5,934,303
7%	$1,747,014	$2,620,521	$3,494,028	$4,367,535	$5,241,042

While these two equations are interesting to note, I would not recommend using them as the backbone of your plans. I would only use them as a very rough idea.

Why are these only rough guidelines to your financial plans for retirement?

- Your investment risk tolerance may not be static throughout the years.
- You need to examine *sequence of returns risk*, as returns are not the same every year (that is, even if you get the same long-term

rate of return, the order or sequence in which you obtain the returns will impact how long your funds will last once you start making withdrawals).

- It is prudent to factor in all the tax implications on all accounts from taxes on withdrawals as a characteristic of returns.
- Additionally, tax laws, tax rates, and government benefits constantly change.

Finally, the problem with the question of how much money you need for a 30-year retirement is that you really shouldn't be picking your life horizon in advance!

While mortality tables will tell you that there is a 50% chance a 65-year-old lives to 85 and an 11.5% chance a 65-year-old lives to 95, *life is random and I wouldn't build a plan this way.*

When working with a financial planner, your written financial plan—and when I say "financial plan," I don't mean an Excel spreadsheet—should capture all that we have discussed in this book and more.

I personally think these are the top questions you should be researching, contemplating, and finding answers to as you think about your finances, your financial plan, and the value proposition of your financial advisor/planner:

- What occurred in the latest federal and provincial budgets that may affect my situation?
- What are your views on future potential upcoming changes?
- Is my dividend and salary mix appropriate given my situation?
- Are my insurance needs covered—both wealth insurance and risk insurance?
- Are my wealth needs covered?
- Is my investment portfolio tax-efficient?
- What is my risk tolerance this year? What was my risk tolerance last year?
- What has been my historical rate of return? What is my projected rate of return?
- What are my fees? How do they compare to the industry and are there other options?
- Are there upcoming thresholds to lower fees or any consolidation of account benefits?

- Is a fee-for-service model more appropriate for my needs?
- Are my fees tax-efficient?
- What is my strategic asset allocation? Does my portfolio need to be rebalanced?
- What is my asset location and is it appropriate?
- What are my RRSP, TFSA, non-registered, and corporate portfolios forecast to be worth at my retirement at the current savings rate? What about projected estate value?
- What is my debt situation and are there any opportunities to turn bad debt into good debt?
- Is there an opportunity to use debt to my advantage, given my ability and willingness to do so?
- Am I making full use of all the trust structures available?
- Is there open communication between my financial planner(s), accountant(s), and lawyer(s)?
- Is my estate plan efficient from a protection standpoint?
- Is my estate plan efficient from a tax standpoint?
- Do I need to update my primary and secondary will?

The Value of a Financial Plan

Although it is an asset to have a written financial plan, getting it in writing should not be the focus nor should it be the conclusion of your planning activities. Instead, the value of your plan is all about its implementation and execution: what gets measured, gets done. With that said, it is important to have a physical plan that you can keep and come back to that is updated at least once a year.

Most financial planners should have access to appropriate planning software that prepares and presents a written financial plan. There are two major benefits to this process:

1. To demonstrate if you are on track with your financial goals, retirement, and estate plans. From there, scenario and sensitivity analyses can be completed, such as the financial impacts of retiring earlier rather than later; different cash flow needs, such as spending more on travel the first 10 years in retirement; different rate of return scenarios; the impact on financials given a death, disability, or illness; and more.

2. To compare current strategies to alternative strategies and what impact they have on your financial plans. (Examples of these would include the many strategies discussed in this book.)

Let's dig into the details of the value of a plan by looking at a sample.

Example

Meet Dr. Michael Jones, 45, and Mrs. Kathryn Jones, 43.

Michael is an incorporated professional drawing a salary of $200,000 per year and paying Kathryn a salary of $50,000 per year.

- They are currently maximizing their RRSPs, RESPs, saving $200,000 per year in their corporation, and not investing in their TFSAs.
- They currently have approximately $2,000,000 saved amongst the different accounts.
- They spend $72,000 per year not including taxes, investment purchases, and debt payments on their $900,000 debt obligations.
- They would both like to retire in 19 years and would like a retirement after-tax cash flow of $180,000 per year indexed with inflation.
- They have two children—Mark, 10, and Chloe, 8—with educational funding needs.
- They have several insurance plans owned personally.
- Their current risk tolerance is moderate aggressive and their financial knowledge is quite high.

Their financial goals are:

1. To have enough funds for that retirement cash flow need.
2. To leave a legacy to their children, and eventually grandchildren, in a tax-efficient and protected manner.

The following pages illustrate a sample current plan and a recommended plan with implementations of strategies.

This is an example of a high-net worth draft financial plan for illustrative purposes. However, many strategies may be applicable to the average professional. Additional sample plans can be provided by contacting us.

Plan Analysis Synopsis

Client Information

	Michael Jones	**Kathryn Jones**
Birth Date	1974/03/04	1976/05/07
Gender	Male	Female
Address	Toronto, Ontario Canada	Toronto, Ontario Canada
Citizenship	Canada	Canada

Family Member Information

Name	Birth Date	Age as of Plan Date	Gender	Relation-ship	Dependant of
Mark Jones	2009/06/06	10	Male	Son	Both
Chloe Jones	2011/07/09	8	Female	Daughter	Both

Advisor Information

Name	Advisor Type	Business Phone	Cell Phone
Andrew Feindel/Kyle Richie	Advisor	(416) 607-5077	

Plan Assumptions

Individual Assumptions	**Michael Jones**	**Kathryn Jones**
Retirement Date	2039/01/01	2039/01/01
Life Expectancy	100	100
Shared Assumptions		
Marital Status	Married	
Income Tax Method	Detailed Tax	
Inflation Rate	2.00%	
Elect to Split Pension Income	Yes	

Estate Assumptions

Detail	Michael	Kathryn
Is there a will?	No	No
Last revised?	n/a	n/a
Where are the wills kept?	n/a	n/a

Income Information

Regular Income Source	Member	Applicable	Current Amount	Indexed By
Corporation Salary	Michael	2020/01/01 to 2038/12/31	$16,667/mo	2.00%
Corporation Salary	Kathryn	2020/01/01 to 2038/12/31	$4,167/mo	2.00%

CPP/QPP & OAS Information

Description	Michael Jones	Kathryn Jones
CPP/QPP Benefits Start On	2039/02/01	2039/02/01
OAS Benefits Start On	2039/04/01	2041/06/01
OAS Deferred Benefit Bonus	0.0%	0.0%
Qualify for % of Max CPP/QPP Benefits	100%	100%
Qualify for % of OAS Benefits	100%	100%

Expense Information

Regular Expenses

Expense Description	Member	Period Applicable	Current Amount	Frequency	Indexed By	Fixed?
Housing (e.g. utilities, repairs)	Joint	2020/01/01 to 2038/12/31	$1,300	Monthly	2.00%	Yes
Food	Joint	2020/01/01 to 2038/12/31	$700	Monthly	2.00%	Yes
Transportation (e.g. gas, insurance)	Joint	2020/01/01 to 2038/12/31	$1,000	Monthly	2.00%	Yes
Entertainment (e.g. restaurants, movies)	Joint	2020/01/01 to 2038/12/31	$1,200	Monthly	2.00%	Yes
Personal (e.g. clothing, hobbies)	Joint	2020/01/01 to 2038/12/31	$500	Monthly	2.00%	Yes
Other (e.g. child care, travel)	Joint	2020/01/01 to 2038/12/31	$1,200	Monthly	2.00%	Yes
Retirement Expense	Joint	2039/01/01 to 2076/12/31	$15,000	Monthly	2.00%	Yes
Mark University Education	Mark	2027/01/01 to 2030/12/31	$20,000	Annual	4.00%	No
Chloe University Education	Chloe	2029/01/01 to 2032/12/31	$20,000	Annual	4.00%	No

Lump-Sum Expenses

Expense Description	Member	Date to Be Incurred	Amount in Current $	Amount to Be Incurred
Final Expenses	Michael	2074/12/31	$25,000	$25,000
Final Expenses	Kathryn	2076/12/31	$25,000	$25,000

Insurance Scenario Lump-Sum Expenses

Expense Description	Applicable To	Member	Date to Be Incurred	Amount in Current $	Amount to Be Incurred
Critical Illness Expense	Critical Illness	Michael	2021/01/01	$100,000	$100,000
Critical Illness Expense	Critical Illness	Kathryn	2021/01/01	$100,000	$100,000

Lifestyle Asset Information

Asset	Asset Type	Owner	Purchase Date	Purchase Amount	Market Value	Value as of	Current Pre-Tax Growth
Cottage	Cottage	Joint	2013/08/01	$350,000	$500,000	2020/01/01	2.00%
Home	Principal Residence	Joint	2006/06/01	$750,000	$2,000,000	2020/01/01	2.00%

Portfolio Assets

Market Value Date	Market Value	Cost Base	Int.	Div.	Cap. Gains	Def. Growth	Total Return	Std. Dev.	Annual Account Fee	Reinvest Income?
Account Name: Bank Savings Account (Joint/Non-Registered)									**Goal: Retirement**	
2020/01/01	$0	$0	0.00%	0.00%	0.00%	0.00%	0.00%	0.00%	0.00%	Yes
Account Name: Bank—NR Stock Account—Joint (Non-Registered)									**Goal: Retirement**	
2020/01/01	$400,000	$390,000	2.00%	2.00%	2.00%	0.00%	6.00%	10.76%	0.00%	Yes
Account Name: Bank—RSP—Michael (RRSP)									**Goal: Retirement**	
2020/01/01	$400,000	$0	1.67%	0.89%	1.51%	1.93%	6.00%	10.76%	0.00%	Yes
Account Name: Bank RSP—Kathryn (RRSP)									**Goal: Retirement**	
2020/01/01	$150,000	$0	1.67%	0.89%	1.51%	1.93%	6.00%	10.76%	0.00%	Yes
Account Name: Bank—Mark RESP (Michael)									**Goal: Mark University Education**	
2020/01/01	$40,000	$33,000	0.00%	0.00%	0.00%	6.00%	6.00%	10.76%	0.00%	Yes
Account Name: Bank—Chloe RESP (Michael)									**Goal: Chloe University Education**	
2020/01/01	$32,000	$25,000	0.00%	0.00%	0.00%	6.00%	6.00%	10.76%	0.00%	Yes
Account Name: New RSP—Michael (RRSP)									**Goal: Retirement**	
2020/01/01	$0	$0	1.67%	0.89%	1.51%	1.93%	6.00%	10.76%	0.00%	Yes
Account Name: New RSP—Kathryn (RRSP)									**Goal: Retirement**	
2020/01/01	$0	$0	1.67%	0.89%	1.51%	1.93%	6.00%	10.76%	0.00%	Yes

Market Value Date	Market Value	Cost Base	Int.	Div.	Cap. Gains	Def. Growth	Total Return	Std. Dev.	Annual Account Fee	Reinvest Income?
Account Name: New TFSA—Michael									**Goal: Retirement**	
2020/01/01	$0	$0	1.67%	0.89%	1.51%	1.93%	6.00%	10.76%	0.00%	Yes
Account Name: New TFSA—Kathryn									**Goal: Retirement**	
2020/01/01	$0	$0	1.67%	0.89%	1.51%	1.93%	6.00%	10.76%	0.00%	Yes
Account Name: New NonReg CC—Joint (Non-Registered)									**Goal: Retirement**	
2020/01/01	$0	$0	0.75%	0.75%	0.75%	4.75%	7.00%	10.76%	1.00%	Yes
Account Name: New Mark Trust—CC Leverage (Non-Registered)									**Goal: Unallocated**	
2020/01/01	$0	$0	0.75%	0.75%	0.75%	4.75%	7.00%	10.76%	1.00%	Yes
Account Name: New Chloe Trust—CC Leverage (Non-Registered)									**Goal: Unallocated**	
2020/01/01	$0	$0	0.75%	0.75%	0.75%	4.75%	7.00%	10.76%	1.00%	Yes
Account Name: Insurance Proceeds (Joint/Non-Registered)									**Goal: Retirement**	
2020/03/19	$0	$0	0.00%	0.00%	0.00%	0.00%	0.00%	0.00%	0.00%	Yes

Note: The Portfolio Assets table includes a breakdown of the return rates by return type for your investment accounts. Interest returns are taxed as ordinary income at the marginal tax rate. Dividends receive preferential tax treatment, while one-half the capital gains are taxed at the marginal tax rate. Income from the deferred growth component is not subject to tax until the asset is sold and is usually taxed as a capital gain. The actual total return rates that you will receive will depend on many factors, including inflation, type of investment, market conditions, and investment performance.

Liabilities

Liability Description	Original Principal	Current Principal	Interest Rate	Payment	Payment Type	End Date	Linked Asset
Home Mortgage	$500,000	$410,159	3.00%	$2,366.00	Principal and Interest	2038/12/31	Home
Cottage Mortgage	$400,000	$307,125	3.00%	$1,770.00	Principal and Interest	2038/12/31	Cottage

Life Insurance Policies

Description	Insured	Payer	Beneficiary	Benefit Amount	Premium Amount	Cash Surrender Value
Policy Type: Life						
Kathyrn 1M Life Insurance	Kathryn	Kathryn	Michael	$1,000,000	$3,250/yr	$0*
Michael 1M Life Insurance	Michael	Michael	Kathryn	$1,000,000	$4,500/yr	$0*

* CSV payable with death benefit

Disability Insurance Policies

Description	Insured	Payer	Effective Date	Benefit Amount	Premium Amount	Waiting Period
Policy Type: Individual Disability						
Michael 5,000/m OMA Individual Disability	Michael	Michael	2010/01/01	$5,000/mo	$1,350/yr	3 months
Kathryn 2,500/m OMA Individual Disability	Kathryn	Kathryn	2010/01/01	$2,500/mo	$750/yr	3 months

Critical Illness Insurance Policies

Description	Insured	Payer	Effective Date	Benefit Amount	Premium Amount	Premium Refund
Policy Type: Cash to Insured Coverage						
100K Michael OMA CI Insurance	Michael	Michael	2010/02/01	$100,000	$200/mo	0.00%
100K Kathryn OMA CI Insurance	Kathryn	Kathryn	2020/02/01	$100,000	$150/mo	0.00%

Education Goals

Mark University Education: Expenses

Member	Start Year	End Year	Annual Amount (at Present)	Total Projected Cost
Mark	2027	2030	$20,000	$111,761

Assets Allocated to Mark University Education

Account	Market Value Date	Value Allocated to This Goal	Growth Rate
Bank—Mark RESP	2020/01/01	$40,000	6.00%

Chloe University Education: Expenses

Member	Start Year	End Year	Annual Amount (at Present)	Total Projected Cost
Chloe	2029	2032	$20,000	$120,881

Assets Allocated to Chloe University Education

Account	Market Value Date	Value Allocated to This Goal	Growth Rate
Bank—Chloe RESP	2020/01/01	$32,000	6.00%

Savings Strategies

Account Saved To	Applicable	Amount	Indexed By
Bank—Mark RESP	2020/01/01 to 2026/12/01	$2,500 /yr	0.00%
Bank—Chloe RESP	2020/01/01 to 2028/12/01	$2,500 /yr	0.00%

Note: A percentage value in the Amount column indicates the portion of salary that is being saved. These income percentages use the salary's index rate.

Surplus Savings Strategies

Account Saved To	Applicable	% of Surplus
Bank Savings Account	2039/01/01 to 2076/12/31	100%

Note: You may still have surplus cash available for investment, after having established a regular savings program and/or maximized your RRSP contributions. Surplus savings strategies specify how unallocated surplus cash is to be invested each year. Unallocated surplus cash may change from year to year based on changes in your income and expenses.

The surplus savings strategies assume that you will invest surplus cash and not spend it on current needs or desires. Be sure to review your plan annually with your financial advisor to determine if these investments are occurring according to plan. If not, your plan should be revised and new projections should be prepared to reflect a realistic savings strategy.

RRSP Maximizer Savings Strategies

Asset Name	Applicable	Constrained by Cash Flow	Time of Year
Bank RSP—Michael (RRSP)	2020/01/01 to 2038/12/31	No	January
Bank RSP—Kathryn (RRSP)	2020/01/01 to 2038/12/31	No	January

Note: The maximum allowable RRSP contribution for a particular taxpayer in a particular year depends on factors such as earned income for the prior year, pension adjustments, and any RRSP carry-forward room that the taxpayer has available. Even with the regular RRSP contributions under your regular savings strategy, there is room for additional contributions. We recommend that you maximize the tax-deferral opportunities available to you by making an additional lump sum RRSP contribution, in order to use your available contribution room.

The RRSP maximizer strategies listed above will project the maximum contributions you can make on an annual basis, based on the assumptions in this plan. If the constrained by cash flow option is YES, then the recommended contributions will take into consideration whether your available cash flow in each year is sufficient to fund the maximum contributions you are allowed to make.

Transfer Strategies

Source Asset	Destination Asset	Amount	When
Michael 1M Life Insurance	New NonReg CC—Joint	100.00%	2074/12/31
Michael 1M Life Insurance	New NonReg CC—Joint	100.00%	2074/12/31
Kathyrn 1M Life Insurance	New NonReg CC—Joint	100.00%	2076/12/31
Kathyrn 1M Life Insurance	New NonReg CC—Joint	100.00%	2076/12/31

Note: Transfers specify a plan for moving your investments from one type of asset to another on specific dates or events such as retirement. Also, transfers will be desirable in some cases to move from one type of investment to another type at a certain point in time.

Deficit Coverage Order During Pre-Retirement

Account	Account Type	Owner
Bank—NR Stock Account—Joint	Non-Registered	Joint
Bank Savings Account	Non-Registered	Joint
Insurance Proceeds	Non-Registered	Joint
New NonReg CC—Joint	Non-Registered	Joint

Note: The assets listed above are available and will be redeemed in the order they appear to meet cash flow needs during the pre-retirement period.

Liquidation Order During Retirement

Account	Account Type	Owner
Bank—NR Stock Account—Joint	Non-Registered	Joint
Bank Savings Account	Non-Registered	Joint
Insurance Proceeds	Non-Registered	Joint
New NonReg CC—Joint	Non-Registered	Joint
New TFSA—Kathryn	TFSA	Kathryn
New TFSA—Michael	TFSA	Michael
New RSP—Kathryn	RRSP	Kathryn
New RSP—Michael	RRSP	Michael
Bank RSP—Kathryn	RRSP	Kathryn
Bank—RSP—Michael	RRSP	Michael

Note: The assets listed above are available and will be redeemed in the order they appear to meet cash flow needs during the retirement period.

Private Corporation Synopsis

Dr. Michael Jones Corp.—Current Plan

The following report presents a summary of the data entered for this private corporation. In addition to this background information, the ownership percentage and valuation information is presented in both a table and chart format to reflect how income is divided among the various shareholders of the private corporation.

Summary

Dr. Michael Jones Corp.	Current Plan
Province of Incorporation	Ontario
Province of Taxation	Ontario
Corporate Year-End	Dec. 31
Total Common Shares Outstanding	100
Value of All Common Shares	$999,901
Total Preferred Shares Outstanding	100
Value of All Preferred Shares	$100
Private Corporation Total Market Value	$1,000,001

Share Ownership

Common Shares	Ownership %*	Ownership $*
Michael	100%	$999,901
Kathryn	0%	$0
Other	0.0%	$0

*Ownership % and $ as of Jan. 1, 2020

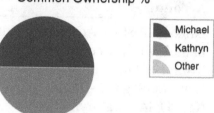

Common Ownership %

- Michael
- Kathryn
- Other

Preferred Ownership

Preferred Shares	Ownership %*	Ownership $*
Michael	0.0%	$0
Kathryn	100.0%	$100
Other	0.0%	$0

*Ownership % and $ as of Jan. 1, 2020
†includes all Preferred Share classes

Preferred Ownership %

- Michael
- Kathryn
- Other

Historical Data

Business Limit Detail	Amount
Adjusted Aggregate Investment Income for 2019	$38,212

Notional Account Detail	Amount
NRDTOH End-of-Year Value for 2019	$0
ERDTOH End-of-Year Value for 2019	$0
GRIP End-of-Year Value for 2019	$24,132
CDA End-of-Year Value for 2019	$64,981
NRDTOH Dividend Refund for 2019	$0
ERDTOH Dividend Refund for 2019	$0
Capital Loss Carryover End-of-Year Value for 2019	$0

Asset Name	Michael	Kathryn	Other
Outstanding Shareholder Loans	$0	$0	$0

Investment Accounts

Asset Name	Valuation Date	Market Value	Cost Base	Int.	Div.	Cap. Gains	Def. Growth	Total	Annual Account Fee
NonReg Stock Account	2020/01/01	$1,000,000	$900,000	2.00%	2.00%	2.00%	0.00%	6.00%	0.00%

Real Estate Assets

Asset Name	Purchase Date	Purchase Amount	Market Value Date	Market Value	Growth Rate	Active Business	Net Rental Income
Property and Equipment	2019/12/31	$1	2020/01/01	$1	2.00%	No	$0

Contributions—Inter-Company Dividends Received

Received From	Type	Amount	GRIP	Frequency	Start Date	End Date	Infl Rate
Cash Savings	Non-taxable	$80,000	$0	Annual	2020/12/01	2039/01/01	0.00%
Investment Savings	Non-taxable	$10,000	$0	Monthly	2020/01/01	2039/01/01	0.00%

Withdrawals—Manual Dividend Distributions

Share Type	Dividend Type	Amount	Frequency	Start Date	End Date	Infl Rate	Direct After-Tax Proceeds To Michael	Kathryn
Michael and Kathryn	Non-Taxable	$120,000	Annual	2039/01/01	2076/12/31	2.00%	Cash Flow	Cash Flow

Estate

Detail	
Share options at first death	Transfer to survivor
Share options at second death and death in the same year	Sold to other shareholder
Enable the 50% solution	No
Estate freeze (information only)	No

Financial Snapshot

Current Plan—Michael and Kathryn Jones

Goal Coverage

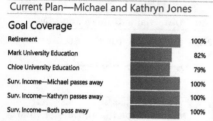

Retirement	100%
Mark University Education	82%
Chloe University Education	79%
Surv. Income—Michael passes away	100%
Surv. Income—Kathryn passes away	100%
Surv. Income—Both pass away	100%

Asset Allocation

Rate of Return		6.00%
Standard Deviation		10.76%

Asset Class	($)	(%)
U.S. Equity	$545,940	27.00%
Canadian Large-Cap Equity	$525,720	26.00%
International Equity	$465,060	23.00%
Emerging Markets Equity	$181,980	9.00%
Canadian Bonds	$161,760	8.00%
Canadian Small-Cap Equity	$101,100	5.00%
Global Bonds	$40,440	2.00%
Total	**$2,022,000**	

© 2019 Morningstar Investment Management LLC. All rights reserved.
Morningstar is a registered investment advisor that develops proprietary asset
allocation tools used for educational purposes only. Morningstar has granted
Advicent Solutions, LP a license to use these asset allocation tools.
Morningstar is not affiliated with Advicent Solutions.

Insurance Coverage

Michael	Benefit Amount
Universal Life	$1,000,000
Individual Disability	$5,000 / month
Cash to Insured Coverage	$100,000
Kathryn	**Benefit Amount**
Universal Life	$1,000,000
Individual Disability	$2,500/month
Cash to Insured Coverage	$100,000

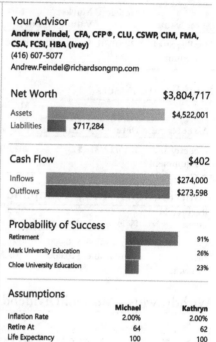

Your Advisor

Andrew Feindel, CFA, CFP®, CLU, CSWP, CIM, FMA, CSA, FCSI, HBA (Ivey)
(416) 607-5077
Andrew.Feindel@richardsongmp.com

Net Worth $3,804,717

Assets	$4,522,001
Liabilities	$717,284

Cash Flow $402

Inflows	$274,000
Outflows	$273,598

Probability of Success

Retirement	91%
Mark University Education	26%
Chloe University Education	23%

Assumptions

	Michael	Kathryn
Inflation Rate	2.00%	2.00%
Retire At	64	62
Life Expectancy	100	100

Net Worth Statement

Current Plan

This report displays a comprehensive list of your assets and liabilities as of **January 1, 2020**. Use this report to better understand your net worth situation.

Note: Term life insurance policies and existing annuities do not appear on this report as they have no cash value.

Assets	Michael	Kathryn	Joint	Total
Non-Registered Investments				
Bank—NR Stock Account—Joint			$400,000	$400,000
Total	$0	$0	**$400,000**	**$400,000**
Registered Investments				
Bank—RSP—Michael	$400,000			$400,000
Bank—Mark RESP	$40,000			$40,000
Bank—Chloe RESP	$32,000			$32,000
Bank RSP—Kathryn		$150,000		$150,000
Total	**$472,000**	**$150,000**	**$0**	**$622,000**
Lifestyle Assets				
Home			$2,000,000	$2,000,000
Cottage			$500,000	$500,000
Total	**$0**	**$0**	**$2,500,000**	**$2,500,000**
Private Corporations				
Dr. Michael Jones Corp.	$500,001			$500,001
Dr. Michael Jones Corp.		$500,001		$500,001
Total	**$500,001**	**$500,001**	**$0**	**$1,000,001**

Liabilities	Michael	Kathryn	Joint	Total
Home Mortgage			$410,159	$410,159
Cottage Mortgage			$307,125	$307,125
Total	**$0**	**$0**	**$717,284**	**$717,284**
Total Net Worth	**$972,001**	**$650,001**	**$2,182,716**	**$3,804,717**

Net Worth Timeline

Current Plan

This report displays net worth data over time according to asset category. The projections show end-of-year values beginning in the year of the analysis until the last surviving client's year of death. Use this report to show how each asset category contributes to total net worth throughout the plan.

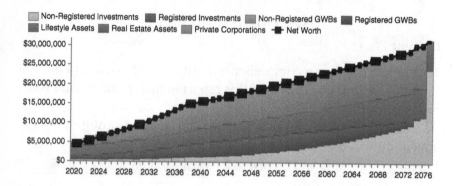

Net Worth Outlook

Current Plan

This report shows changes in your net worth over time. These projected end-of-year values begin with the analysis year and end with the death of the last surviving client. Furthermore, assets included in this report are categorized to show how changes in net worth occur. Use this report to assess your total net worth by asset category through the duration of the analysis.

Year and Age	Non-Registered Investments	Registered Investments	Lifestyle Assets	Private Corporations	Total Liabilities	Total Net Worth
2020 (46/44)	$424,000	$704,109	$2,550,000	$1,239,708	$688,648	**$4,229,168**
2021 (47/45)	$449,440	$791,696	$2,601,000	$1,485,369	$659,147	**$4,668,359**
2022 (48/46)	$476,406	$885,319	$2,653,020	$1,737,207	$628,753	**$5,123,198**
2023 (49/47)	$504,991	$985,354	$2,706,080	$1,995,451	$597,442	**$5,594,434**
2024 (50/48)	$535,290	$1,091,778	$2,760,202	$2,260,341	$565,183	**$6,082,427**
2025 (51/49)	$567,408	$1,205,309	$2,815,406	$2,532,124	$531,950	**$6,588,296**
2026 (52/50)	$601,452	$1,326,072	$2,871,714	$2,811,057	$497,713	**$7,112,583**
2027 (53/51)	$637,539	$1,424,288	$2,929,148	$3,097,407	$462,440	**$7,625,943**
2028 (54/52)	$675,792	$1,528,158	$2,987,731	$3,391,451	$426,101	**$8,157,031**
2029 (55/53)	$716,339	$1,605,172	$3,047,486	$3,693,475	$388,665	**$8,673,807**
2030 (56/54)	$759,319	$1,706,657	$3,108,436	$4,003,777	$350,096	**$9,228,094**
2031 (57/55)	$804,879	$1,823,938	$3,170,604	$4,322,665	$310,362	**$9,811,725**
2032 (58/56)	$853,171	$1,975,014	$3,234,017	$4,650,460	$269,427	**$10,443,235**
2033 (59/57)	$904,362	$2,142,952	$3,298,697	$4,987,493	$227,254	**$11,106,250**
2034 (60/58)	$958,623	$2,321,956	$3,364,671	$5,334,110	$183,807	**$11,795,552**
2035 (61/59)	$1,016,141	$2,512,708	$3,431,964	$5,690,666	$139,047	**$12,512,432**
2036 (62/60)	$1,077,109	$2,715,933	$3,500,604	$6,057,534	$92,934	**$13,258,247**

Year and Age	Non-Registered Investments	Registered Investments	Lifestyle Assets	Private Corporations	Total Liabilities	Total Net Worth
2037 (63/61)	$1,141,736	$2,932,402	$3,570,616	$6,435,097	$45,427	$14,034,424
2038 (64/62)	$1,210,240	$3,162,929	$3,642,028	$6,823,755	$0	$14,838,951
2039 (* 65/63 *)	$1,282,854	$3,273,573	$3,714,868	$6,846,679	$0	$15,117,975
2040 (66/64)	$1,359,825	$3,395,502	$3,789,166	$6,873,479	$0	$15,417,972
2041 (67/65)	$1,441,415	$3,531,200	$3,864,949	$6,904,361	$0	$15,741,925
2042 (68/66)	$1,527,900	$3,675,980	$3,942,248	$6,944,369	$0	$16,090,498
2043 (69/67)	$1,619,574	$3,760,311	$4,021,093	$7,034,090	$0	$16,435,068
2044 (70/68)	$1,716,748	$3,845,967	$4,101,515	$7,131,013	$0	$16,795,243
2045 (71/69)	$1,819,753	$3,933,055	$4,183,545	$7,235,295	$0	$17,171,649
2046 (72/70)	$1,929,263	$4,016,148	$4,267,216	$7,347,266	$0	$17,559,893
2047 (73/71)	$2,048,489	$4,094,840	$4,352,561	$7,459,241	$0	$17,955,131
2048 (74/72)	$2,202,495	$4,117,363	$4,439,612	$7,572,134	$0	$18,331,604
2049 (75/73)	$2,363,835	$4,134,910	$4,528,404	$7,686,118	$0	$18,713,268
2050 (76/74)	$2,532,881	$4,146,984	$4,618,972	$7,801,176	$0	$19,100,013
2051 (77/75)	$2,709,998	$4,153,101	$4,711,351	$7,917,286	$0	$19,491,737
2052 (78/76)	$2,895,547	$4,152,796	$4,805,579	$8,034,428	$0	$19,888,349
2053 (79/77)	$3,089,877	$4,145,632	$4,901,690	$8,152,578	$0	$20,289,777
2054 (80/78)	$3,293,758	$4,130,351	$4,999,724	$8,271,709	$0	$20,695,543
2055 (81/79)	$3,507,277	$4,107,026	$5,099,718	$8,391,795	$0	$21,105,817
2056 (82/80)	$3,731,156	$4,074,507	$5,201,713	$8,512,804	$0	$21,520,180
2057 (83/81)	$3,965,854	$4,032,151	$5,305,747	$8,634,705	$0	$21,938,457
2058 (84/82)	$4,211,785	$3,979,415	$5,411,862	$8,757,464	$0	$22,360,525
2059 (85/83)	$4,469,730	$3,915,045	$5,520,099	$8,881,043	$0	$22,785,917
2060 (86/84)	$4,740,163	$3,838,382	$5,630,501	$9,005,404	$0	$23,214,450
2061 (87/85)	$5,023,673	$3,748,560	$5,743,111	$9,130,503	$0	$23,645,848
2062 (88/86)	$5,321,110	$3,644,203	$5,857,973	$9,256,297	$0	$24,079,584
2063 (89/87)	$5,632,934	$3,524,696	$5,975,133	$9,382,738	$0	$24,515,501
2064 (90/88)	$5,959,970	$3,388,734	$6,094,636	$9,509,775	$0	$24,953,115
2065 (91/89)	$6,303,083	$3,234,931	$6,216,528	$9,637,353	$0	$25,391,895
2066 (92/90)	$6,663,053	$3,062,064	$6,340,859	$9,765,417	$0	$25,831,393
2067 (93/91)	$7,040,435	$2,869,041	$6,467,676	$9,893,905	$0	$26,271,057
2068 (94/92)	$7,435,673	$2,654,426	$6,597,029	$10,022,754	$0	$26,709,882
2069 (95/93)	$7,852,733	$2,409,732	$6,728,970	$10,151,895	$0	$27,143,330
2070 (96/94)	$8,294,817	$2,127,866	$6,863,549	$10,281,258	$0	$27,567,490
2071 (97/95)	$8,763,426	$1,805,373	$7,000,820	$10,410,766	$0	$27,980,384
2072 (98/96)	$9,260,151	$1,439,859	$7,140,837	$10,540,339	$0	$28,381,186
2073 (99/97)	$9,786,680	$1,028,364	$7,283,654	$10,669,895	$0	$28,768,592
2074 (100/98)	$11,344,800	$515,557	$7,429,327	$10,799,343	$0	$30,089,026
2075 (–/99)	$11,864,042	$0	$7,577,913	$10,928,590	$0	$30,370,546
2076 (–/100)	$24,021,024	$0	$7,729,471	$0	$0	$31,750,495

* = year of retirement

Cash Flow Outlook

Current Plan

This report projects itemized cash flow information over the duration of the selected years. Cash inflows and outflows are categorized by source and summarized as aggregate totals. This provides an overview of your cash flow projections.

	Year				
Age	**2020** 46/44	**2021** 47/45	**2022** 48/46	**2023** 49/47	**2024** 50/48
Cash Inflows					
Earned Income					
Corporation Salary (Michael)	$200,000	$204,000	$208,080	$212,242	$216,486
Corporation Salary (Kathryn)	$50,000	$51,000	$52,020	$53,060	$54,122
Total	$250,000	$255,000	$260,100	$265,302	$270,608
Investment Income					
Bank—NR Stock Account—Joint	$24,000	$25,440	$26,966	$28,584	$30,299
Total	$24,000	$25,440	$26,966	$28,584	$30,299
Total Cash Inflows	**$274,000**	**$280,440**	**$287,066**	**$293,886**	**$300,907**
Cash Outflows					
Lifestyle Expenses					
Housing (e.g. utilities, repairs) (Joint)	$15,600	$15,912	$16,230	$16,555	$16,886
Food (Joint)	$8,400	$8,568	$8,739	$8,914	$9,092
Transportation (e.g. gas, insurance) (Joint)	$12,000	$12,240	$12,485	$12,734	$12,989
Entertainment (e.g. restaurants, movies) (Joint)	$14,400	$14,688	$14,982	$15,281	$15,587
Personal (e.g. clothing, hobbies) (Joint)	$6,000	$6,120	$6,242	$6,367	$6,495
Other (e.g. child care, travel) (Joint)	$14,400	$14,688	$14,982	$15,281	$15,587
Home Mortgage (Joint)	$28,392	$28,392	$28,392	$28,392	$28,392
Cottage Mortgage (Joint)	$21,240	$21,240	$21,240	$21,240	$21,240
Total	$120,432	$121,848	$123,292	$124,766	$126,268
Registered Contributions					
Bank—RSP—Michael	$27,230	$27,775	$28,330	$28,897	$29,475
Bank RSP—Kathryn	$8,824	$9,000	$9,180	$9,364	$9,551
Bank—Mark RESP (Michael)	$2,500	$2,500	$2,500	$2,500	$2,500
Bank—Chloe RESP (Michael)	$2,500	$2,500	$2,500	$2,500	$2,500
Total	$41,054	$41,775	$42,510	$43,260	$44,025
Non-Registered Savings					
Bank—NR Stock Account—Joint	$24,000	$25,440	$26,966	$28,584	$30,299
Total	$24,000	$25,440	$26,966	$28,584	$30,299

	Year				
	2020	**2021**	**2022**	**2023**	**2024**
Age	**46/44**	**47/45**	**48/46**	**49/47**	**50/48**
Cash Inflows					
Employment Expenses					
CPP/QPP Contributions— Employment	$5,339	$5,661	$6,047	$6,447	$6,762
EI Premiums	$1,687	$1,721	$1,756	$1,791	$1,827
Total	$7,027	$7,382	$7,803	$8,238	$8,589
Miscellaneous Expenses					
Michael 5,000/m Individual Disability	$1,350	$1,350	$1,350	$1,350	$1,350
Kathryn 2,500/m Individual Disability	$750	$750	$750	$750	$750
Michael 1M Life Insurance	$4,500	$4,500	$4,500	$4,500	$4,500
Kathyrn 1M Life Insurance (Kathryn)	$3,250	$3,250	$3,250	$3,250	$3,250
100K Michael CI Insurance (Michael)	$2,400	$2,400	$2,400	$2,400	$2,400
100K Kathryn CI Insurance (Kathryn)	$1,650	$1,800	$1,800	$1,800	$1,800
Total	$13,900	$14,050	$14,050	$14,050	$14,050
Taxes					
Federal Income Tax	$42,043	$42,923	$43,819	$44,741	$45,777
Provincial Income Tax	$25,142	$25,673	$26,211	$26,764	$27,490
Total	$67,186	$68,596	$70,030	$71,505	$73,267
Total Cash Outflows	**$273,598**	**$279,091**	**$284,652**	**$290,403**	**$296,499**
Surplus/(Deficit)	**$402**	**$1,349**	**$2,414**	**$3,483**	**$4,409**

Retirement Cash Flow Timeline

Current Plan

This report shows your annual inflows and outflows during the retirement period. Positive inflows are shown in bold whereas negative values are shown in gray and in parentheses. Other Incomes will include such things as Earned Salary, Pension, and Investment incomes. Withdrawals from Assets include Registered proceeds and Non-Registered proceeds. Growth and Reinvestments include growth, reinvestments, and annual contributions made to all assets. Age of retirement is marked with an asterisk.

Year	Age	Total Needs	CPP/ QPP/ OAS	Other Income	With- drawal from Assets	Taxes	Surplus/ (Shortfall)	Growth and Reinves- tments	EOY Assets
2039	*65/63*	$346,790	$50,614	$247,432	$79,132	$30,387	$0	$262,390	$11,403,106
2040	66/64	$356,392	$58,308	$255,285	$74,486	$31,687	$0	$273,386	$11,628,806
2041	67/65	$366,359	$65,984	$263,469	$68,032	$31,125	$0	$285,320	$11,876,976
2042	68/66	$376,711	$72,046	$272,002	$67,092	$34,429	$0	$298,357	$12,148,250
2043	69/67	$387,466	$73,487	$280,902	$136,229	$103,151	$0	$312,233	$12,413,975
2044	70/68	$398,643	$74,956	$290,187	$139,963	$106,463	$0	$322,793	$12,693,728
2045	71/69	$410,264	$76,456	$299,878	$143,669	$109,738	$0	$333,763	$12,988,104
2046	72/70	$422,675	$77,985	$309,995	$148,123	$113,428	$0	$340,725	$13,292,677
2047	73/71	$438,416	$79,545	$320,563	$157,216	$118,907	$0	$355,135	$13,602,570
2048	74/72	$479,340	$81,135	$331,603	$216,208	$149,606	$0	$392,737	$13,891,992
2049	75/73	$492,943	$82,758	$343,143	$222,338	$155,296	$0	$401,225	$14,184,864
2050	76/74	$507,041	$84,413	$355,207	$228,661	$161,240	$0	$409,780	$14,481,041
2051	77/75	$521,633	$86,101	$367,825	$235,134	$167,427	$0	$418,368	$14,780,385
2052	78/76	$536,716	$87,824	$381,026	$241,710	$173,845	$0	$426,954	$15,082,771
2053	79/77	$552,282	$89,580	$394,842	$248,337	$180,477	$0	$435,504	$15,388,087
2054	80/78	$568,753	$91,371	$409,306	$255,786	$187,710	$0	$444,386	$15,695,819
2055	81/79	$585,449	$93,199	$424,453	$262,690	$194,893	$0	$452,884	$16,006,098
2056	82/80	$603,009	$95,063	$440,321	$270,242	$202,617	$0	$461,602	$16,318,467
2057	83/81	$621,171	$96,964	$456,948	$277,881	$210,623	$0	$470,223	$16,632,710
2058	84/82	$639,895	$98,903	$474,378	$285,476	$218,863	$0	$478,671	$16,948,663
2059	85/83	$659,549	$100,882	$492,654	$293,681	$227,667	$0	$487,256	$17,265,818
2060	86/84	$679,831	$102,899	$511,822	$301,850	$236,740	$0	$495,620	$17,583,949
2061	87/85	$700,856	$104,957	$531,933	$310,141	$246,175	$0	$503,830	$17,902,737
2062	88/86	$722,891	$107,056	$553,038	$319,002	$256,206	$0	$512,082	$18,221,611
2063	89/87	$745,548	$109,197	$575,194	$327,614	$266,456	$0	$519,931	$18,540,368
2064	90/88	$769,196	$111,381	$598,458	$336,608	$277,252	$0	$527,683	$18,858,479
2065	91/89	$793,876	$113,609	$622,893	$345,990	$288,616	$0	$535,299	$19,175,367
2066	92/90	$819,510	$115,881	$648,565	$355,519	$300,455	$0	$542,622	$19,490,534
2067	93/91	$845,874	$118,199	$675,543	$364,998	$312,866	$0	$549,357	$19,803,381
2068	94/92	$872,861	$120,563	$703,901	$374,697	$326,300	$0	$555,320	$20,112,852
2069	95/93	$903,996	$122,974	$733,718	$391,578	$344,274	$0	$563,945	$20,414,360
2070	96/94	$938,520	$125,434	$765,074	$413,776	$365,764	$0	$573,993	$20,703,940
2071	97/95	$974,734	$127,942	$798,059	$437,295	$388,562	$0	$583,411	$20,979,564
2072	98/96	$1,012,734	$130,501	$832,765	$462,214	$412,745	$0	$593,425	$21,240,349
2073	99/97	$1,052,619	$133,111	$869,289	$488,616	$438,397	$0	$603,651	$21,484,938
2074	100/98	$1,119,494	$138,273	$1,907,736	$567,889	$494,404	$0	$1,613,202	$22,659,700
2075	-/99	$1,022,235	$73,929	$970,593	$543,171	$565,458	$0	$678,568	$22,792,632
2076	-/100	$11,693,479	$77,907	$16,887,461	$0	$4,271,889	$0	$12,156,982	$24,021,024

Retirement Need and Investable Assets

Current Plan

This report displays a yearly summary of your incomes, expenses, asset withdrawal needs, and asset balances for the selected plan scenario. The amounts included in the withdrawal amounts and the end-of-year balances of the investable accounts include values from accounts specifically designated to the retirement goal.

	Retirement Needs				Pre-Tax Annual Withdrawals/(Contributions/Reinvestments)				EOY Investable Account Balances			
Year and Age	Pre-Tax Income	Private Corporation and Other Inflows	Total Expenses (incl. taxes)	Withdrawals Needed	Non-Registered Accounts	Registered Accounts	Locked-In Accounts	TFSA	Non-Registered Accounts	Registered Accounts	Locked-In Accounts	TFSA
2039 (*65/63*)	$50,614	$174,817	$304,563	$79,132	$0	$79,132	$0	$0	$1,282,854	$3,273,573	$0	$0
2040 (66/64)	$58,308	$178,314	$311,108	$74,486	$0	$74,486	$0	$0	$1,359,825	$3,395,502	$0	$0
2041 (67/65)	$65,984	$181,880	$315,895	$68,032	$0	$68,032	$0	$0	$1,441,415	$3,531,200	$0	$0
2042 (68/66)	$72,046	$185,518	$324,655	$67,092	$0	$67,092	$0	$0	$1,527,900	$3,675,980	$0	$0
2043 (69/67)	$73,487	$189,228	$398,943	$136,229	$0	$136,229	$0	$0	$1,619,574	$3,760,311	$0	$0
2044 (70/68)	$74,956	$193,012	$407,932	$139,963	$0	$139,963	$0	$0	$1,716,748	$3,845,967	$0	$0
2045 (71/69)	$76,456	$196,873	$416,997	$143,669	$0	$143,669	$0	$0	$1,819,753	$3,933,055	$0	$0
2046 (72/70)	$77,985	$200,810	$426,594	$147,799	($324)	$148,123	$0	$0	$1,929,263	$4,016,148	$0	$0
2047 (73/71)	$79,545	$204,826	$438,097	$153,726	($3,490)	$157,216	$0	$0	$2,048,489	$4,094,840	$0	$0
2048 (74/72)	$81,135	$208,923	$474,940	$184,882	($31,325)	$216,208	$0	$0	$2,202,495	$4,117,363	$0	$0
2049 (75/73)	$82,758	$213,101	$486,898	$191,038	($31,299)	$222,338	$0	$0	$2,363,835	$4,134,910	$0	$0
2050 (76/74)	$84,413	$217,363	$499,235	$197,459	($31,202)	$228,661	$0	$0	$2,532,881	$4,146,984	$0	$0
2051 (77/75)	$86,101	$221,711	$511,943	$204,131	($31,003)	$235,134	$0	$0	$2,709,998	$4,153,101	$0	$0
2052 (78/76)	$87,824	$226,145	$525,012	$211,044	($30,667)	$241,710	$0	$0	$2,895,547	$4,152,796	$0	$0
2053 (79/77)	$89,580	$230,668	$538,429	$218,181	($30,156)	$248,337	$0	$0	$3,089,877	$4,145,632	$0	$0
2054 (80/78)	$91,371	$235,281	$552,581	$225,929	($29,857)	$255,786	$0	$0	$3,293,758	$4,130,351	$0	$0

* = year of retirement

Year and Age	Retirement Needs			Pre-Tax Annual Withdrawals/(Contributions/Reinvestments)					EOY Investable Account Balances			
	Pre-Tax Income	Private Corporation and Other Inflows	Total Expenses (incl. taxes)	Withdrawals Needed	Non-Registered Accounts	Registered Accounts	Locked-In Accounts	TFSA	Non-Registered Accounts	Registered Accounts	Locked-In Accounts	TFSA
2055 (81/79)	$93,199	$239,987	$566,823	$233,638	($29,053)	$262,690	$0	$0	$3,507,277	$4,107,026	$0	$0
2056 (82/80)	$95,063	$244,786	$581,747	$241,897	($28,345)	$270,242	$0	$0	$3,731,156	$4,074,507	$0	$0
2057 (83/81)	$96,964	$249,682	$597,097	$250,450	($27,431)	$277,881	$0	$0	$3,965,854	$4,032,151	$0	$0
2058 (84/82)	$98,903	$254,676	$612,827	$259,247	($26,229)	$285,476	$0	$0	$4,211,785	$3,979,415	$0	$0
2059 (85/83)	$100,882	$259,769	$629,271	$268,620	($25,061)	$293,681	$0	$0	$4,469,730	$3,915,045	$0	$0
2060 (86/84)	$102,899	$264,965	$646,137	$278,273	($23,577)	$301,850	$0	$0	$4,740,163	$3,838,382	$0	$0
2061 (87/85)	$104,957	$270,264	$663,521	$288,300	($21,841)	$310,141	$0	$0	$5,023,673	$3,748,560	$0	$0
2062 (88/86)	$107,056	$275,669	$681,660	$298,935	($20,068)	$319,002	$0	$0	$5,321,110	$3,644,203	$0	$0
2063 (89/87)	$109,197	$281,183	$700,181	$309,800	($17,813)	$327,614	$0	$0	$5,632,934	$3,524,696	$0	$0
2064 (90/88)	$111,381	$286,806	$719,411	$321,224	($15,385)	$336,608	$0	$0	$5,959,970	$3,388,734	$0	$0
2065 (91/89)	$113,609	$292,543	$739,380	$333,228	($12,762)	$345,990	$0	$0	$6,303,083	$3,234,931	$0	$0
2066 (92/90)	$115,881	$298,393	$759,995	$345,721	($9,798)	$355,519	$0	$0	$6,663,053	$3,062,064	$0	$0
2067 (93/91)	$118,199	$304,361	$781,358	$358,798	($6,200)	$364,998	$0	$0	$7,040,435	$2,869,041	$0	$0
2068 (94/92)	$120,563	$310,448	$803,922	$372,911	($1,786)	$374,697	$0	$0	$7,435,673	$2,654,426	$0	$0
2069 (95/93)	$122,974	$316,657	$831,210	$391,578	$0	$391,578	$0	$0	$7,852,733	$2,409,732	$0	$0
2070 (96/94)	$125,434	$322,991	$862,200	$413,776	$0	$413,776	$0	$0	$8,294,817	$2,127,866	$0	$0
2071 (97/95)	$127,942	$329,450	$894,687	$437,295	$0	$437,295	$0	$0	$8,763,426	$1,805,373	$0	$0
2072 (98/96)	$130,501	$336,039	$928,754	$462,214	$0	$462,214	$0	$0	$9,260,151	$1,439,859	$0	$0
2073 (99/97)	$133,111	$342,760	$964,488	$488,616	$0	$488,616	$0	$0	$9,786,680	$1,028,364	$0	$0
2074 (100/98)	$138,273	$349,615	$1,055,777	$567,889	$0	$567,889	$0	$0	$11,344,800	$515,557	$0	$0
2075 (-/99)	$73,929	$356,608	$1,105,420	$674,883	$131,712	$543,171	$0	$0	$11,864,042	$0	$0	$0
2076 (-/100)	$77,907		$4,847,549	($10,474,912)	($10,474,912)	$0	$0	$0	$24,021,024	$0	$0	$0
Total	$15,244,554											

* = year of retirement

Detailed Estate Analysis

Current Plan

This report is designed to show the effects of dying in a given year, and the resulting impact of taxation on the estate.

	2020	2034	2048	2062	2076
Non-Registered Investments					
Bank Savings Account	$0	$0	$35,140	$420,928	$484,671
Bank—NR Stock Account—Joint	$424,000	$958,623	$2,167,355	$4,900,182	$10,539,982
New NonReg CC—Joint	$0	$0	$0	$0	$1,122,215
Subtotal	$424,000	$958,623	$2,202,495	$5,321,110	$12,146,868
Registered Investments					
Bank—RSP—Michael	$452,864	$1,716,796	$3,188,148	$2,821,771	$0
Bank RSP—Kathryn	$168,353	$605,160	$929,215	$822,432	$0
Bank—Mark RESP	$45,686	$0	$0	$0	$0
Bank—Chloe RESP	$37,206	$0	$0	$0	$0
Subtotal	$704,109	$2,321,956	$4,117,363	$3,644,203	$0
Private Corporations					
Dr. Michael Jones Corp.	$1,247,921	$5,927,899	$9,233,358	$11,966,925	$14,880,814
Subtotal	$1,247,921	$5,927,899	$9,233,358	$11,966,925	$14,880,814
Lifestyle Assets					
Home	$2,040,000	$2,691,737	$3,551,689	$4,686,379	$6,183,577
Cottage	$510,000	$672,934	$887,922	$1,171,595	$1,545,894
Subtotal	$2,550,000	$3,364,671	$4,439,612	$5,857,973	$7,729,471
Real Estate Assets					
Subtotal	$0	$0	$0	$0	$0
Liabilities					
Home Mortgage	($393,773)	($104,891)	($0)	($0)	($0)
Cottage Mortgage	($294,875)	($78,916)	($0)	($0)	($0)
Subtotal	($688,648)	($183,807)	($0)	($0)	($0)
Pro-Forma Net Worth	**$4,237,381**	**$12,389,341**	**$19,992,828**	**$26,790,212**	**$34,757,153**
Insurance Proceeds					
Kathryn 1M OMA UL Life Insurance	$1,000,000	$1,000,000	$1,000,000	$1,000,000	$1,000,000
Michael 1M OMA UL Life Insurance	$1,000,000	$1,000,000	$1,000,000	$1,000,000	$0
Subtotal	$2,000,000	$2,000,000	$2,000,000	$2,000,000	$1,000,000

	2020	2034	2048	2062	2076
Death Benefits					
CPP/QPP Death Benefits	$5,000	$5,000	$5,000	$5,000	$2,500
Subtotal	$5,000	$5,000	$5,000	$5,000	$2,500
Change in Value of Private Corporations	$0	$0	$0	$0	$0
Estate Before Taxes and Expenses	$6,242,381	$14,394,341	$21,997,828	$28,795,212	$35,759,653
Additional Income Taxes	($705,746)	($2,897,504)	($4,815,651)	($5,375,019)	($4,332,705)
Transfers on Death	$0	$0	$0	$0	$0
Charitable Bequests	($0)	($0)	($0)	($0)	($0)
Estate Expenses					
Final Expenses	($25,000)	($25,000)	($25,000)	($25,000)	$0
Final Expenses	($25,000)	($25,000)	($25,000)	($25,000)	($25,000)
Subtotal	($50,000)	($50,000)	($50,000)	($50,000)	($25,000)
Net Estate	**$5,486,635**	**$11,446,838**	**$17,132,177**	**$23,370,193**	**$31,401,949**
Net Estate (Today's $)	**$5,486,635**	**$8,675,272**	**$9,840,287**	**$10,173,141**	**$10,359,695**

Utilizing Tax-Efficient Strategies

Recommendations

Net Worth

Proposed Recommendations—Utilizing Tax Efficient Strategies Available for Corporations

Starting 2021—Personal Strategies:

- Stop corporation salaries and begin splitting dividends evenly, $105,000 each (today's dollars)—saving remaining net income in corporation
- Stop maximizing RRSP and begin maximizing TFSA until death—with planned revision of retirement asset liquidation order, to spend RRSP funds first to incur less taxes upon estate
- Debt swap with Non-Reg to make mortgage tax deductible on home
- Formulate estate plan with both primary and secondary wills, along with appropriate trust structures for protection and tax purposes

Starting 2021—Corporate Strategies

- Transfer existing life and CI insurance into corporation
- Utilize corporate-class ETFs in corporation (6% tax-deferred capital gains)
- Implement $150,000 leverage in corporation, utilizing corporate class investment structure—benefiting from interest deduction and tax deferral
- Put in force corporate joint-last-to-die whole life PAR policy— $30,000/year premium for 10 years
- Creation of estate plan for intergenerational wealth transfer

Starting 2024:

- Increase corporation leverage loan principal to $300,000
- Leverage of $500,000 ($250,000 for each child) into trusts for Mark and Chloe, utilizing corporate-class investments (taking advantage of gains growing tax-free in children's hands) with tax-deductible advisory fees
- Utilize trusts to protect wealth and ultimately have children pay less taxes on their investments

Cash Flow Outlook

Proposed Plan

This report projects itemized cash flow information over the duration of the selected years. Cash inflows and outflows are categorized by source and summarized as aggregate totals. This provides an overview of your cash flow projections.

	Year				
Age	**2020** 46/44	**2021** 47/45	**2022** 48/46	**2023** 49/47	**2024** 50/48
Cash Inflows					
Earned Income					
Corporation Salary (Michael)	$200,000	$0	$0	$0	$0
Corporation Salary (Kathryn)	$50,000	$0	$0	$0	$0
Total	$250,000	$0	$0	$0	$0
Non-Registered Proceeds					
Bank—NR Stock Account—Joint	$0	$424,000	$0	$0	$0
Total	$0	$424,000	$0	$0	$0
Investment Income					
Bank—NR Stock Account—Joint	$24,000	$0	$0	$0	$0
New NonReg CC —Joint	$0	$8,959	$9,490	$10,053	$10,650
New Mark Trust CC Leverage	$0	$0	$0	$0	$5,599
New Chloe Trust CC Leverage	$0	$0	$0	$0	$5,599
Total	$24,000	$8,959	$9,490	$10,053	$21,848
Private Corporation Inflows					
Dr. Michael Jones Corp.	$0	$214,200	$218,484	$222,854	$227,311
Total	$0	$214,200	$218,484	$222,854	$227,311
Miscellaneous Income					
Debt Swap—Leverage (Joint)	$0	$400,000	$0	$0	$0
Mark Leverage Loan (Joint)	$0	$0	$0	$0	$250,000
Chloe Leverage Loan (Joint)	$0	$0	$0	$0	$250,000
Total	$0	$400,000	$0	$0	$500,000
Total Cash Inflows	**$274,000**	**$1,047,159**	**$227,974**	**$232,907**	**$749,159**

			Year		
Age	**2020** 46/44	**2021** 47/45	**2022** 48/46	**2023** 49/47	**2024** 50/48
Cash Outflows					
Lifestyle Expenses					
Housing (e.g. utilities, repairs) (Joint)	$15,600	$15,912	$16,230	$16,555	$16,886
Food (Joint)	$8,400	$8,568	$8,739	$8,914	$9,092
Transportation (e.g. gas, insurance) (Joint)	$12,000	$12,240	$12,485	$12,734	$12,989
Entertainment (e.g. restaurants, movies) (Joint)	$14,400	$14,688	$14,982	$15,281	$15,587
Personal (e.g. clothing, hobbies) (Joint)	$6,000	$6,120	$6,242	$6,367	$6,495
Other (e.g. child care, travel) (Joint)	$14,400	$14,688	$14,982	$15,281	$15,587
Home Mortgage (Joint)	$28,392	$393,805	$0	$0	$0
Cottage Mortgage (Joint)	$21,240	$21,240	$21,240	$21,240	$21,240
Debt Swap—Leverage (Joint)	$0	$32,640	$32,640	$32,640	$32,640
Mark Leverage Loan (Joint)	$0	$0	$0	$0	$22,281
Chloe Leverage Loan (Joint)	$0	$0	$0	$0	$22,281
Total	$120,432	$519,901	$127,540	$129,014	$175,078
Registered Contributions					
Bank—RSP—Michael	$27,230	$0	$0	$0	$0
Bank RSP—Kathryn	$8,824	$0	$0	$0	$0
Bank—Mark RESP (Michael)	$2,500	$2,500	$2,500	$2,500	$2,500
Bank—Chloe RESP (Michael)	$2,500	$2,500	$2,500	$2,500	$2,500
New TFSA—Michael	$0	$31,000	$6,000	$6,000	$6,000
New TFSA—Kathryn	$0	$31,000	$36,000	$36,000	$6,000
Total	$41,054	$67,000	$47,000	$47,000	$17,000
Non-Registered Contributions					
New NonReg CC—Joint	$0	$400,000	$0	$0	$0
New Mark Trust CC Leverage	$0	$0	$0	$0	$250,000
New Chloe Trust CC Leverage	$0	$0	$0	$0	$250,000
Total	$0	$400,000	$0	$0	$500,000

	Year				
	2020	**2021**	**2022**	**2023**	**2024**
Age	**46/44**	**47/45**	**48/46**	**49/47**	**50/48**
Cash Outflows					
Non-Registered Savings					
Bank—NR Stock Account—Joint	$24,000	$0	$0	$0	$0
New NonReg CC—Joint	$0	$8,959	$9,490	$10,053	$10,650
New Mark Trust CC Leverage	$0	$0	$0	$0	$5,599
New Chloe Trust CC Leverage	$0	$0	$0	$0	$5,599
Total	$24,000	$8,959	$9,490	$10,053	$21,848
Employment Expenses					
CPP/QPP Contributions— Employment	$5,339	$0	$0	$0	$0
EI Premiums	$1,687	$0	$0	$0	$0
Total	$7,027	$0	$0	$0	$0
Miscellaneous Expenses					
Michael 5,000/m Individual Disability	$1,350	$1,350	$1,350	$1,350	$1,350
Kathryn 2,500/m Individual Disability	$750	$750	$750	$750	$750
Michael 1M Life Insurance	$4,500	$0	$0	$0	$0
Kathryn 1M Life Insurance (Kathryn)	$3,250	$0	$0	$0	$0
100K Michael CI Insurance (Michael)	$2,400	$0	$0	$0	$0
100K Kathryn CI Insurance (Kathryn)	$1,650	$0	$0	$0	$0
Total	$13,900	$2,100	$2,100	$2,100	$2,100
Taxes					
Federal Income Tax	$42,043	$17,075	$16,233	$16,514	$11,759
Provincial Income Tax	$25,142	$13,658	$13,355	$13,518	$10,263
Total	$67,186	$30,733	$29,587	$30,032	$22,021
Total Cash Outflows	**$273,598**	**$1,028,692**	**$215,718**	**$218,199**	**$738,048**
Surplus/(Deficit)	**$402**	**$18,466**	**$12,256**	**$14,708**	**$11,111**

Net Worth Timeline

Proposed Plan

This report displays net worth data over time according to asset category. The projections show end-of-year values beginning in the year of the analysis until the last surviving client's year of death. Use this report to show how each asset category contributes to total net worth throughout the plan.

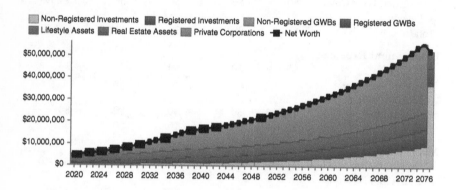

Net Worth Outlook

Proposed Plan

This report shows changes in your net worth over time. These projected end-of-year values begin with the analysis year and end with the death of the last surviving client. Furthermore, assets included in this report are categorized to show how changes in net worth occur. Use this report to assess your total net worth by asset category through the duration of the analysis.

Year and Age	Non-Registered Investments	Registered Investments	Lifestyle Assets	Private Corporations	Total Liabilities	Total Net Worth
2020 (46/44)	$424,000	$704,109	$2,550,000	$1,203,186	$688,648	**$4,192,647**
2021 (47/45)	$424,092	$815,678	$2,601,000	$1,456,786	$667,309	**$4,630,247**
2022 (48/46)	$449,260	$913,845	$2,653,020	$1,717,024	$638,676	**$5,094,474**
2023 (49/47)	$475,922	$1,017,901	$2,706,080	$1,996,701	$608,931	**$5,587,674**
2024 (50/48)	$504,167	$1,097,631	$2,760,202	$2,287,659	$1,053,012	**$5,596,646**
2025 (51/49)	$534,087	$1,182,039	$2,815,406	$2,590,660	$994,871	**$6,127,321**
2026 (52/50)	$565,783	$1,271,087	$2,871,714	$2,906,402	$934,419	**$6,680,568**
2027 (53/51)	$599,360	$1,334,825	$2,929,148	$3,235,622	$871,560	**$7,227,396**
2028 (54/52)	$634,930	$1,401,271	$2,987,731	$3,579,101	$806,197	**$7,796,837**
2029 (55/53)	$672,611	$1,437,597	$3,047,486	$3,937,665	$738,228	**$8,357,131**
2030 (56/54)	$712,528	$1,495,051	$3,108,436	$4,342,188	$667,547	**$8,990,657**
2031 (57/55)	$754,814	$1,564,525	$3,170,604	$4,765,371	$594,043	**$9,661,271**
2032 (58/56)	$799,609	$1,664,889	$3,234,017	$5,208,295	$517,602	**$10,389,208**
2033 (59/57)	$847,063	$1,777,502	$3,298,697	$5,672,107	$438,104	**$11,157,266**
2034 (60/58)	$897,333	$1,896,872	$3,364,671	$6,158,021	$355,423	**$11,961,475**
2035 (61/59)	$950,587	$2,023,405	$3,431,964	$6,667,318	$269,429	**$12,803,845**
2036 (62/60)	$1,007,001	$2,157,529	$3,500,604	$7,201,359	$179,988	**$13,686,505**
2037 (63/61)	$1,066,763	$2,299,701	$3,570,616	$7,761,581	$86,958	**$14,611,703**
2038 (64/62)	$1,130,071	$2,450,403	$3,642,028	$8,349,506	$0	**$15,572,008**
2039 (*65/63*)	$1,197,137	$2,483,406	$3,714,868	$8,576,265	$0	**$15,971,676**
2040 (66/64)	$1,268,183	$2,511,062	$3,789,166	$8,822,987	$0	**$16,391,397**
2041 (67/65)	$1,343,445	$2,538,721	$3,864,949	$9,090,973	$0	**$16,838,087**
2042 (68/66)	$1,423,173	$2,569,422	$3,942,248	$9,381,604	$0	**$17,316,447**
2043 (69/67)	$1,507,633	$2,601,976	$4,021,093	$9,696,345	$0	**$17,827,047**
2044 (70/68)	$1,597,106	$2,636,603	$4,101,515	$10,036,749	$0	**$18,371,972**
2045 (71/69)	$1,691,888	$2,673,546	$4,183,545	$10,404,462	$0	**$18,953,441**
2046 (72/70)	$1,792,296	$2,710,948	$4,267,216	$10,801,229	$0	**$19,571,689**
2047 (73/71)	$1,898,662	$2,757,343	$4,352,561	$11,226,099	$0	**$20,234,665**
2048 (74/72)	$2,011,341	$2,844,554	$4,439,612	$11,627,184	$0	**$20,922,691**
2049 (75/73)	$2,130,707	$2,935,084	$4,528,404	$12,047,076	$0	**$21,641,271**
2050 (76/74)	$2,257,156	$3,030,341	$4,618,972	$12,483,173	$0	**$22,389,642**
2051 (77/75)	$2,391,110	$3,130,062	$4,711,351	$12,935,650	$0	**$23,168,173**
2052 (78/76)	$2,533,014	$3,234,474	$4,805,579	$13,405,268	$0	**$23,978,335**
2053 (79/77)	$2,683,339	$3,343,820	$4,901,690	$13,892,825	$0	**$24,821,674**
2054 (80/78)	$2,842,586	$3,458,349	$4,999,724	$14,399,154	$0	**$25,699,813**
2055 (81/79)	$3,011,283	$3,578,381	$5,099,718	$14,925,130	$0	**$26,614,513**
2056 (82/80)	$3,189,992	$3,704,198	$5,201,713	$15,471,670	$0	**$27,567,572**
2057 (83/81)	$3,379,306	$3,836,101	$5,305,747	$16,039,733	$0	**$28,560,887**
2058 (84/82)	$3,579,856	$3,974,411	$5,411,862	$16,630,325	$0	**$29,596,454**

* = year of retirement

Year and Age	Non-Registered Investments	Registered Investments	Life-style Assets	Private Corporations	Total Liabilities	Total Net Worth
2059 (85/83)	$3,792,307	$4,119,458	$5,520,099	$17,244,502	$0	$30,676,366
2060 (86/84)	$4,017,367	$4,271,598	$5,630,501	$17,883,366	$0	$31,802,832
2061 (87/85)	$4,255,783	$4,431,205	$5,743,111	$18,548,076	$0	$32,978,176
2062 (88/86)	$4,508,348	$4,598,669	$5,857,973	$19,239,845	$0	$34,204,836
2063 (89/87)	$4,775,902	$4,774,408	$5,975,133	$19,959,944	$0	$35,485,387
2064 (90/88)	$5,059,731	$4,958,270	$6,094,636	$20,709,704	$0	$36,822,339
2065 (91/89)	$5,361,267	$5,149,949	$6,216,528	$21,490,520	$0	$38,218,265
2066 (92/90)	$5,681,505	$5,349,865	$6,340,859	$22,303,856	$0	$39,676,085
2067 (93/91)	$6,021,450	$5,558,528	$6,467,676	$23,151,245	$0	$41,198,899
2068 (94/92)	$6,382,228	$5,776,389	$6,597,029	$24,034,291	$0	$42,789,938
2069 (95/93)	$6,765,036	$6,003,918	$6,728,970	$24,954,680	$0	$44,452,605
2070 (96/94)	$7,171,159	$6,241,585	$6,863,549	$25,914,176	$0	$46,190,470
2071 (97/95)	$7,601,795	$6,490,131	$7,000,820	$26,914,629	$0	$48,007,375
2072 (98/96)	$8,051,319	$6,761,026	$7,140,837	$27,957,977	$0	$49,911,159
2073 (99/97)	$8,527,522	$7,046,456	$7,283,654	$29,046,254	$0	$51,903,885
2074 (100/98)	$9,031,985	$7,394,499	$7,429,327	$30,182,746	$0	$54,038,556
2075 (-/99)	$9,566,386	$7,597,298	$7,577,913	$31,375,919	$0	$56,117,516
2076 (-/100)	$37,083,576	$8,031,398	$7,729,471	$0	$0	$52,844,445

* = year of retirement

Retirement Cash Flow Timeline

Proposed Plan

This report shows your annual inflows and outflows during the retirement period. Positive inflows are shown in bold whereas negative values are shown gray and in parentheses. Other Incomes will include such things as Earned Salary, Pension, and Investment incomes. Withdrawals from Assets include Registered proceeds and Non-Registered proceeds. Growth & Reinvestments include growth, reinvestments and annual contributions made to all assets. Age of retirement is marked with an asterisk.

Year	Age	Total Needs	CPP/ QPP/ OAS	Other Income	With-drawal from Assets	Taxes	Sur-plus/ (Short-fall)	Growth and Reinve-stments	EOY Assets
2039	*65/63*	$299,514	$29,329	$200,106	$126,741	$56,661	$0	$226,810	$12,256,808
2040	66/64	$306,260	$34,624	$205,103	$134,068	$67,535	$0	$232,770	$12,602,231
2041	67/65	$313,199	$41,826	$210,259	$135,725	$74,611	$0	$238,646	$12,973,138
2042	68/66	$320,340	$47,405	$215,581	$134,342	$76,989	$0	$244,772	$13,374,199
2043	69/67	$327,689	$48,353	$221,075	$134,332	$76,071	$0	$251,345	$13,805,954
2044	70/68	$335,256	$49,320	$226,750	$134,211	$75,025	$0	$258,311	$14,270,457
2045	71/69	$343,049	$50,306	$232,612	$133,973	$73,843	$0	$265,699	$14,769,896
2046	72/70	$351,076	$51,313	$238,671	$133,607	$72,515	$0	$271,417	$15,304,472
2047	73/71	$359,347	$52,339	$244,934	$126,782	$64,708	$0	$279,544	$15,882,105
2048	74/72	$367,872	$53,386	$251,411	$88,456	$25,381	$0	$288,346	$16,483,079
2049	75/73	$376,661	$54,453	$258,111	$90,319	$26,221	$0	$300,214	$17,112,867
2050	76/74	$385,725	$55,543	$265,044	$90,971	$25,832	$0	$312,678	$17,770,670
2051	77/75	$395,076	$56,653	$272,221	$92,168	$25,966	$0	$325,843	$18,456,821
2052	78/76	$404,725	$57,786	$279,652	$93,404	$26,118	$0	$339,720	$19,172,756
2053	79/77	$414,685	$58,942	$287,351	$94,678	$26,286	$0	$354,349	$19,919,984
2054	80/78	$424,969	$60,121	$295,328	$95,991	$26,471	$0	$369,766	$20,700,089
2055	81/79	$435,591	$61,323	$303,597	$97,299	$26,629	$0	$386,029	$21,514,794
2056	82/80	$446,565	$62,550	$312,172	$98,650	$26,806	$0	$403,175	$22,365,859
2057	83/81	$457,908	$63,801	$321,067	$100,044	$27,003	$0	$421,261	$23,255,140
2058	84/82	$469,635	$65,077	$330,297	$101,482	$27,221	$0	$440,342	$24,184,592
2059	85/83	$481,763	$66,378	$339,878	$102,967	$27,461	$0	$460,466	$25,156,267
2060	86/84	$494,310	$67,706	$349,828	$104,500	$27,724	$0	$481,700	$26,172,331
2061	87/85	$507,295	$69,060	$360,163	$106,082	$28,010	$0	$504,105	$27,235,065
2062	88/86	$520,739	$70,441	$370,904	$107,714	$28,321	$0	$527,743	$28,346,863
2063	89/87	$534,660	$71,850	$382,069	$109,399	$28,658	$0	$552,692	$29,510,254
2064	90/88	$549,479	$73,287	$393,680	$111,726	$29,214	$0	$579,416	$30,727,704
2065	91/89	$565,314	$74,753	$405,759	$114,840	$30,038	$0	$608,056	$32,001,737
2066	92/90	$581,691	$76,248	$418,329	$118,003	$30,888	$0	$638,156	$33,335,227
2067	93/91	$598,591	$77,773	$431,414	$121,149	$31,745	$0	$669,757	$34,731,223
2068	94/92	$616,099	$79,328	$445,041	$124,368	$32,639	$0	$703,007	$36,192,908
2069	95/93	$634,246	$80,915	$459,238	$127,664	$33,571	$0	$738,002	$37,723,635
2070	96/94	$653,082	$82,533	$474,033	$131,069	$34,554	$0	$774,859	$39,326,921
2071	97/95	$672,475	$84,184	$489,456	$134,344	$35,509	$0	$813,526	$41,006,555
2072	98/96	$685,561	$85,868	$505,541	$127,247	$33,095	$0	$847,666	$42,770,322
2073	99/97	$705,701	$87,585	$522,321	$129,571	$33,776	$0	$891,203	$44,620,231
2074	100/98	$751,641	$91,837	$1,539,833	$84,737	$20,140	$944,625	$937,243	$46,609,230
2075	–/99	$742,418	$59,147	$558,114	$244,903	$119,746	$0	$982,103	$48,539,603
2076	–/100	$27,741,148	$62,830	$37,535,537	$27,221	$9,884,440	$0	$27,978,511	$45,114,974

Retirement Need and Investable Assets

Proposed Plan

This report displays a yearly summary of your incomes, expenses, asset withdrawal needs, and asset balances for the selected plan scenario. The amounts included in the withdrawal amounts and the end of year balances of the investable accounts include values from accounts specifically designated to the retirement goal.

| Year and Age | Retirement Needs | | | | Pre-Tax Annual Withdrawals/ (Contributions/Reinvestments) | | | | EOY Investable Account Balances | | | |
	Pre-Tax Other Income Inflows	Private Corporation and Other Inflows	Total Expenses (incl. taxes)	Withdrawals Needed	Non-Registered Accounts	Registered Accounts	Locked-In Accounts	TFSA	Non-Registered Accounts	Registered Accounts	Locked-In Accounts	TFSA
2039 (65/63)	$29,329	$174,817	$318,887	$114,741	$0	$126,741	$0	($12,000)	$1,197,137	$1,752,812	$0	$730,594
2040 (66/64)	$34,624	$178,314	$335,005	$122,068	$0	$134,068	$0	($12,000)	$1,268,183	$1,723,913	$0	$787,150
2041 (67/65)	$41,826	$181,880	$347,431	$123,725	$0	$135,725	$0	($12,000)	$1,343,445	$1,691,623	$0	$847,099
2042 (68/66)	$47,405	$185,518	$355,265	$122,342	$0	$134,342	$0	($12,000)	$1,423,173	$1,658,777	$0	$910,644
2043 (69/67)	$48,353	$189,228	$359,913	$122,332	$0	$134,332	$0	($12,000)	$1,507,633	$1,623,972	$0	$978,003
2044 (70/68)	$49,320	$193,012	$364,544	$122,211	$0	$134,211	$0	($12,000)	$1,597,106	$1,587,199	$0	$1,049,403
2045 (71/69)	$50,306	$196,873	$369,152	$121,973	$0	$133,973	$0	($12,000)	$1,691,888	$1,548,458	$0	$1,125,088
2046 (72/70)	$51,313	$200,810	$373,730	$121,607	$0	$133,607	$0	($12,000)	$1,792,296	$1,505,635	$0	$1,205,313
2047 (73/71)	$52,339	$204,826	$371,948	$114,782	$0	$126,782	$0	($12,000)	$1,898,662	$1,466,992	$0	$1,290,352
2048 (74/72)	$53,386	$208,923	$338,765	$76,456	$0	$88,456	$0	($12,000)	$2,011,341	$1,464,062	$0	$1,380,493
2049 (75/73)	$54,453	$213,101	$345,874	$78,319	$0	$90,319	$0	($12,000)	$2,130,707	$1,459,042	$0	$1,476,042
2050 (76/74)	$55,543	$217,363	$351,877	$78,971	$0	$90,971	$0	($12,000)	$2,257,156	$1,453,016	$0	$1,577,325
2051 (77/75)	$56,653	$221,711	$358,532	$80,168	$0	$92,168	$0	($12,000)	$2,391,110	$1,445,377	$0	$1,684,684
2052 (78/76)	$57,786	$226,145	$365,335	$81,404	$0	$93,404	$0	($12,000)	$2,513,014	$1,435,989	$0	$1,798,485
2053 (79/77)	$58,942	$230,668	$372,288	$82,678	$0	$94,678	$0	($12,000)	$2,683,339	$1,424,706	$0	$1,919,114
2054 (80/78)	$60,121	$235,281	$379,393	$83,991	$0	$95,991	$0	($12,000)	$2,842,586	$1,411,367	$0	$2,046,981

* = year of retirement

	Retirement Needs				Pre-Tax Annual Withdrawals/ (Contributions/Reinvestments)				EOY Investable Account Balances			
Year and Age	Pre-Tax Income	Private Corporation and Other Inflows	Total Expenses (incl. taxes)	Withdrawals Needed	Non-Registered Accounts	Registered Accounts	Registered Locked-In Accounts	TFSA	Non-Registered Accounts	Registered Accounts	Registered Locked-In Accounts	TFSA
2055 (81/79)	$61,323	$239,987	$386,609	$85,299	$0	$97,299	$0	($12,000)	$3,011,283	$1,395,861	$0	$2,182,520
2056 (82/80)	$62,550	$244,786	$393,986	$86,650	$0	$98,650	$0	($12,000)	$3,189,992	$1,378,007	$0	$2,326,191
2057 (83/81)	$63,801	$249,682	$401,527	$88,044	$0	$100,044	$0	($12,000)	$3,379,306	$1,357,618	$0	$2,478,483
2058 (84/82)	$65,077	$254,676	$409,235	$89,482	$0	$101,482	$0	($12,000)	$3,579,856	$1,334,499	$0	$2,639,912
2059 (85/83)	$66,378	$259,769	$417,115	$90,967	$0	$102,967	$0	($12,000)	$3,792,307	$1,308,431	$0	$2,811,026
2060 (86/84)	$67,706	$264,965	$425,171	$92,500	$0	$104,500	$0	($12,000)	$4,017,367	$1,279,190	$0	$2,992,408
2061 (87/85)	$69,060	$270,264	$433,406	$94,082	$0	$106,082	$0	($12,000)	$4,255,783	$1,246,533	$0	$3,184,673
2062 (88/86)	$70,441	$275,669	$441,825	$95,714	$0	$107,714	$0	($12,000)	$4,508,348	$1,210,196	$0	$3,388,473
2063 (89/87)	$71,850	$281,183	$450,432	$97,399	($396)	$109,399	$0	($12,000)	$4,775,902	$1,169,906	$0	$3,604,501
2064 (90/88)	$73,287	$286,806	$459,424	$99,330	($1,284)	$111,726	$0	($12,000)	$5,059,731	$1,124,778	$0	$3,833,491
2065 (91/89)	$74,753	$292,543	$468,852	$101,556	($2,166)	$114,840	$0	($12,000)	$5,361,267	$1,073,729	$0	$4,076,221
2066 (92/90)	$76,248	$298,393	$478,478	$103,837	($2,996)	$118,003	$0	($12,000)	$5,681,505	$1,016,351	$0	$4,333,514
2067 (93/91)	$77,773	$304,361	$488,287	$106,153	($3,834)	$121,149	$0	($12,000)	$6,021,450	$952,283	$0	$4,606,245
2068 (94/92)	$79,328	$310,448	$498,311	$108,535	($4,679)	$124,368	$0	($12,000)	$6,382,228	$881,049	$0	$4,895,340
2069 (95/93)	$80,915	$316,657	$508,557	$110,985	($5,554)	$127,664	$0	($12,000)	$6,765,036	$802,138	$0	$5,201,780
2070 (96/94)	$82,533	$322,991	$519,039	$113,516	($6,294)	$131,069	$0	($12,000)	$7,171,159	$714,978	$0	$5,526,607
2071 (97/95)	$84,184	$329,450	$529,685	$116,051	$0	$134,344	$0	($12,000)	$7,601,795	$619,208	$0	$5,870,923
2072 (98/96)	$85,868	$336,039	$537,154	$115,247	$0	$127,247	$0	($12,000)	$8,051,319	$525,127	$0	$6,235,899
2073 (99/97)	$87,585	$342,760	$547,916	$117,571	$0	$129,571	$0	($12,000)	$8,527,522	$423,683	$0	$6,622,772
2074 (100/98)	$91,837	$1,349,615	$569,564	($871,888)	$0	$84,737	$0	($12,000)	$9,031,985	$361,640	$0	$7,032,859
2075 (-/99)	$59,147	$356,608	$654,657	$238,903	$0	$244,903	$0	($6,000)	$9,566,386	$136,107	$0	$7,461,190
2076 (-/100)	$62,830	$37,322,072	$10,455,050	($26,929,852)	($26,951,073)	$27,221	$0	($6,000)	$37,083,576	$116,176	$0	$7,915,222

* = year of retirement

Detailed Estate Analysis

Proposed Plan

This report is designed to show the effects of dying in a given year, and the resulting impact of taxation on the estate.

	2020	2034	2048	2062	2076
Non-Registered Investments					
Bank Savings Account	$0	$0	$0	$0	$27,201
Bank—NR Stock Account—Joint	$424,000	$0	$0	$0	$0
New NonReg CC—Joint	$0	$897,333	$2,011,341	$4,508,348	$10,076,488
Subtotal	$424,000	$897,333	$2,011,341	$4,508,348	$10,103,689
Registered Investments					
Bank—RSP—Michael	$452,864	$0	$0	$0	$0
Bank RSP—Kathryn	$168,353	$0	$0	$0	$0
New RSP—Michael	$0	$1,023,882	$1,350,405	$1,152,423	$0
New RSP—Kathryn	$0	$380,630	$113,657	$57,773	$0
New TFSA—Michael	$0	$187,238	$556,983	$1,392,941	$3,241,048
New TFSA—Kathryn	$0	$305,123	$823,509	$1,995,532	$4,645,361
Bank—Mark RESP	$45,686	$0	$0	$0	$0
Bank—Chloe RESP	$37,206	$0	$0	$0	$0
Subtotal	$704,109	$1,896,872	$2,844,554	$4,598,669	$7,886,409
Private Corporations					
Dr. Michael Jones Corp.	$1,201,764	$5,976,493	$11,020,911	$18,861,536	$33,152,951
Subtotal	$1,201,764	$5,976,493	$11,020,911	$18,861,536	$33,152,951
Lifestyle Assets					
Home	$2,040,000	$2,691,737	$3,551,689	$4,686,379	$6,183,577
Cottage	$510,000	$672,934	$887,922	$1,171,595	$1,545,894
Subtotal	$2,550,000	$3,364,671	$4,439,612	$5,857,973	$7,729,471
Real Estate Assets					
Subtotal	$0	$0	$0	$0	$0
Liabilities					
Home Mortgage	($393,773)	($0)	($0)	($0)	($0)
Cottage Mortgage	($294,875)	($78,916)	($0)	($0)	($0)
Debt Swap—Leverage	($0)	($115,203)	($0)	($0)	($0)
Mark Leverage Loan	($0)	($80,651)	($0)	($0)	($0)

	2020	2034	2048	2062	2076
Chloe Leverage Loan	($0)	($80,652)	($0)	($0)	($0)
Subtotal	($688,648)	($355,423)	($0)	($0)	($0)
Pro-Forma Net Worth	**$4,191,224**	**$11,779,948**	**$20,316,417**	**$33,826,527**	**$58,872,521**
Insurance Proceeds					
Kathryn 1M Life Insurance	$1,000,000	$0	$0	$0	$0
Michael 1M Life Insurance	$1,000,000	$0	$0	$0	$0
Subtotal	$2,000,000	$0	$0	$0	$0
Death Benefits					
CPP/QPP Death Benefits	$5,000	$5,000	$5,000	$5,000	$2,500
Subtotal	$5,000	$5,000	$5,000	$5,000	$2,500
Change in Value of Private Corporations	$2,608,765	$3,067,495	$3,307,725	$3,919,600	$3,805,381
Estate Before Taxes and Expenses	$8,804,989	$14,852,443	$23,629,142	$37,751,127	$62,680,402
Additional Income Taxes	($1,391,623)	($3,334,591)	($5,045,494)	($7,685,878)	($11,984,558)
Transfers on Death	$0	$0	$0	$0	$0
Charitable Bequests	($0)	($0)	($0)	($0)	($0)
Estate Expenses					
Final Expenses	($25,000)	($25,000)	($25,000)	($25,000)	$0
Final Expenses	($25,000)	($25,000)	($25,000)	($25,000)	($25,000)
Subtotal	($50,000)	($50,000)	($50,000)	($50,000)	($50,000)
Net Estate	**$7,363,366**	**$11,467,852**	**$18,533,648**	**$30,015,249**	**$50,670,845**
Net Estate (Today's $)	**$7,363,366**	**$8,691,198**	**$10,645,256**	**$13,065,762**	**$16,716,622**

Closing Thoughts: Your Next Steps

As I noted at the outset, I wrote this book because I felt compelled to capture my thinking about the best financial paths and principles for incorporated professionals.

My experience over the past decade-plus has shown me, sometimes quite vividly, that the financial rules of thumb many incorporated professionals will encounter as they're trying to organize and optimize their financial lives fall woefully short of what's needed.

My hope is that you will take the information and insights from this book into your own financial life. But I didn't write this as a cut-and-paste, one-size-fits-all guide.

Instead, many of the examples in this book will need to be tested to be sure they work for you. The right strategies will depend on a myriad of different factors, including your goals, preferences, circumstances, needs, time horizon, and much more. Importantly, these factors will also change over time—meaning that what works, or doesn't work, for you today might become a fit later.

With these thoughts in mind, here are my three key takeaways for you:

1. **This book is intended to start a dialogue, not end it.**

   Advice works best when it's part of a conversation, and conversations work best when both parties are engaged and committed. You can use the information in this book to help get informed, and then explore strategies, opportunities, and scenarios to put what you've read into practice.

   In many cases, you'll be seeking a professional financial advisor to help you implement what you've learned here. Perhaps the most important facet of that relationship is your advisor's willingness to listen and engage. If there are ideas in this book that resonate with you, take them to your advisor—and use them to create the best plan for you and your situation.

2. **Don't let yourself get anchored to strategies that no longer work.**

   The reality is that change is constant, especially in the financial world. Everything changes: tax rates, your age, your personal circumstances, government programs and services, expected return on asset classes, market opportunities, and more. What this means is that your strategies, too, need to remain dynamic and flexible, so that you can accommodate these changing variables.

   What this also means is that the insights in this book will change over time. What works today may not work tomorrow. As you're planning your financial future, you will need to keep checking and verifying that you're not relying on outdated approaches and ways of thinking.

   Instead, you should always be asking yourself and your advisors, "Am I taking the best and most appropriate actions today? How are my plans adjusting for the changing variables that will affect my success?" Use this book as inspiration, but not as an instruction manual.

3. What are you waiting for?

You've had me as your financial coach throughout these pages, but now we're at the end—and it's time for you to put these insights into action.

If you read these last few sentences and put the book down, taking no further steps, you will gain no benefit, and I will have failed in my objective of helping you improve your outcomes as an incorporated professional.

Let's not let that happen. Instead, invest in yourself and your future by getting started on the conversations outlined here. Whether that means scheduling an appointment with your accountant, resolving to interview a few potential financial advisors, or dusting off your financial plan for a second opinion, moving your plans into the realm of action is your best shot at designing the future you deserve.

As the old proverb goes, "Fortune favours the bold"—so get started with a bold action today.

Index